The Teaching for Social

William Ayers
Series Editor

The Public Assault on America's Children:
Poverty, Violence, and Juvenile Injustice
VALERIE POLAKOW, EDITOR

Walking the Color Line:
The Art and Practice of Anti-racist Teaching
MARK PERRY

Construction Sites:
Excavating Race, Class, and Gender Among Urban Youths
LOIS WEIS AND MICHELLE FINE, EDITORS

A Simple Justice:
The Challenge of Small Schools
WILLIAM AYERS, MICHAEL KLONSKY, AND GABRIELLE H. LYON, EDITORS

Holler If You Hear Me:
The Education of a Teacher and His Students
GREGORY MICHIE

WITHDRAWN

The Public Assault on America's Children

POVERTY, VIOLENCE, AND JUVENILE INJUSTICE

VALERIE POLAKOW
Editor

Teachers College, Columbia University
New York and London

Published by Teachers College Press, 1234 Amsterdam Avenue, New York, NY 10027

Library of Congress Cataloging-in-Publication Data

The Public assault on America's children : poverty, violence, and juvenile injustice / Valerie Polakow, editor.
    p. cm. — (The Teaching for social justice series)
    Includes bibliographical references (p.) and index.
    ISBN 0-8077-3984-7 (cloth : alk. paper) — ISBN 0-8077-3983-9 (pbk. : alk. paper)
    1. Children and violence—United States. 2. Poor children—Government policy—United States. I. Polakow, Valerie. II. Series.
HQ784.V55 P86 2000
305.23'0973—dc21   00-055204

ISBN 0-8077-3983-9 (paper)
ISBN 0-8077-3984-7 (cloth)

Printed on acid-free paper
Manufactured in the United States of America

08 07 06 05 04 03 02 01   8 7 6 5 4 3 2 1

Contents

Foreword   vii

Jonathan Kozol

Introduction
Savage Policies: Systemic Violence and the Lives of Children   1

Valerie Polakow

Part I: Poverty, Violence, and the Lived Realities of Children

1. A Crucible of Contradictions:
Historical Roots of Violence Against Children
in the United States   21

Barbara Finkelstein

2. Poverty and Environmentally Induced Damage to Children   42

Sue Books

3. Poverty and Youth Violence:
Not All Risk Factors Are Created Equal   59

Joseph A. Vorrasi and James Garbarino

4. Framing Children in the News:
The Face and Color of Youth Crime in America   78

LynNell Hancock

Part II: Schools, Violence, and Zero-Tolerance Policies

5. America's Least Wanted:
Zero-Tolerance Policies and the Fate of Expelled Students   101

Sasha Polakow-Suransky

6. Listen First: How Student Perspectives on Violence
    Can Be Used to Create Safer Schools   130

    Pedro A. Noguera

Part III: Juvenile Injustice

7. "Look Out, Kid, It's Something You Did":
    The Criminalization of Children   157

    Bernadine Dohrn

8. Throwaway Children:
    Conditions of Confinement and Incarceration   188

    James Bell

Afterword   211

    Maxine Greene

About the Editor and the Contributors   213

Index   217

Foreword

As the wheels go down beneath an airplane landing at LaGuardia Airport in New York City, passengers on the right side of the plane get a bird's eye view of Rikers Island, which, with 20,000 inmates—virtually all of them black or Hispanic—is the largest and most racially consistent penal colony in the entire world. Across the water from the prison island one can also see a very large and rather modernistic structure, blue and white, which, from the air, looks like a cruise ship of some sort but is, in fact, a multi-story prison barge to which, from 1996 to 1999, thousands of juveniles were brought in chains to be incarcerated pending their assignment to more permanent facilities.

One hundred children at a time were held in cells at water level, or below, for periods of ten days or more while waiting for the gears of bureaucratic law to finalize their disposition. Very few people looking from the window of a plane would have believed that they were looking at a prison barge for children—in New York!—a city once regarded as a bastion of humanitarian ideas about the nurturing of youth. Fewer still could have imagined how much money our society was spending to entomb these children on a floating structure without windows.

The barge is no longer home to children now. Three secure facilities, all land-based, two in the South Bronx, now hold the city's juvenile detainees. The cost per child for a year's detention: $93,000. Cost per child for a year of public school in the South Bronx: about $8,000. The underfinanced and overcrowded public schools hold kids in classes as large as 35 or 40. Class size in the newest of the three detention centers, which I visited this spring, is typically 12 children.

A teenage boy from the South Bronx whom I have known for many years—one of very few in his impoverished neighborhood who has graduated high school and is on his way to college—came with me the day I visited the costly new detention center in his neighborhood. He was amazed to see its beautiful facilities and to learn how much it costs to keep a child there. He's a sophisticated boy. Thank God he also has a sense of irony.

"Is this what it takes," he asked, "for kids to get some real attention in New York?"

He's Hispanic and he noticed too that every child in the children's prison was a child of color. There was not a single White kid behind bars.

At issue are the values of a nation that writes off so many of its poorest children in deficient urban schools starved of all the riches found in good suburban schools nearby, criminalizes those it has short-changed and cheated, and then willingly expends ten times as much to punish them as it has ever spent to teach them when they were still innocent and clean. The moral and political questions that this poses about national priorities lie at the heart of every chapter in this book.

Children's advocates and educators everywhere will find the contributions here assembled of tremendous value in their daily struggle to resist the present tide of punitive and often vengeful social policy that seems to value children more and more as clients of the growing prison industry, and less and less as future citizens of a republic. My favorite sections of this book are both by people I have known for many years—Valerie Polakow and Bernardine Dohrn, both of whom are fervent and persistent advocates for children; but the entire volume presents powerful and compelling voices for children and has a cumulative impact that should force debate and raise important questions for all readers. I hope it will be widely read and that the questions that it raises will be given the political response that they demand.

Jonathan Kozol

The Public Assault on America's Children

POVERTY, VIOLENCE, AND JUVENILE INJUSTICE

Introduction

Savage Policies

Systemic Violence and the Lives of Children

VALERIE POLAKOW

The time has come to decide what we want to do. I'm convinced the entire population is blind, at least that is my impression from observing the behavior of the people I have seen so far . . . .

I cannot say whether there will be a future, what matters for the moment is to see how we can live in the present. Without a future the present serves no purpose, it's as if it did not exist. Perhaps humanity will manage to live without eyes, but then it will cease to be humanity.

—José Saramago, *Blindness*, pp. 228–229

This book examines systemic violence against children in the United States: the violence of poverty and homelessness, the violence of environmentally induced childhood diseases, the violence confronting children in schools and communities, the media and legislative "criminalization" of children, and a national drumbeat of "zero-tolerance" leading to the increasing confinement and incarceration of youthful offenders. The dominant discourse of punishment and retribution, the role of the state in terms of private or public responsibility, and the developmental needs and rights of the child set against the backdrop of a withered welfare state are all themes that frame the multiple advocacy perspectives presented by the authors in this volume.

Grave violations of children's human rights in a juvenile justice system run amuck; rapidly eroding social-citizenship rights to a childhood free from poverty, destitution, hunger, and homelessness; the deprivation of educational rights by mandatory expulsion policies—all are part of the postmodern terrors of a vulnerable childhood. Whose children do we see when we construct the meaning of childhood at the dawn of the new century in the United States? Which young lives matter and which young lives do not?

THE WITHERED WELFARE STATE AND ITS YOUNG VICTIMS

Public policies make and unmake young lives. The United States stands alone among all industrialized democratic societies in failing to provide social insurance polices for parents and children. While social security for elderly Americans is still considered an earned entitlement, a social security system for children, who in turn must depend on their parents' benefits, forms part of a completely different discourse. Poor parents, and specifically poor single mothers, are constructed as "moral threats" undeserving of government support. The federal welfare program AFDC (Aid to Families with Dependent Children), established in 1935 as Title 1VA of the Social Security Act, guaranteed means-tested federal assistance to children in poor families. This limited federal entitlement has now been gutted as a result of the passage of the Personal Responsibility and Work Opportunity Reconciliation Act (PL 104-193) which President Clinton signed on August 22, 1996, proclaiming "the end of welfare as we know it." Thus the residual social safety net was decisively shredded, effectively ending poor children's entitlement to minimal forms of public assistance.[1]

Temporary Assistance to Needy Families (TANF) block grants to states replaced the former AFDC and were tied to a set of mandatory work requirements that custodial parents, predominantly single mothers, were required to meet in order for the family to qualify for public assistance. The mandatory work requirements have escalated yearly: from 20 hours in fiscal years 1997 and 1998, to 25 in 1999, and 30 in 2000. While the federal welfare law grants waivers for mandatory work requirements for single mothers with children younger than one year old, many states have adopted more stringent requirements. In Michigan, Massachusetts, New York, and Wisconsin, the waiver from work requirements only applies to mothers with infants younger than 12 weeks, exacerbating an acute national crisis in child care for infants and toddlers. After 2 consecutive years, states may choose to cut all benefits whether or not welfare recipients have found employment, and there is a lifetime limit of 5 years on public assistance for the entire family. In addition, there have been sweeping cuts of services to legal immigrants, their children, and their aging parents, as well as cuts to thousands of disabled poor children who have lost their disability payments due to far more stringent eligibility requirements. And despite recent amend- ments to reinstate certain classes of disabled children, thousands continue to suffer from the benefit cuts. Food stamps continue to be denied to many legal immigrants, to single unemployed adults after 3 months, and to single- parent households who are sanctioned for noncompliance with work re- quirements (Super, Parrot, Steinmetz, & Mann, 1996; Children's Defense Fund, 1998).

As states rush to demonstrate "the end of welfare," there has been a precipitous drop in the number of people receiving welfare across the na- tion. As of March 1999, welfare rolls (two thirds of welfare recipients were dependent children) declined by 47%—from a high of 14 million in 1994 to 7 million in 1999 (DeParle, 1999). Recipients who left welfare for work averaged only about $6.60 an hour in wages with 75% lacking health bene- fits, and the poorest 20% of families lost more in benefits (approximately $1,400 a year) than they actually gained in earnings (Weinstein, 1999).

There is also growing evidence that most recipients who are cut from assistance do not actually find jobs, but that rather welfare caseload declines are due to the widespread imposition of sanctions for noncompliance. In New York City, for example, when Rudolph Giuliani took office as mayor, he promised to end welfare completely by the end of the century. Conse- quently New York City has eliminated 400,000 clients, the majority of whom are single mothers with children, from the welfare rolls since 1996 (DeParle, 1998).

As the number of families with children on welfare continues to de- cline across the nation, there is little evidence of increasing economic self- sufficiency or family viability. Rather, many critics see this as a corporate "business-politics" strategy for coercing cheap labor from women in an ex- panding low-wage service sector economy that offers neither benefits, job security, nor a living wage (Piven, 1998). In Michigan, for example, a state study tracking welfare recipients found that only 11% of "Work First" clients were considered successful "graduates," working at least 20 hours a week 3 months after starting a job. The Jobs Commission reported that those recipients who do find jobs make about $8,560 per year ("Eighty Percent Work First Graduates," 1998), which for a family of three is about 75% of the federal poverty line.

The Children's Defense Fund and the National Coalition for the Home- less have released a joint report on family hardship and well-being (Sherman et al., 1998) that cites disturbing findings that also fly in the face of media and legislative claims celebrating the rapid drops in welfare caseloads. The report documents that as more and more families are being pushed off welfare into the low-wage work force, 71% of workers earn below the federal poverty level for a family of three. The authors also report a proliferation of low-wage, short-term employment, and multiple child care problems in terms of access, quality, and affordability. With more than 14 million children living in poverty, the number of destitute children living below one half of the poverty line (less than $6,401 for a three-person family in 1997) has grown by almost half a million children since welfare "reforms" were instituted. In addition to the increase in extreme child poverty among families who were already impoverished, there is increasing hunger and homelessness in poor urban and rural communities, and decreasing access to Medicaid and food stamps (Sherman et al., 1998). The damage of welfare "reform" in terms of the violence done to young children is yet to be made visible as families' lives unravel in a ravaging market economy, where public infrastructures are crumbling and income inequality is soaring. For the children at the bottom of the well, the booming economy neither splashes nor trickles down.

Given these grim realities, what happens to young children whose single mothers are forced into mandatory work requirements without access to affordable and good-quality child care? What family stresses and developmental scars result? Consider the case of Kathy, a young mother of a 4-year-old child in Michigan. She tells:

> I was working as a cashier for $5.25 an hour. . . . I had no money for day care and then I lost my job because they said I had to work the night shift and who was there to care for my daughter? So they fired me and then the eviction notice came . . . and then they cut me off (welfare) because I didn't meet the work requirements—and we lost food stamps and Medicaid, some days we ran out of food—it was terrible . . . and soon after we ended up in a shelter and my daughter was traumatized . . . and that's when the nightmare began . . . [2]

Kathy's abrupt fall into homelessness with her young daughter, 2 years after a traumatic experience of domestic violence, was the final straw as her shattered life continued to spiral downward, eventually causing her to lose her daughter to foster care. However, her tragic story is not unusual; rather, it reflects the pernicious cycle of sanctions, public assistance cuts, and destitution that characterize the nuts and bolts of daily life for many poor mothers under the systemic violence of the new welfare regime, which wreaks untold damage on single mothers and their children. Further, what developmental damage has been done to Kathy's young daughter, Sarah, whose childhood has fallen victim to a public policy assault on her vulnerable family?

Consider the situation of Chris, the 16-month-old son of another single mother in Michigan. Mary was told she had to work 30 hours a week in exchange for benefits, despite the federal law that explicitly limits the mandatory work requirements of mothers with children under 6 to a maximum of 20 hours per week. Mary reluctantly placed her son in an unsatisfactory child care center and received a state child care subsidy, but it only covered actual hours of care. Most child care centers charge part- or full-time rates. Mary found herself still having to pay an additional co-pay of $55 per week, $220 per month, out of a welfare benefit and low-wage job that brought her a combined monthly income of $700. As she was unable to find subsidized housing (there was a 2-year wait in her county), she paid $400 a month for the top floor of a house in a dangerous neighborhood. After paying child care and housing costs, and using up her food stamp allowance, Mary was left with $80 a month to take care of all their other expenses including additional food, transportation, utilities, clothing, and other personal needs. When Chris developed asthma, her anxieties about the substandard care he was receiving at his day care increased, and she had frequent absences from work due to his respiratory illnesses. When she was fired, her welfare benefits were cut, she was unable to pay the rent, and her child care subsidies were terminated, resulting in her removal of Chris from his child care center. Thus she and Chris began their descent into the increasingly familiar netherworld of welfare's discards.

However, Chris and Mary's story was still an existential cut above stories of infants placed in developmentally dangerous child care. One young mother, Shari, described removing her 20-week-old infant from an unlicensed home where her baby was neither held nor changed regularly; he, together with seven other infants, was strapped in an infant seat and fed by a propped-up bottle, and Shari describes how "the floor was filthy and there were roaches and her refrigerator didn't work right so I worried about his milk being bad." Shari chose to quit her mandatory low-wage job and take care of her own son. However, as a poor mother dependent on state assistance, she did not have the right to exercise that choice without severe penalties, and state retribution was swift: She and her son lost their benefits for noncompliance, and with no network of family in the area, mother and child faced the prospect of homelessness.

From Michigan to New York and across the country, the crisis of child care follows a recognizable pattern of damaged young lives and closed access. *The New York Times* reported that in New York City in 1997 there were 47,871 children of welfare mothers in need of care, but only 18,638 slots were available. And in Manhattan, there were no licensed infant slots at all! One young woman describes her fears when a caseworker threatened to reduce and cut her benefits unless she accepted a work assignment.

Wendy Verso tells of leaving her 17-month-old with a woman who kept the infant strapped to a dirty stroller all day "for safety" as she cared for additional children (Swarns, 1998).

The personal narratives of desperate mothers placing their children in developmentally damaging care are confirmed by systematic national studies that have documented the acute crisis of affordable quality care that began prior to welfare "reform" and that has only worsened in the years since 1996. These national reports on child care documented widespread problems in many states for low-income children: unsafe, unsanitary centers, poor-quality care—with particular concerns raised about substandard and dangerous care for infants and toddlers—and lack of regulation, closed access, and chronic unavailability to low-income families (Children's Defense Fund, 1996; Ebb, 1994; U.S. General Accounting Office, 1993). Findings from the 1995 *Cost, Quality, and Outcomes Study* raised urgent concerns about the level of care for infants and toddlers: Child care at most centers was rated as poor to mediocre, and only 8% of the infant/toddler rooms received a rating of "good" quality, with more than 40% receiving a rating of less than minimal quality—and these ratings were of licensed settings! (Helburn, 1995).

In the absence of a comprehensive national child care system, child care must be sought on the private market, which at licensed centers is prohibitive, ranging from $5,000 to $12,000 per year, more than the cost of annual tuition at many universities. Decades of research have consistently confirmed the benefits of high-quality early education intervention programs for low-income "at-risk" children, particularly in terms of elementary school outcomes (Federal Interagency Forum on Child and Family Statistics, 1997; Zigler & Styfco, 1993), yet only about 36% of income-eligible children are currently served by Head Start (Children's Defense Fund, 1998). Such lack of access to early intervention programs and high-quality child care constitutes an ongoing chronic problem for poor mothers. The new *Cost, Quality, and Outcomes Study* (Frank Porter Graham Child Development Center, 1999) reiterates the links between quality child care and school readiness, and the developmental damage that results from poor-quality care. Children who had received poor-quality child care during early childhood showed damaging impacts in terms of school success as early as second grade. Poor children also have limited access to school-age care and after-school programs (see Brayfield, Deich, & Hofferth, 1993; Caspar, Hawkins, & O'Connell, 1994). The absence of adequate after-school care, late-hour-shift care, sick-child care, and supervision of adolescents creates additional burdens, as mothers who require these services must constantly juggle work and family demands, with frequent high costs to their children's safety and well-being (Polakow, 1993).

Inaccessible and unaffordable care has resulted in a proliferation of nonregulated, nonlicensed care across the country. No monitoring and no standards are enforced and many such providers are poor themselves and live in dangerous neighborhoods marked by ongoing poverty, domestic violence, and histories of abuse (Ebb, 1994). In Michigan such informal care accounted for 88.8% of all child care provided for welfare recipients receiving subsidies in August 1999 (Kahn & Polakow, 2000). Unlicensed day care aides enrolled by FIA may be paid as little as $1.35 per hour per child. So lax are the screening procedures that a recent State audit revealed that the FIA enrolled and paid 274 day care aides and relative providers with convictions for crimes against children, including criminal sexual conduct. An additional 6220 enrolled aides and providers were found to have committed other crimes serious enough to warrant termination of enrollment in other states. Crimes ranged from homicide to armed robbery to delivery of drugs (State of Michigan Office of the Auditor General, 2000). The acute child care crisis for low-income mothers in Michigan is replicated across the country: poor screening and monitoring of aides and providers in non-licensed settings, low rates of child care subsidy reimbursement, late payments by state agencies—all create desperate decisions and ominous outcomes for poor children.

Gwendolyn Mink (1998) argues that the new welfare law "removes poor single mothers from the welfare state to a police state . . . as they are forced to purchase their families' long-term survival by sacrificing basic rights the rest of us take for granted" (p. 133). It is emblematic that such antimaternalism first emerged from a right-wing "family values" Republican assault on single mothers, who were publicly denounced in Congress and demonized on national television as "breeding mules," "alligators," and "monkeys" (Polakow, 1997). Representative Clay Shaw, Jr., who shepherded welfare legislation through the House, stated that "it may be like hitting a mule with a two by four but you've got to get their attention" (DeParle, 1994, p. 1).

This public assault took place against a backdrop of increasing poverty, destitution, and homelessness for the poorest children. During the 1990s, as welfare was being dismantled, single mothers constituted 70–90% of homeless families nationwide (Bassuk, 1990; Bassuk et al., 1996; Steinbock, 1995); more than 50% of homeless families became homeless because the mother fled domestic violence (National Clearinghouse for the Defense of Battered Women, 1994); and one in four homeless persons was a child younger than 18 (National Coalition for the Homeless, 1996). Furthermore, reports from the Food and Research Action Center indicated that 13.6 million children younger than 12 were hungry for part of each month (Children's Defense Fund, 1996), and that by 1997, despite increasing federal attempts to insure children, 11.6 million children remained without health insurance and two thirds of uninsured children were without coverage for more than 6 months (Children's Defense Fund, 1999). Despite the record of the United States in failing to develop social insurance policies that provide for the basic health, shelter, and daily living needs of its most vulnerable citizens—poor children—poverty was cast as a "moral" problem, tied to public rhetoric about "family values" and "family breakdown," which in turn was used to rationalize the demise of "welfare as we knew it." Mink (1998) points out that "welfare law now forbids mothers who remain single to work inside the home caring for their own children" (p. 30), thereby infringing on the rights of poor mothers to mother their own children and violating their family liberty, which includes "a constitutionally protected right 'to the care, custody, management, and companionship' of one's own children" (*May vs. Anderson,* quoted in Mink, 1998, p. 30).

Such is the path of systemic violence concealed under the discourse of "welfare reform" as millions of poor infants and young children become early state discards, shunted off to deplorable child care settings; and early developmental damage takes its silent toll in the form of social and cognitive impairments, post-traumatic stress disorders, and academic failure as the youngest of the poor are consigned to the "other childhood."

RIGHTS DENIED: THE MARGINALIZATION AND CRIMINALIZATION OF VULNERABLE CHILDREN

For poor school-age children, who are disproportionately children of color, clustered in neglected and underfinanced schools districts, an unequal education is, as Kozol (1991) puts it, "simply not contested" (p. 116). Similarly, educational intervention strategies are often framed in cost-benefit terms: "How much is it worth investing in this child as opposed to that one? Where will we see the best return?" (p. 117). Poor children are rarely seen as deserving beneficiaries of public money, and the older they are the less crumbs there are to spread around. Educational outcomes for poor children are significantly worse, and as race and poverty intersect—40% of African American and Latino children are living in poverty compared with 11% for Whites—the social capital of children of color is vastly diminished in comparison with that of White students. Underresourced schools—fewer books, fewer supplies, no Internet access, teachers lacking certification and training, lower teacher salaries, and buildings in need of repair—all characterize the school lives of children living in the poorest communities. Not only do the richest school districts spend 56% more per student than their poorest counterparts, but the physical and environmental conditions in many poor schools are in dire shape (Children's Defense Fund, 1999).

In *Amazing Grace,* Kozol (1995) documents the school lives of children in the South Bronx taught by "provisionals" or permanent substitutes, in overcrowded schools where classes take place on stair landings, in bathrooms, and in coat closets. With the added complication of neurological impairments from lead poisoning in dilapidated schools and homes, many of the children "suffer the emotional and physical attrition that results from chronic illnesses like asthma and anxiety, as well as the steady and low-level misery of rotting teeth, infected gums, and festering untreated sores" (p. 154). Yet as Kozol points out, such "socially created injuries" to intellect rarely feature in the debates about poor and minority children's academic achievements. What does predominate, however, is an "at-risk" discourse that pathologizes poor children and their families, ignores vast economic inequalities, and fails to confront the cumulative impact of racial and economic discrimination on children. As Swadener (1995) argues in her work deconstructing the ideology of risk, "The problem of locating pathology in the victim is the most objectionable tenet of the dominant rhetoric . . . placing yet another repressive label on an ever-widening group of young people and their families" (pp. 18–19). For children disenfranchised by poverty, the classroom is often a landscape of condemnation, where rigid drill routines and coercive teaching foster compliance and disengagement, resulting in the marginalization of students who do not "fit" (Polakow, 1993). And marginalization increases as children move into middle and high school, where national studies have consistently documented the failure of schools to educate "disadvantaged youth" (Knapp, 1995). More than a decade ago, Kenneth Clark (1988) indicted "this pattern of inferior education, of low standards and expectations [that] continues through secondary schools and culminates in failures, drop-outs and pushouts" (p. iv). In 1997, the racial disparity in high school drop-out rates remained stark at 7.6% for Whites, 13.4% for Blacks, and 25.3% for Hispanics (National Center for Education Statistics, 1997), where major factors contributing to such disparities are family poverty and underresourced schools (Children's Defense Fund, 1999). Suspension and expulsion too play a role as disproportionate numbers of poor adolescents and youth of color are suspended and expelled, increasing the likelihood of ultimate failure, which has only been exacerbated since the passage of the 1994 Gun Free Schools Act mandating a one-year expulsion for students who carry weapons onto school property. This law has further damaged the educational possibilities of marginal youth, resulting in mandatory expulsions of thousands of students for perceived weapons violations — without any provisions for educational alternatives or supportive therapeutic interventions (Education Commission of the States, 1996).

Homeless children form another marginalized youth constituency. Despite the reauthorization of the Stuart B. McKinney Act (1990) mandating that homeless children have the same access to public education and services that all other resident children receive, approximately 23% of the 750,000 homeless school-age children do not attend school regularly. When they do squeeze through the schoolhouse door, they encounter a plethora of obstacles that have been extensively documented: problems encountered with transfer of records, chronic health problems, lower scores on standardized tests, grade retention, lack of remediation and special services, and multiple emotional impairments related to the stress, the shame, and the disrupted daily lives that form part of the terrors of homelessness (National Law Center on Homelessness and Poverty, 1995; Polakow, 1998; Rafferty, 1995).

Hence for both preschool and school-age children, the multiple systemic assaults encountered as part of childhood on the edges have a cumulative effect where, as the Norwegian researcher Johan Galtung (1969) put it, "the violence is built into the structure and shows up as unequal power and consequently as unequal life chances" (p. 169).

These unequal life chances take an even more sinister turn as current policies commit vast numbers of juvenile offenders to zones of indifference and invisibility—where the most troubled children are demonized as predatory criminals beyond the reach of rehabilitation, intervention, and education. Public discourse reflects the shift in public attitudes about children as more and more states are clamoring to adopt lowered minimum ages at which children may be tried and sentenced as adults; and in Texas, legislator Jim Pitts has called for lowering the minimum age for the death penalty to 11-year-olds. Furthermore, racial disparities among white youth and youth of color are dramatic, revealing pervasive discrimination at all stages of the juvenile process (Butterfield, 2000).

Such disturbing policy trends, perpetrated in state after state, serve to "criminalize" youth; yet they fail to address the systemic violence, the abuse, the domestic violence, the neighborhood violence, and the developmental damage that so many children have experienced as part of their "socially toxic environments" (Garbarino, 1995). The public outcry about juvenile crime and the federal and state responses have focused on "zero-tolerance" policies and moving children into adult courts and prisons; yet there is little legislative support to reduce the wide availability and access to guns or to fund community prevention and after-school efforts on any large scale, in order to avert the "deadly consequences" (Prothrow-Stith, 1991) that ensue when violence prevention is seen neither as an educational nor as a public health issue. Most juvenile crime occurs between 3 and 7 p.m., yet child care, school-age care, and adolescent extracurricular activities are vastly underfunded. Significant too is the fact that children and youth are 10 times more likely to be victims than perpetrators of violence (an average of 14 children die each day from gunfire) and that most children who suffer violence are victims of adults (Children's Defense Fund, 1998).

The shift from rehabilitation to incarceration, the growth of punk prisons, and the increase in prison budgets and decrease in education budgets, have created an alarming industry of incarceration. As increasing numbers of ever younger children are placed in the adult criminal system, alarming violations of their human rights have taken place. Amnesty International (1998) reports that children who are in juvenile custody "have been subjected to brutal physical force and cruel punishments . . . [and that] once they enter the juvenile justice system of the USA, many children experience violations of their fundamental human rights" (p. 1); that 200,000 children a year are prosecuted in general criminal courts; that 7,000 are held in jails before trial; and that more than 11,000 are in prisons and other long-term adult correctional facilities in violation of international human rights treaties. The United States has also failed to implement certain provisions of the ICCPR (International Covenant on Civil and Political Rights) that protect the human rights of children, such as the prohibition of the death penalty for crimes committed by children before age 18, and the United States has still not ratified the Convention on the Rights of the Child. Alone among 192 governments, the United States and Somalia are the only two members of the United Nations not to ratify the Convention.

As we explore the violations of the human rights of children, the pernicious public policies that have targeted our most vulnerable children and youth, the shredded social safety net that has wreaked existential havoc in so many young lives, there is much to be confronted, and more important, much to be done. One of the purposes of this volume is to document and inform—to serve as an urgent wake-up call about the rights of vulnerable children who are most often poor and members of minority communities. It is clear that there are also other toxic forms of violence that take place: physical and sexual abuse and domestic violence, which create private and intimate horrors that assault and damage all children's lives; and other forms of systemic violence that target nonpoor and affluent children. These forms of violence have not been specifically addressed in this volume. *The Public Assault on America's Children* explicitly focuses on systemic violence in the public space, and the authors of this volume all confront public policies and public discourses in those public spaces that shape and imperil vulnerable young lives.

ORGANIZATION OF THE BOOK

In Part I, "Poverty, Violence, and the Lived Realities of Children," both historical and contemporary forms of violence are discussed. Barbara Finkelstein, in Chapter 1, grounds our understanding of systemic violence against children in three "time-honored traditions": the religious, the political, and the socioeconomic, and points out the myriad of contradictions "that have made the United States a beacon of human rights for other nations, but have not guaranteed safe havens for children here at home." Each of these traditions has in turn protected the privacy of the family, impeded the development of social insurance policies for children, curtailed the scope of child intervention and protection, and rendered poor children vulnerable to adverse circumstances and consigned them to zones of public invisibility; and ultimately each has "provided sanctuary for the nurture of violence against children and youth." Confronting violence against children, Finkelstein argues, forces us "to grapple with the contradictory character of our most cherished beliefs and practices."

In Chapter 2, Sue Books analyses the social etiology of environmentally induced damage to children, pointing out that poor children are 50% more likely to die during childhood and arguing that this is not merely an unfortunate occurrence but an inevitable consequence of the systemic violence that besets poor children's lives. She discusses the alarming rise in tuberculosis and asthma, and the disproportionate exposure of poor children to lead poisoning—all inextricably linked to poverty, bad housing conditions, and gross inequities in health care and delivery. Too often, Books points out, environmentally induced damage is decontextualized and construed as an affliction of "other people's children," as a private responsibility, or as an unintended consequence, rather than as "the predictable consequence of social injustice," which she argues demands recognition as a "moral and social horror."

Joseph Vorrasi and James Garbarino in Chapter 3 explore the intricate interrelationship between poverty and youth violence and point to the damage incurred in environments "filled with threats such as violence, racism, unstable care arrangements, economic deprivation, and community insecurity." Such "socially toxic" worlds, in which poverty is a central element, poison children's development and create debilitating outcomes. The authors present an illuminating case study of Malcolm, a young boy trapped in a socially toxic world in which economic inequality, drugs, the illicit economy, and youth violence converge—as Malcolm attempts, unsuccessfully, to ensure the physical and psychological survival of his family. The tragic consequences are emblematic of yet another discarded poor young life.

In Chapter 4, LynNell Hancock examines the media framing of youth crime in America and the role that the media plays in shaping "the fear of other people's children." In her analysis of the media coverage of the two "littlest murder suspects" in Chicago, Hancock raises disturbing issues of dehumanized, objectified reporting, where unquestioned credibility is accorded to the police version of events. The framing of two 8-year-olds as "remorseless thugs" is very much in keeping with the larger public framing of "superpredator" youth, particularly youth of color, as living in "fatherless, godless, jobless" families. Hancock points out that juvenile crime is decontextualized and racialized, largely disconnected from adult crime and social or family conditions; for "adults kill children at a far more astonishing rate than kids do, but the crimes are not always given equal column inches. Ninety percent of the murders of children under 12, and three fourths of the murders of 12- through 17-year-olds are committed by adults." In the wake of recent school shootings, Hancock raises further disturbing questions about the face and geography of youth crime, and the damage done to children's rights.

Part II, "Schools, Violence, and Zero-Tolerance Polices," shifts the spotlight to American schools, the impact of expulsion policies, and school violence. The authors also present the voices of students who describe their own experiences of marginalization and their perceptions of violence and safety in school. In Chapter 5, Sasha Polakow-Suransky analyzes zero-tolerance legislation against the backdrop of the federal Gun Free Schools Act of 1994. He points out that within one year after passage of the law, every state had introduced zero-tolerance legislation with mandatory expulsion policies to punish students bringing weapons, drugs, or any other dangerous artifacts into school. Under such zero-tolerance policies, students are expelled for seemingly innocuous childish offenses such as that of a third grader bringing a 1-inch plastic gun to school. Such mandatory expulsion policies give schools license to exclude students for indefinite periods of time. A case study of the state of Michigan is presented as illustrative of one of the harshest zero-tolerance states in the nation. The case study reveals disproportionately racialized expulsions and a deplorable lack of alternative education placements, depriving hundreds of school-age children of their right to an education, which, Polakow-Suransky argues, amounts to legally sanctioned truancy: "Such is the sad irony of a society in which we condemn those parents who abandon their children but condone those schools that abandon theirs."

Pedro Noguera, focusing on school violence and school safety in Chapter 6, argues that American schoolchildren live in a violence-suffused society that fails to recognize the connections between the "deplorable social conditions under which large numbers of children live and the increased likelihood that these same children will become victims or perpetrators of violence." In the aftermath of school shootings, many school districts have rushed to high-tech surveillance measures, armed security guards, and increased suspensions and expulsions. Noguera criticizes these social-control measures as ineffective, and argues that very little effort has been undertaken to explore youth attitudes and perceptions about violence, to understand the school's social climate, or to listen to students' voices. Noguera presents illustrative findings from his own action research conducted at two California middle schools and points out that ultimately schools that do succeed in producing safe environments are schools that repudiate intimidation and coercion and foster supportive relationships between students and adults.

The third and final part of the book, "Juvenile Injustice," focuses on the criminalization of children and the conditions of confinement and incarceration for youth. Both Bernadine Dohrn and James Bell present us with the grim realities of throwaway children and the injustices meted out to them as juvenile offenders who are increasingly crimimalized. In Chapter 7 Dohrn notes that between 1985 and 1994, 25,000 children were murdered in the United States, so that "there is the equivalent of a Columbine every day in America." Furthermore, the racially coded public perceptions of children in trouble with the law is evident in both the starkly differentiated constructions of youth of color as deadly thugs and superpredators, contrasted with the alienated-loner imagery that permeated the highly sensationalized schoolyard massacres by white youth. As zero-tolerance for troubled children becomes a national drumbeat, Dohrn shows how there has been an escalating trend of criminalizing children for offenses once viewed through a prism of juvenile misbehavior: From policing schools and school-based arrests, to school expulsions, to the lowering of termination age in foster care, to the revival of status offenses, to the expansion of adult-court jurisdiction through trying more children as adult criminals, we see there are increasing numbers of court cases, more and more detained and incarcerated youth in overcrowded facilities, and vast shifts in fiscal priorities from education to incarceration. All this, Dohrn reminds us, heralds "an erosion of civic responsibility for children" as society continues "on its current course of escalating punishments for children and increasing adult abdication of responsibility."

Dohrn's indictment of the injustices meted out to troubled children, the violations of their rights, and the abdication of adult responsibility is amplified by James Bell in Chapter 8 as he describes the often brutal conditions of incarceration and confinement experienced by "throwaway children" where "the nexus of color and adolescence have converged . . . that has juveniles being confined in numbers that cannot be accounted for by criminal activity alone and should give pause to any civil society." He points out that although juvenile crime has decreased, the confinement of juveniles continues to increase, resulting in violations of their rights and overcrowding in a juvenile justice system rife with institutional racism. Bell urges juvenile justice professionals to oppose the "get tough on juvenile crime" legislation that has so demonized young people of color. After describing juvenile facilities, Bell systematically analyzes conditions of confinement drawing from his many years of experience in monitoring facilities, conducting inspections, and litigating cases. Key problems encountered are insufficient resources, overcrowding, poor medical screening, untrained mental health personnel, delayed access to educational programming, lack of safety of the physical surroundings, and the use of isolation and of chemical agents such as pepper spray. Bell advocates strongly for individualized and comprehensive interventions that support juvenile offenders with a focus on their strengths rather than their deficits. He argues that our punitive and retributive policies and practices are "worse than those of any other industrialized nation and are simply unacceptable."

In *The Public Assault on America's Children,* the authors trace the multiple contours of systemic violence: from the deep historical roots that sustain it, to the poverty and developmental damage, to schools as sites of marginalization and exclusion, to the injustices that inhere in the juvenile justice system. To render visible the injustices meted out to our youngest and most vulnerable members of our society, to uncover what has been concealed, and to confront the all-encompassing blindness that has permitted such systemic violence against children to sprout in so many corners of our public space forms an underlying rationale for this book: As the doctor's wife reminds us in José Saramago's prophetic novel (1997), failure to "see" creates a terrifying "white" blindness whose translucence permits the abrogation of human rights and poisons the possibility of our human future.

NOTES

1. The research on the impact of recent federal welfare legislation on the lives of single mothers and their children is part of a larger ongoing study conducted in partnership with Peggy Kahn, University of Michigan, Flint.

2. The interviews cited here were conducted in 1998 and 1999. All names have been changed to protect confidentiality.

REFERENCES

Amnesty International. (1998, November). *Betraying the young: Children in the U.S. justice system.* Washington, DC: Author.

Bassuk, E. L. (1990). Who are the homeless families?: Characteristics of sheltered mothers and children. *Community Mental Health Journal, 26,* 425–434.

Bassuk, E. L., Bassuk, S. S., Browne, A., Buckner, J. C., Salomon, A., & Weinreb, L. F. (1996). Caring for the uninsured and underinsured: The characteristics and needs of sheltered homeless and low-income housed mothers. *Journal of the American Medical Association, 276*(8), 640–646.

Brayfield, A. A., Deich, S., & Hofferth, S. L. (1993). *Caring for children in low-income families*. Washington, DC: Urban Institute Press.

Butterfield, F. (2000, April 26). Racial disparities seen as pervasive in juvenile justice. *The New York Times,* pp. A1, A18.

Caspar, L. M., Hawkins, M., & O'Connell, M. (1994). *Who's minding the kids? Child care arrangements: Fall 1991*. U.S. Bureau of the Census. Current Population Reports, P-70, no. 36. Washington, DC: U.S. Government Printing Office.

Children's Defense Fund. (1996). *The state of America's children: Yearbook*. Washington, DC: Author.

Children's Defense Fund. (1997). *The state of America's children: Yearbook*. Washington, DC: Author.

Children's Defense Fund. (1998). *The state of America's children: Yearbook*. Washington, DC: Author.

Children's Defense Fund. (1999). *The state of America's children: Yearbook*. Washington, DC: Author.

Clark, K. (1988). Foreword. In R. C. Smith & C. Lincoln (Eds.), *America's shame, America's hope: Twelve million youth at risk* (pp. iv–v). Chapel Hill, NC: MDC.

DeParle, J. (1994, November 13). Momentum builds for cutting back welfare system. *The New York Times,* pp. A1, A30.

DeParle, J. (1998, December 20). What welfare to work really means. *The New York Times Magazine,* pp. 50–59, 70, 72, 74, 88–89.

DeParle, J. (1999, August 29). States struggle to use windfall born of shifts in welfare law. *The New York Times,* pp. A1, A30–A31.

Ebb, N. (1994). *Child care tradeoffs: States make painful choices*. Washington, DC: Children's Defense Fund.

Education Commission of the States. (1996, May). *Clearinghouse notes*. Denver: Author.

Eighty percent Work First graduates still working. (1998, March 9). *Ann Arbor News,* p. C3.

Federal Interagency Forum on Child and Family Statistics. (1997). *America's children: Key national indicators of well-being*. Washington, DC: Author.

Frank Porter Graham Child Development Center. (1999). *Cost, quality, and outcomes study*. Chapel Hill: University of North Carolina.

Galtung, J. (1969). Violence, peace, and peace research. *Journal of Peace Research, 6*(1), 167–191.

Garbarino, J. (1995). *Raising children in a socially toxic environment*. San Francisco: Jossey-Bass.

Gun Free Schools Act of 1994, 20 U.S.C. § 8921(e).

Helburn, S. (Ed.). (1995). *Cost, quality, and child outcomes in child care centers*. Denver: University of Colorado (Eric Document Reproduction Service No. ED 386 297).

Kahn, P., & Polakow, V. (2000). Mothering denied: Commodification and caregiving under new U.S. welfare laws. *Sage Race Relations Abstracts, 25*(1), 7–25.

Knapp, M. S. (1995). *Teaching for meaning in high poverty classrooms.* New York: Teachers College Press.

Kozol, J. (1991). *Savage inequalities: Children in America's schools.* New York: Crown.

Kozol, J. (1995). *Amazing grace: The lives of children and the conscience of a nation.* New York: HarperCollins.

Mink, G. (1998). *Welfare's end.* Ithaca: Cornell University Press.

National Center for Education Statistics. (1997). *Dropout rates in the United States, 1997.* Washington, DC: U.S. Department of Education.

National Clearinghouse for the Defense of Battered Women. (1994, February). *Statistics packet* (3rd ed.). Philadelphia: Author.

National Coalition for the Homeless. (1996). *Welfare repeal: Moving Americans off welfare into homelessness.* Washington, DC: Author.

National Law Center on Homelessness and Poverty. (1995). *A foot in the schoolhouse door.* Washington, DC: Author.

Personal Responsibility and Work Opportunity Reconciliation Act of 1996, Pub. Law No. 104-193, H.R. 3734.

Piven, F. F. (1998). Welfare and work. *Social Justice: A Journal of Crime, Conflict, and World Order, 25*(2), 67–81.

Polakow, V. (1993). *Lives on the edge: Single mothers and their children in the other America.* Chicago: University of Chicago Press.

Polakow, V. (1997). The shredded net: The end of welfare as we knew it. *Sage Race Relations Abstracts, 22*(3), 3–22.

Polakow, V. (1998). Homeless children and their families: The discards of the postmodern 1990s. In S. Books (Ed.), *Invisible children in the society and its schools* (pp. 3–22). Mahwah, NJ: Lawrence Erlbaum.

Prothrow-Stith, D. (1991). *Deadly consequences.* New York: HarperCollins.

Rafferty, Y. (1995). The legal rights and educational problems of homeless children and youth. *Educational Foundations and Policy Analysis, 17*(1), 39–61.

Saramago, J. (1997). *Blindness* (G. Pontiero, Trans.). New York: Harcourt Brace. (Original work published in Portuguese in 1995)

Sherman, A., et al. (1998, December). *Welfare to what? Early findings on family hardship and well-being.* Washington, DC: Children's Defense Fund.

State of Michigan Office of the Auditor General. (2000, January). *Performance and financial related audit of the child development and care program, Family Independence Agency.* Lansing, MI: Author.

Steinbock, M. (1995). Homeless female-headed families: Relationships at risk. *Marriage and Family Review, 20*(1/2), 143–159.

Stewart B. McKinney Act Homeless Assistance Amendments Act of 1990, Pub. Law No. 101-645.

Super, D., Parrot, S., Steinmetz, S., & Mann, C. (1996). *The new welfare law.* Washington, DC: Center on Budget and Policy Priorities.

Swadener, B. B. (1995). Children and families "at promise": Deconstructing the discourse of risk. In B. B. Swadener & S. Lubeck (Eds.), *Children and families "at promise": Deconstructing the discourse of risk* (pp. 17–49). Albany: State University of New York Press.

Swarns, R. (1998, April 14). Mothers poised for Workfare face acute lack of daycare. *The New York Times,* pp. A1, A20.

U.S. General Accounting Office. (1993). *Review of health and safety standards at child care facilities.* Washington, DC: Department of Health and Human Services.

Weinstein, J. (1999, August 26). When work is not enough. *The New York Times,* pp. C1, C6.

Zigler, E., & Styfco, S. J. (Eds.). (1993). *Head Start and beyond: A national plan for extended early childhood intervention.* New Haven: Yale University Press.

PART I

Poverty, Violence, and the Lived Realities of Children

A Crucible of Contradictions
Historical Roots of Violence Against Children in the United States

BARBARA FINKELSTEIN

SITUATING THE PROBLEM

The practice of violence against children is a time-honored tradition in the United States. Indeed, the roots of violence are planted deeply in the soil of religious beliefs, in the bedrock of public law, and in the disciplinary practices, child-rearing beliefs, and authority structures of families across the social and racial spectrum (deMause, 1974; Garbarino, 1997; Gordon, 1988; Petersen del Mar, 1996). Violence against children has been visible in the informal spaces of children's lives in neighborhoods, streets, playgrounds, and schools (Greven, 1991; Schlossman, 1977; Weis & Marusza, 1998); in the grounded routines and practices of legally constituted educational institutions (Books, 1998; Finkelstein, 1989; Greven, 1991; Wollons, 1988); in the deep structures of gender, class, and race relations in the United States (Fine & Weis, 1998; Gordon, 1988; Michel, 1999); and in the cultural messages that have been projected through popular literature and the mass media.

If traditions of violence against children are time honored in the United States, so too are an array of dialectically linked countertraditions that serial generations of social reformers have organized in an attempt to elevate the status of children; envelop them in blankets of legal, moral, social, cultural, and ideological protection; and root out violence from the arsenal of permissible disciplinary actions taken against them.

21

The attempt to exorcise violence from children's lives is expressed in a series of social discoveries that, over the course of time, have unpeeled an array of once invisible forms of violence that have beset the lives of children. There was the discovery of childhood innocence among Romantic poets and transcendental philosophers who, in the early decades of the nineteenth century, projected childhood as a divine rather than a corrupt condition and called for, among other things, a physical and moral liberation of children's minds and bodies (Ariès, 1962; deMause, 1974; Plotz, 1979). Attempts to reveal the social sources of violence are also reflected in nineteenth-century discoveries of street children as a class of people in need of protection and benevolent "moral" tutors (Brace, 1872; Finkelstein, 1985a, b); of child neglect as a deplorable social condition; of child labor as a form of assault; and of child abuse as a legally punishable social offense. In the late nineteenth century and early decades of the twentieth, violence against children was revealed with the discovery of adolescence as a vulnerable and bombastic period of youth development, of juvenile delinquency as a specialized category of curable criminality, and of children's rights as a construct, requiring legal protection (Finkelstein, 1985b; Hawes, 1991; Kett, 1977; Schlossman, 1977).

Over the course of the twentieth century, the attempt to root out violence against children has taken new forms as scholars, feminists, theologians, journalists, and educators have discovered and revealed the existence of long traditions of incest and other sexual abuse and of child beating in families across the social spectrum and across centuries (Ascione & Arkow, 1999; Books, 1998; deMause, 1974; Jenkins, 1998). As Weis and Marusza (1998) have suggested of today's world: "Violent outbursts are not isolated instances as an overwhelming number of men lash out toward females in the public and private corners of their lives" (p. 25; see also Korbin, 1997). Recently, with the public outing of child pornography, prostitution, and pedophilia, once invisible and silenced realities have become visible (Helfer, Kemp, & Krugman, 1997; Jenkins, 1998; Petersen del Mar, 1996). Through the efforts of contemporary child advocates, the omnipresence of institutional punishments—such as physical beatings, sexual violence, and the harsh treatment of incarcerated juveniles—has claimed the attention of the public, as have statistics documenting the existence of incest and other forced sex. Yet continuing violence against children is reflected in mandatory "zero-tolerance" expulsion laws, in incidences of school failure, in teen violence, and in the structured silences that result from the array of incest taboos that serve to shield as well as to condemn assaults against young children, male and female (Children's Defense Fund, 1999; Fine & Weis, 1998; Huston, 1991; Males, 1996).

Efforts to transform the status of children and of childhood are reflected not only in the discovery of abusive acts and conditions, but also in the discovery of child advocacy as an approach to social action and a strategy for political and organizational development. The emergence of the Children's Aid Society and religiously based protectories in the latter decades of the nineteenth century, the National Federation of Day Nurseries and the Children's Bureau during the Progressive Era, the emergence of child-centered physicians and psychologists in the early twentieth century (Crenson, 1998; Kett, 1977; Lasch, 1979; Schlossman, 1977); the creation of the United Nations Declaration of Human Rights at midcentury (Bellamy, 1996); and institutions such as UNICEF and the Children's Defense Fund in the latter half of the twentieth century—all reflect continuing efforts to identify violence and protect children from its more draconian expressions.[1]

Finally, the attempt to exorcise violence from the lives of children has found expression in a gradual, if limited, involvement of local government agencies in the business of child protection over the course of two centuries (Finkelstein, 1985b; Haubrich & Apple, 1975; Ten Bensel, Rheinberger, & Radbill, 1997). There is a corpus of law creating alternative institutions for the rearing of children considered to be victims of neglect, malnutrition, battering, and sexual abuse (Finkelstein, 1985b; Grubb & Lazerson, 1982). Orphanages came and went in the nineteenth century, to be replaced by substitute families outside of cities, and ultimately by a limited welfare system (Crenson, 1998). There were specialized public institutions to serve the young: juvenile reformatories in the early twentieth century, foster care systems, and child abuse prevention centers among others at century's end (Jenkins, 1998; Schlossman, 1977).

An evolving corpus of law has established specialized public agencies for the protection of the young—Children's Aid societies in the nineteenth century, the Children's Bureau in the early twentieth century, child protective services, family court, and the National Center for Missing and Exploited Children in the latter decades of the twentieth century (Jenkins, 1998). There are legal traditions regulating the conditions of child labor and laws in more than 30 states, limiting, if not prohibiting, the use of corporal punishment in public schools (Finkelstein, 1970/1989; Glenn, 1983, 1984; Raichle, 1977). There are laws limiting the power of patriarchal authority within families, defining children's rights, and assessing penalties for spousal and child abuse (Books, 1998; Finkelstein, 1970/1989; Hawes, 1991; Hyman & Wise, 1977; Jenkins, 1998; Vardin & Brody, 1979).

Notwithstanding a historically evolving concept of childhood, child abuse, and children's needs; notwithstanding the gradual discovery of child innocence, child neglect, child abuse, child rights, baby battery, and date rape as social conditions in need of remediation; notwithstanding a 200-year history of child advocacy; notwithstanding the expansion of government involvement in the business of child protection and the involvement of

physicians in its identification; notwithstanding the emergence of institutional mechanisms for the reporting of abuse; notwithstanding the presence
of thousands of people who, over the course of two centuries, have condemned violence in all of its forms—traditions of violence against children
have persisted. Indeed, they have recently emerged with new vigor as children are recriminalized, as they are bound over as adults for sentencing at
age 13, incarcerated at increasing rates, and penalized as adults might be.
(See chapter 7, this volume; Finkelstein, 1985a, b; Haubrich & Apple, 1975).

How is it possible that in the birthplace of human rights, violence
against children has persisted? How is it possible that in the home of the
"free and the brave," thousands of what Marian Wright Edelman (1993) has
called "tiny tragedies" beset the lives of children and youth who are abused,
bullied, and killed daily? How is it possible that a nation that has spawned
passionate child advocates, that has institutionalized child advocacy, and
that has defined children's rights on a grand and pathbreaking scale has
also failed to institutionalize practices that protect the weakest and most
vulnerable of our citizens?

This chapter constitutes a modest attempt to make sense of these persistent contradictions by situating the phenomenon of violence against children and youth where it properly belongs, if we are to constitute the means
to eliminate it—in the religious, political, socioeconomic, and cultural traditions that govern life in the United States.

In my view, the persistence of violence against children is bound
within three time-honored traditions. First, there are powerful religious traditions that join the virtues of corporal punishment, physical discipline, and
hard labor to spiritual and moral salvation and to a view that the will of
children needs to be broken, bent, or at least subdued (Ariès, 1962; de-
Mause, 1974; Finkelstein, Mourad, & Doner, 1998; Greven, 1991). Second,
there are traditions of political association—a faith in the power of constitutional government, the value of democratic processes, the protection of
individual rights, the privacy of the family, religious diversity, a free press,
and free expression—that have made the United States a beacon of human
rights for other nations, but have not guaranteed safe havens for children
here at home. In the United States, there is an equally powerful distaste for
the exercise of public authority, the imposition of uniform social standards,
and the redistribution of human and material resources to those in need.
Indeed, the very qualities of political association that guarantee individual
rights also result in the privatization of life in families and churches and
provide blankets of protection for those who might abuse, mishandle, and
violate children and youth (Finkelstein, Mourad, & Doner, 1998). Within
this political tradition, responsibility for personal morality has been situated

within the individual family and the church, rather than in the larger community of public caregivers, such as government-funded and -sponsored, universally available child care centers, health clinics, recreational facilities, and the like.

Finally, there are powerful socioeconomic traditions that project mothers as the appropriate moral guardians of the young, the principal caretakers of children, a specialized group of social actors to whom child care is delegated and in whom responsibility for children's well-being is lodged (Kerber, 1980; Norton, 1980)—no matter what the force of economic, social, cultural, or family circumstance might be, nor what support services individual parents might be able to muster or purchase.

Taken singly, each of these traditions—religious, political, socioeconomic—offers refuge for some of our most cherished political, economic, cultural, and social beliefs. Ironically, however, each tradition has also protected family privacy, prevented the development of universally available health and education benefits, limited the power of child protection agencies, and provided sanctuary for the nurture of violence against children and youth.

What follows is an elaboration of each of these traditions. Intended to be suggestive rather than definitive, these minihistorical renderings call attention to the ways in which traditions of religious belief, moral authority, political culture, and socioeconomic action have anchored and sustained violence against children in subtle and often unexplored ways. Although the traditions are overlapping and interconnected, it is helpful to analyze them singly, since, as we shall see, traditions that sustain violence against children are deep, complex, and multiply anchored.

RELIGIOUS TRADITIONS

The durability of religious traditions that sustain and rationalize the use of violence against children is well illustrated by the incantations of ministers, priests, and moral reformers who have extolled the virtues of corporal punishment as they tendered advice to parents, conceptualized educationally sound practice, and explicitly rationalized the use of violence in particular circumstances. Lyman Cobb, for example, a moral reformer in the middle decades of the nineteenth century, despised thoughtless and frequent whippings and championed the use of moral persuasion to control children; yet he described in graphic detail the uses to which corporal punishment could be legitimately put—when, as he suggested, all other means had been exhausted. Bernard Wishy (1968), the historian of childhood, describes the uses of physical punishment by an idealized mother figure named Mrs. Robinson who, having used all means of moral persuasion with a disobedient and ungovernable son, finally resorted to corporal punishment:

> Although Mrs. Robinson used the best methods in raising her children, a moment arrived when a disobedient son had gone too far. She thought whipping was vindictive, but she was at her wits end. After explaining why he needed caning, Mrs. Robinson made an appointment for the event with her little boy for the next day and sent the sister for a whip. When the sister showed it to him, she cried and kissed her brother. The mother then hung the rod where he could see it and meditate upon it. Next day she again explained why the whipping was necessary and read an appropriate story from the bible. After explaining the story she asked, "Would you rather have God punish your mother or have her punish you?" The poor child's choice was a foregone conclusion but before this torture finally ended both knelt and prayed. (pp. 45–46)

Notwithstanding the emergence of pressures against the use of corporal punishment by parents, support for its uses have persisted to this day. D. Ross Campbell's *How to Really Love Your Child* (1977), written from the perspective of a moderate, nonfundamentalist Christian psychiatrist seeking to provide an alternative to what Philip Greven has called "the ardent advocacy of the rod," and broadcasting its detrimental effects, nonetheless will not rule it out. "Let's face it, corporal punishment is sometimes necessary to break a pronounced belligerent defiance, but only as a last resort" (quoted in Greven, 1991, p. 94).

Commitments to the use of corporal punishment are revealed not only in the forms that advice to parents has taken, but also in the voices of successive generations of pedagogues who, as they visited an array of physical punishments on disobedient students, commonly invoked biblical texts and stories as they engaged in what many of them playfully called instances of "muscular Christianity." The following recollection of Lamar Fontaine, a southern gentleman who attended schools in mid-nineteenth-century Georgia, is typical of the voices of hundreds of students and teachers who had similar tales to tell (Finkelstein, 1970/1989; Hyman & Wise, 1977).

> [The teacher] . . . carried me down to the spring . . . in the shadow of an old cottonwood log; he repeated a verse from the Bible, about sparing the rod and spoiling the child; he often knelt, and prayed a short prayer, in which he asked his Heavenly Father to forgive the awful crime of which I had been guilty, and then rose, and catching me by my long hair, almost lifting me from the ground, he administered an awful whipping. (Fontaine, 1908, pp. 14–15)

Indeed, a certain taken-for-grantedness characterizes the attitudes of teachers toward corporal punishment throughout the nineteenth and well into the twentieth century. In hundreds of recollections, physical coercion was looked upon as natural and necessary, as biblically sanctioned, as the mark of a good teacher. The observations of one student who had attended schools in New York City in the 1830s are typical of many others:

> It must not be inferred that he was a brutal tyrant. It was only that the funda-
> mental law of the school was obedience to rules, and seldom did any fellow
> incur chastisement, that he did not also have to listen to the quotation of Solo-
> mon's proverb. "The way of the Transgressor is Hard!" With all his severe
> discipline, there was no teacher in the school who was so generously loved.
> (Redfield, 1900, p. 23)

The persuasive power of Judeo-Christian religious beliefs is visible not only in the rhetoric that teachers deployed as they punished students but also in the assumption that corporal punishment and good teaching were inextricably bound together. It was evident as well in the continuing use of corporal punishment in the face of systematic opposition to its use. In 1867, New Jersey teachers successfully petitioned their legislature to rein-state corporal punishment, citing biblical authority to reinforce their position (Raichle, 1977). Educators were undeterred by specific regulations such as those issued by the Bureau of Indian Affairs in the 1920s and 1930s suggesting that corporal punishment must be resorted to only in cases of "grave violations of rules" (Trennert, 1989, p. 5). Citing biblical authority and the need for order and discipline, missionary-school administrators in an array of institutions for Native American boys and girls nonetheless continued its use, and sometimes with excessive force.

Gradually, over the course of the nineteenth and twentieth centuries, invocations of biblical authority have served to suppress as well as to justify the continuing use of physical force in schools (Finkelstein, 1970/1989; Glenn, 1983, 1984; Raichle, 1977). The power of "old-fashioned" religious traditions is alive and well in the private, unregulated spaces of homes, in religious schools, in many public schools where corporal punishment is still legally sanctioned, and in a variety of neighborhood associations—where corporal punishment is a daily occurrence and invocations of biblical authority a commonplace justification for it. Indeed, the newspaper accounts of abusive situations, the observations of caseworkers, and the reasoning of parents suffuse with a fund of biblical allusion and sentiment. Indeed, this kind of rhetorical justification continues to inform, if not entirely to overwhelm, the public dialogue governing the discipline of young people at home and in school.

POLITICAL TRADITIONS

There is a second tradition in U.S. life within which violence against children is comfortably nested—in forms of political practice that cultivate sharp divisions between public and private life. From the founding of the American nation and the public school system in the late-eighteenth and middle decades of the nineteenth centuries to the present day, generations of American political, social, and education reformers have anchored the concept of a flourishing democracy in a bedrock of belief about the value of high walls of separation between church and state, contractual and personal relations, and the public and the private spheres of life. As an array of contemporary political philosophers and historians have observed, the history of the United States can be understood in part as a history of tensions between public need and private interest, communal bonds and individual rights, liberty and equality, rights and needs, and unity and diversity (Finkelstein, 1988; Noddings, 1987; Stanley, 1983a, 1983b; Sullivan, 1981).

They have called attention to the existence of two distinct spheres of action—a private or moral sphere over which the government has no authority, and a public or civic sphere where Americans negotiate conflict and difference and invoke government authority to assure individual rights and freedoms. There is an assumption that there are certain values that should remain outside the reach of public authorities, including matters of religious belief, child-rearing practices, character training, and family authority. It is within the private sphere that Americans claim rights to independence and freedom. It is within the public sphere that they negotiate their political and economic interests and identify commonalities and differences of belief and commitment (Brown, 1987; Finkelstein, 1989; Noddings, 1987; Stanley, 1983a, 1983b; Sullivan, 1981).

The consequences of this bifurcation are reflected in public policies that, among things, privatize norms of child rearing, define the authority of families and churches as outside the legitimate sphere of public regulation, and limit the forms that public responsibility and support for children and child rearing has taken. The first of these limitations center, as Norton Grubb and Marvin Lazerson (1982) have observed, on a historic doctrine that government responsibility must be limited to include only those instances when parents have failed their children rather than expanded to include support for children universally across the social spectrum. Edward Everett Hale, a nineteenth-century Massachusetts minister, expressed this sentiment precisely: "Wherever there are parents, incompetent to make their homes fit training places for their children, the State should be glad, should be eager to undertake their care" (quoted in Grubb and Lazerson, 1982, p. 38). It was just such an assumption that inspired the reasoning of the Pennsylvania Court of Appeals when they denied a writ of habeas corpus to the father of Mary Ann Crouse, who had petitioned the managers of the House of Refuge in Philadelphia to return custody of his daughter. The Pennsylvania court, in the doctrine of parens patriae, defined moral education to be a public as well as a private concern, and rationalized government removal of children from failing families to state institutions.

> The object of charity is reformation, by training its inmates to industry; by imbuing their minds with principles of morality and religion; by furnishing them with means to earn a living; and above all, separating them from the corrupting influence of improper associates. To this end, may not the natural parents, when unequal to the task of education, or unworthy of it, be superseded by the parens patriae, or common guardians of the community? It is to be remembered that the public has a paramount interest in the virtue and knowledge of its members and that, of strict right, the business of education belongs to it. That parents are ordinarily entrusted with it, is because it can seldom be put in better hands; but where they are incompetent or corrupt, what is there to prevent the public from withdrawing their faculties, held as they obviously are, at its sufferance. The right of parental control is a natural, but not an inalienable one. (*Ex parte Crouse*, 1838, quoted in Bremner, 1970, p. 695)

As Grubb and Lazerson (1982) have observed, "Rather than affirming broad public responsibility for the welfare of children, *parens patriae* has taken on the negative cast of intervention only in exceptional cases of parental failure" (p. 45).

A second limitation on government involvement is driven by a related assumption: that government involvement in the lives of children has been justified only when the "best interest of the child" is abridged. This kind of reasoning has formed the foundation for an evolving series of legal actions designed to rescue children from recalcitrant and violent parents, while at the same time to circumscribe occasions for government action. Commitments to "child saving" inspired Congress in the period from 1810 to 1895 not only to appropriate money for the army to create reservations for Native Americans, but also to build boarding schools for Native American children intended, in the parlance of congressional debate, "to dissolve all tribal relations"; in the parlance of Protestant theology, to remove children from the demoralizing influence of families; in the parlance of modern sociology, to transform the social network of Indian parents and replace the home with the school acting *in loco parentis* (Finkelstein, 1985b; Grubb & Lazerson, 1982).

Child-saving rationales have also animated the passage of laws limiting child labor, requiring school attendance, providing child-support payments to fatherless families—e.g., widows of war veterans, husbandless house-holders, and abandoned children. A commitment to child-saving has justi-fied the construction of orphanages in the early nineteenth century, the juvenile justice system, child protective services in the early twentieth cen-tury, and a contemporary disposition to rediscover the utility of orphanages as alternative environments for abused children.

No matter how humanitarian their intention or successful the outcome for the welfare of the young, child-saving approaches to children's welfare have effectively defined government responsibility as an emergency condi-tion, a kind of social rescue operation fit primarily for the child victims of adverse family circumstance. Through the prism of child-saving ideologies, public approaches to child welfare have done little to contradict the pre-sumption of private responsibility for children, invite a more universal ap-proach to their needs, or provide support systems for overburdened par-ents. In fact, they have stigmatized families in need and affixed a series of status-degrading labels to them. On matters of child protection, especially for children under 5 years of age, the United States is historically a hands-off nation. When the government has become involved in social rescue operations and efforts to support children, it has typically generated poli-cies that label the need for welfare and child support as symptoms of profli-gacy, constructed dependence as a form of moral and social weakness, constituted interdependence as an abnormal if not undesirable state, and delegated responsibility to private agencies (e.g., the church, the temper-ance society, the mother's aid societies, the enormous array of institutions that constitute a volunteer sector).

The commitment to private responsibility for children is revealed not only by the limited scope of child welfare, but also in the structure and purposes of publicly supported education as well. Public school teachers in the United States, from the time in the 1840s when they began their work to the present moment, have typically proceeded on an assumption that their primary role was academic. Generations of teachers have defined themselves as intellectual overseers, drillmasters, cultivators of cognition, assuming or at least noting that teacher authority has been limited and fo-cused primarily on the academic features of schooling (Cuban, 1993; Fin-kelstein, 1970/1989). Teachers have commonly acted out of a conviction that there are high walls of separation between the public lives of children in school and the private lives of children at home. Parental authority pre-dominates, for all but very poor, low-status families, as hundreds of adminis-trators and teachers have learned when they have tried to suspend or expel students for non-school-related offenses such as dress, hairstyles, cosmetic preferences, or dating practices or when they have tried to control the uses of leisure time (Finkelstein, 1985a, 1970/1989).

Out of respect for privacy and family authority, teachers have never institutionalized home visits, nor, as schooling has become urbanized and bureaucratized, typically mingled socially with students and their families—especially in less privileged neighborhoods. Their contacts have revolved around academic matters, taking the form of parent conferences focusing typically on matters of academic placement and grades. In fact, U.S. educators typically regard matters of private morality and personal belief as the legitimate province of the family or church (Lewis, 1994; Tsuneyoshi, 1994).

Ironically, the separation of public and private life in the United States has protected children from certain forms of government intrusion while at the same time obscured the daily ravages of abuse and neglect and undermined the capacity of teachers to help. With teachers thus disjoined from all but token interventions, the limits of teachers' authority and roles have, indirectly, contributed to the endurance of violence against children.

SOCIOECONOMIC TRADITIONS

The nurture of violence against children resides not only in religious traditions, historic commitments to family privacy, limited government, and high walls of separation between the private and public sphere. It is situated as well in a historic disposition of social planners, humanitarian reformers, policy makers, and traditional child advocates to conceive of child rearing as a moral rather than an economic enterprise, an avocation rather than a legitimate source of paid labor, a way of life rather than a form of gainful employment, a form of education rather than a site for the use of resources, the specialized concern of social volunteers and low-paid wage laborers. To put it another way, there is a historic disposition to create templates of experience that exalt the virtues of family nurture and elevate the symbolic importance of mothers, child workers, and teachers while, at the same time, to limit public investments in children and child rearing, provide only minimal and selective support for child and health care, generate disincentives to maternal employment, limit the access of women to high-paying jobs, and otherwise intensify the pressures of motherhood and child rearing.

This pattern of socioeconomic doublespeak has created a tradition of policy making that, until the 1960s, had limited public support for all but very poor, low-status groups, substituted moral prescription for financial support, obscured socioeconomic inequities, ignored the hidden costs of humane child rearing, underestimated the value of community involvement in child rearing, and provided few enforceable regulatory pressures for environments serving children under 5 (Books, 1998; Finkelstein, 1985b, 1970/1989; Grubb & Lazerson, 1982; Huston, 1991; Michel, 1999).

One reflection of this preference for moral over economic support resides in a century-long tradition of powerful opposition to maternal employment and the construction of community-based child care facilities by all but a small group of African American philanthropists—members of the National Association of Colored Women—who throughout the twentieth century have proceeded on an assumption that maternal employment was an inevitable condition, that community support for safe, loving child care was important, and that the object of their own charitable efforts was best directed at the creation of urban day nurseries (Michel, 1999).

Their socially more privileged and powerful counterparts have differed. Opposition to day nurseries originated at the end of the nineteenth century, at a time when the practices of day nurseries, orphan asylums, infant schools, and Sunday schools constituted a justifiably criticized network of undersupported, sometimes violent, quasi-public, and unregulated tutorial complexes for the children of the poor, widowed, orphaned, or fatherless.

An array of elite reformers and reformer groups and individuals, in the depths of despair about the cruelties visited upon children on "baby farms" and day nurseries, attacked the child care principle as an approach to child protection. Simultaneously, they lamented the need of mothers to work. Jane Addams expressed deep reservations about the capacity of widows and divorced, deserted, or never married women to manage physically demanding jobs and the requirements of family life simultaneously: "How far the wife can be both wife and mother and mother and supporter of the family raises the question of whether the day nursery should tempt her to attempt the impossible. . . . The earnings of working women are very small at the best" (quoted in Michel, 1999, p. 72).

Less ambivalent in her opposition, Florence Kelley, an outspoken advocate of protective labor legislation for women and children, denounced day nurseries as crucibles for the separation of mothers and children: "No money earned in the United States costs so dear, dollar for dollar, as the money earned by the mother of young children. . . . Family life is sapped in its foundations when the mothers of young children work for wages" (quoted in Michel, 1999, p. 73).

In their critique of day nurseries, elite social reformers not only attacked the forms that child protection had taken, but at the same time sustained an ethic of domesticity that was to dominate public policy discourse and delimit the forms that public assistance was to take for almost three quarters of a century. At the center of this ethic was a household over which women would preside. Female influence, as reformers defined it, was to be centered in the household rather than the polling place or marketplace. Women would exercise power differently from men. Men would engage public issues, whereas women's influence would remain

unobtrusive, bounded within small domestic and community circles. Elite social reformers envisioned the household as a place apart, a protected enclave
that would protect children from moral danger and "social contagion." The
domestic environment of the reformers' imaginations was genteel, nonviolent, health giving, socially necessary, and economically dependent on husbands or fathers as specialized wage earners. Reformers' visions of domesticity lodged responsibility for child rearing and child care in female hands and
economic power in the hands of wage-earning spouses and fathers.

With this gender-differentiated vision of family nurture, coalitions of
moral reformers, including ministers, physicians, education reformers, and
an array of child advocates, launched an ultimately successful campaign to
bar children from the labor force, discouraged women with children from
entering it, and unwittingly constituted an isolated family environment of
explosive intimacy where the challenges, responsibilities, and pressures
of child rearing fell almost exclusively on women. For mothers who had
been widowed, deserted, divorced, or inadequately supported, elite social
reformers proposed to provide the means for them to stay home through
the mechanism of mother's pensions. For children who were abandoned,
neglected, unsupervised, or "corrupted," reformers conceived of the truant
officer; expanded the reach of compulsory school laws; substituted commitments to family-style alternative environments for family-less, unsupervised,
neglected, and abused children; and otherwise aimed to disengage children
from labor in factory and field (Crenson, 1998). They discovered "delinquency," defined juvenile justice as a new form of adjudication, and aimed
to transform the court and the prison into parentlike environments for young
people (Kett, 1977; Schlossman, 1977).

When these efforts are taken together, they constitute a systematic approach to child welfare that incorporated five premises: that the best interests of children were well served if they were immersed in networks of
good influence either at home with their mothers or, after 6 years of age,
in school with teachers (Finkelstein, 1985b), that the welfare of children
was compromised by maternal employment, that "child care should be offered only on a temporary basis, that day nurseries should remain objects
of private charity, and that upper class volunteers should set policies for
low income families" (Michel, 1999, p. 67).

When these five premises are taken together, they constitute a tradition
of child protection that progressive reformers called "child saving," but that
historians have characterized variously as "maternalist," "class-biased," "child-
centered," "moralistic," "imperial," or unjust (Finkelstein, 1985a; Finkelstein, Mourad, & Doner, 1998; Gordon, 1988; Grubb & Lazerson, 1982;
Michel, 1999). No matter what the label, the strategy was one that provided
for modest sums of money, disseminated large amounts of advice, and

aimed to standardize class- and culture-specific norms of appropriate child rearing. It was a strategy that defined children as victims of neglect rather than of poverty, incest, or other abuse, and their mothers as fit objects for advice rather than for child-support services. Linda Gordon (1988) has characterized the approach as individual rather than social, moralistic rather than environmental. It constituted, among other things, a form of gender entrapment with the power to reveal and address neglect, but to deny, obscure, and cover up wife beating and incest as sources of violence against children within families.

This approach to child protection became institutionalized in programs of the federal government for more than a half century. It was evident in the work of the Children's Bureau, a federal agency founded in 1902, which tendered advice on maternal and child health and lobbied for mother's pensions and health services for children. Its staff of social workers and psychologists successfully generated congressional support for maternal and child health services, diffused the latest medical intelligence to thousands of mothers, and revealed the deleterious effects of maternal employment. Working mothers, seeking advice from the Bureau, revealed the wrath of intemperate husbands, the pressures of poverty, and the force of adverse circumstance on their capacity to protect their children. Officials of the Children's Bureau responded by expanding their capacity to disseminate good advice, provide blueprints for the preparation of high-quality nurseries in homes, and share the insights of a new generation of mental health professionals. They were not inspired to organize campaigns against violent and incestuous fathers, relatives, and neighbors. Nor were they inclined to support the expansion of child care facilities for children under 5 years of age.

The same approach was also institutionalized in the provisions of the Social Security Act of 1935. The act prohibited child labor during school hours; provided modest amounts of financial assistance for fatherless children in its Aid to Dependent Families provision; imposed a surveillance strategy that would enable state and local agencies to monitor the work habits of mothers and the whereabouts of fathers; and expanded the regulatory reach of the Children's Bureau. But the original Social Security Act made no provisions for the construction of child care facilities to support mothers; to make publicly supported educational services available to children under age 5; to conceptualize a role for fathers as child rearers, nurturers, and tutors; or to impose guidelines for the skimpy numbers of child care facilities outside the family. Nor did the bill structure a means to levy fines, set punishments, or identify fathers who withheld money or perpetrated violence against children and wives (Finkelstein, Mourad, & Doner, 1998; Gordon, 1988; Huston, 1991; Michel, 1999).

These measures have emerged only gradually and unsystematically over the past 40 years as new coalitions of working women; feminists; social reformers; health, education, and welfare rights advocates; social work professionals; and an array of politicians have responded to the pressures of war, social inequity, poverty, racism, and the demands of increasingly greater numbers of working mothers who harbored new conceptions of gender roles and new assumptions about the sources of violence in society. Rights activists formed coalitions and did battle for an expansion of children's rights, women's rights, civil rights, and gender equity and lobbied for the construction of model educational environments for children under five (Gordon, 1988; Grubb & Lazerson, 1982; Michel, 1999). They called attention to links between poverty and abuse, abandonment, neglect, and battery, and to the ways in which constructions of gender and race undermined the capacity of mothers to protect children from assaults by fathers, friends, and marauding drug dealers. They revealed the existence of incest and other abuse, rape, and sexual harassment, and aimed to reconstruct the dialogue and the politics of child protection (Children's Defense Fund, 1999; Giroux, 1988; Gordon, 1988; Hyman & Wise, 1977; Jenkins, 1998; Michel, 1999).

From 1962, when Congress amended the Social Security Act to include provisions for child care, until August 22, 1996, when the Personal Responsibility and Work Opportunity Reconciliation Act was signed into law, the architects of the War against Poverty proceeded on new assumptions about the needs of children. Unlike their Progressive Era forebears, they viewed children of poverty as victims of economic and social inequity rather than of moral degeneracy and/or familial pathology, except, that is, if their mothers were welfare dependent or mired in poverty. Reformers of the 1960s provided for income supports and child care provisions. They saw fewer tensions between commitments to compensatory education and maternal employment; nor did they necessarily look upon working mothers as deranged, neglectful, or abnormal. In recognition of the economic needs of mothers, they introduced job-training programs. They constructed a family-tutoring legislative strategy that identified the interests of children with the interests of their mothers and led Congress to design services to poverty-stricken families in the form of parent-education programs and nursery schools as well as cash payments (Finkelstein, 1985b). The establishment of child care provisions in an amended Social Security Act in 1962; of Head Start and Even Start programs in the 1960s, 1970s, and 1980s; of parent-education programs; and child care service provisions in the Child Development Block Grants of the early 1990s all signaled changes in the approach to child protection and an expansion of the regulations governing safety, health, and welfare in government-supported child care programs (Grubb & Lazerson, 1982; Michel, 1999).

All this is not to say that there was a systematically planned nor successfully implemented program of child protection put in place, nor one that was without stigmatizing elements and draconian forms of means testing.

During the period from 1962 to the early 1980s, income support maintenance was diversified and expanded as Congress continued to identify the interests of children with the economic well-being of their families and channeled modest amounts of income directly into their homes. With the passage of the Family Leave Act in 1994, and the provision of an earned income tax credit to defray the costs of child care, Congress signaled a new if not generous attitude toward working mothers.

In the past three decades, until 1996, new realms of possibility for the support of children and their families have been discovered. As the federal government deployed what some have called a "safety net," what others have called a 60-year commitment to America's poorest children, what still others have criticized as "the nation's social bargain with the poor" (Clinton, 1996), these approaches represent the cumulative efforts of a generation of child advocates to engage the power of the federal government to right social wrongs, protect the dependent, minister to the economically needy, and publicize the effects and extent of abuse, neglect, prejudice, and discrimination against children and youth. These measures were, however, short-lived.

So powerful were the coalitions arrayed against them and so fleeting was the commitment to a social safety net that it ended on August 22, 1996, when President Clinton signed the Personal Responsibility and Work Opportunity Reconciliation Act. Through its rhetorical emphases and regulatory provisions, the Act eliminated child protection as a legitimate rationalization for federal involvement and substituted moral reconstruction and economic oversight instead. The goal of welfare reform according to President Clinton was to "make work and responsibility the law of the land." Senator Mikulski (1996) put it this way: "Welfare reform is about ending the cycle and culture of poverty. . . . [E]nding the culture of poverty is about personal responsibility."

The Act does not provide support directly to poor families in the form of child care services, parent-education programs, and child care centers; nor does it provide unemployment insurance, maternity or paternity leaves, or education allowances. Unlike its predecessors, the 1996 Personal Responsibility and Work Opportunity Act invokes no rhetoric of child protection or child rights. Poor children come into view not as an economically bereft, educationally vulnerable, dependent class of victimized young people, but as the progeny of a morally profligate class of unmarried, undeserving, sexually promiscuous, irresponsible women and absentee fathers in need of moral reclamation, social reconstruction, publicly administered discipline, and paid or unpaid work.

The Act is less about child welfare than about women on welfare; less about child protection than about family regulation. It deploys the disciplinary power of the federal government to bring child rearing under the unbending control of market requirements. It is rationalized as an instrument of deficit reduction, streamlining services to children, cutting medical and social benefits, and redefining the levels of care to which children are entitled. It diverts direct cash payments from families, and through a labyrinthine series of highly regulated federal block grant allocations to the states in the form of Temporary Assistance to Needy Families (TANF) grants, aims to establish the two-parent family as a social norm, the working couple as a social ideal, and state social service agencies as regulatory channels for the administration of child care services, social security insurance, and medical benefits. In short, the Personal Responsibility and Work Opportunity Act transforms childhood policies into economic policies and state-mandated prescriptions for right living—an approach that privatizes children into invisibility and renders them vulnerable to the force of adverse circumstance (Finkelstein, Mourad, & Doner, 1998). Some social critics have characterized it as an important reflection of a war against children (Chomsky, 1995). Sylvia Hewitt and Cornell West (1998) have situated it as a chapter in a 30-year-old "silent war against parents," which has stripped parents of their authority and children of the protective armor that in the past was provided by parents and communities (p. xiii).

CONCLUSION

The historical legacy of child protection is, as we have seen, mired in contradictions. It reflects the efforts of many generations of reformers to protect children's well-being, but at the same time honor family privacy and exempt churches from regulatory oversight—even of its facilities for young children. It reveals a commitment to moral nurture and tutorial environments for children, but has not resulted in systematic efforts to universalize and regulate extrafamilial child care and early learning initiatives. A rhetoric of equal educational opportunity for all classes of children has inspired almost all child welfare initiatives, but schooling for children under 5 has remained privatized and unregulated. Funding and support of public schools has reflected huge disparities in wealth. Notwithstanding the stated importance of early learning environments for children under 5 years of age, preschool child care providers have been among the lowest paid and lowest status class of workers in the country. Commitments to the value of wage labor have proceeded simultaneously with policies that discourage mothers from acquiring or seeking suitable financial rewards for child rearing. Nor do these policies provide child care centers to which mothers could turn with confidence. An elaborate commitment to children's rights and entitlements exists simultaneously with an equally powerful distrust of government authority and financial commitments to high-quality child care. Finally, a commitment to protected environments that can shield young people from physical, mental, and emotional excesses proceeds simultaneously with a public environment that is suffused with violence, conflict, excesses of hate talk, and unmediated brutality.

Violence against children is sustained in a crucible of contradictions. It is embedded in an array of cultural, moral, political, and economic beliefs and practices that buttress much of what is good in America and sustain most of what is bad as well. To address the horrors of violence against children and address the contradictions of our commitments, we will, as a public, have to grapple with the contradictory character of our most cherished beliefs and practices. Whether we are willing to face the hard choices that such an effort entails remains to be seen. It will require new acts of social and educational imagining; it will be expensive. I, for one, am not optimistic about the possibilities.

NOTE

1. However, the United States has still not ratified the most important treaty protecting the human rights of children—the Convention on the Rights of the Child.

REFERENCES

Ariès, P. (1962). *Centuries of childhood: A social history of family life* (R. Baldick, Trans.). New York: Knopf.

Ascione, F. R., & Arkow, P. (Eds.). (1999). *Child abuse, domestic violence, and animal abuse: Linking the circles of compassion for prevention and intervention.* West Lafayette, IN: Purdue University Press.

Bellah, R. N. (1975). *The broken covenant: American civil religion in a time of trial.* New York: Seabury.

Bellah, R. N., Madsden, R., Sullivan, W. M., Swidler, A., & Tipton, S. M. (1985). *Habits of the heart: Individualism and commitment in American life.* New York: Harper and Row.

Bellamy, C. (Ed.). (1996). *The state of the world's children, 1997.* London: Published for UNICEF by Oxford University Press.

Books, S. (Ed.). (1998). *Invisible children in the society and its schools.* Mahwah, NJ: Lawrence Erlbaum.

Brace, C. L. (1872). *The dangerous classes of New York and twenty years' work among them.* New York: Wynkoop and Hallenbeck.

Bremner, R. H. (1970). *Children and youth in America: A documentary history* (Vol. 1.). Cambridge, MA: Harvard University Press.

Brown, R. H. (1987). *Society as text: Essays on rhetoric, reason, and reality.* Chicago: University of Chicago Press.

Campbell, D. R. (1977). *How to really love your child.* Wheaton, IL: Victor Books.

Children's Defense Fund. (1999). *The state of America's children: Yearbook.* Washington, DC: Author.

Chomsky, N. (1995). A dialogue with Noam Chomsky. *Harvard Educational Review, 65*(2), 127–144.

Clinton, W. J. (1996, August 22). *Remarks at the signing of the Welfare Reform Bill.*

Crenson, M. H. (1998). *Building the invisible orphanage: A prehistory of the American Welfare System.* Cambridge: Harvard University Press.

Cuban, L. (1993). *How teachers taught: Constancy and change in American classrooms: 1890–1990* (2nd ed.). New York: Teachers College Press.

deMause, L. (1974). The evolution of childhood. *History of Childhood Quarterly, 1,* 503–575.

Edelman, M. W. (1993). *The state of America's children yearbook.* Washington, DC: Children's Defense Fund.

Ex parte Crouse. (1838). Vol. 4, Pennsylvania. Cited in Bremner, R. (1970). *Children and youth in America: A documentary history.* Cambridge, MA: Harvard University Press.

Fine, M., & Weis, L. (1998). *The unknown city: The lives of poor and working-class young adults.* Boston: Beacon Press.

Finkelstein, B. (1985a). Casting networks of good influence: The reconstruction of childhood in the United States, 1790–1870. In J. M. Hawes & N. Ray Hiner (Eds.), *American childhood: A research guide and historical handbook* (pp. 111–153). Westport, CT: Greenwood Press.

Finkelstein, B. (1985b). Uncle Sam and the children: A history of government involvement in child rearing. In J. M. Hawes & N. R. Hiner (Eds.), *Growing up in America: Children in historical perspective* (pp. 155–265). Champaign-Urbana: University of Illinois Press.

Finkelstein, B. (1988). Rescuing civic learning: Some prescriptions for the 1990s. *Theory into Practice, 27,* 250–256.

Finkelstein, B. (1989). *Governing the young: Teacher behavior in popular primary schools in nineteenth century United States.* New York and London: Taylor and Francis. (Original work doctoral dissertation, Columbia University, 1970)

Finkelstein, B., Mourad, R., & Doner, E. (1998). Where have all the children gone? The transformation of children into dollars in public law 104-193. In S. Books (Ed.), *Invisible children in the society and its schools* (pp. 169–183). Mahwah, NJ: Lawrence Erlbaum.

Fontaine, L. (1908). *My life and lectures.* New York: Neale.

Garbarino, J. J. (1997). The role of economic deprivation in the social context of child maltreatment. In M. E. Helfer, R. S. Kemp, & R. Krugman (Eds.), *The battered child* (5th ed., pp. 49-61). Chicago: University of Chicago Press.

Giroux, H. (1988). *Schooling and the struggle for public life: Critical pedagogy in the modern age.* Minneapolis: University of Minnesota Press.

Glenn, M. C. (1983). Corporal punishment: The need for a historical perspective. *History of Education Quarterly, 23,* 91-97.

Glenn, M. C. (1984). *Campaigns against corporal punishment: Prisoners, sailors, women, and children in ante-bellum America.* Albany: State University of New York Press.

Gordon, L. (1988). *Heroes of their own lives: The politics and history of family violence, Boston, 1880-1960.* New York: Viking.

Greven, P. (1991). *Spare the child: The religious roots of punishment and the psychological impact of physical abuse.* New York: Knopf.

Grubb, W. N., & Lazerson, M. (1982). *Broken promises: How Americans have betrayed their children.* Chicago: University of Chicago Press.

Hawes, J. M. (1991). *The children's rights movement: A history of advocacy and protection.* Boston: Twayne.

Haubrich, V. F., & Apple, M. W. (1975). *Schooling and the rights of children.* Berkeley, CA: McCutchan.

Helfer, M. E., Kempe, R. S., & Krugman, R. (Eds.). (1997). *The battered child* (5th ed.). Chicago: University of Chicago Press.

Hewlett, S. A., & West, C. (1998). *The war against parents: What we can do for America's beleaguered moms and dads.* Boston: Houghton Mifflin.

Huston, A. C. (Ed.). (1991). *Children in poverty: Child development and public policy.* Cambridge: Cambridge University Press.

Hyman, I. A., & Wise, J. H. (Eds.). (1977). *Corporal punishment in American education: Readings in history, practice, and alternatives.* Philadelphia: Temple University Press.

Jenkins, P. (1998). *Moral panic: Changing concepts of the child molester in modern America.* New Haven: Yale University Press.

Kett, J. J. (1977). *Rites of passage: Adolescence in America, 1790-1970.* New York: Basic Books.

Kerber, L. K. (1980). *Common of the Republic: Intellect and ideology in Revolutionary America.* Chapel Hill: University of North Carolina Press.

Korbin, J. E. (1997). Culture and child maltreatment. In M. E. Helfer, R. S. Kempe, & R. Krugman (Eds.), *The battered child* (5th ed., pp. 29-49). Chicago: University of Chicago Press.

Lasch, C. (1979). *The culture of narcissism.* New York: Norton.

Lewis, C. (1994). *Educating hearts and minds: Perspectives on pre-schools and elementary education.* Cambridge: Cambridge University Press.

Males, M. A. (1996). *The scapegoat generation: America's war on adolescents.* Monroe, ME: Common Courage Press.

Mikulski, B. (1996, July 25). *Congressional Record* (unpaged).

Michel, S. (1999). *Children's interest/mothers' rights: The shaping of America's child care policy.* New Haven, CT: Yale University Press.

Noddings, N. (1987). Creating rivals and making enemies. *Journal of Thought,* *22*(3), 23–32.

Norton, M. B. (1980). *Liberty's daughter: The revolutionary experience of American women, 1750–1800.* Boston, Toronto: Little Brown.

Petersen del Mar, D. (1996). *What trouble I have seen: A history of violence against wives.* Cambridge, MA: Harvard University Press.

Plotz, J. (1979). The perpetual messiah: Romanticism, childhood, and the paradoxes of human development. In B. Finkelstein (Ed.), *Regulated children/liberated children: Education in psychohistorical perspective* (pp. 63–96). New York: Psychohistory Press.

Raichle, D. R. (1977). The abolition of corporal punishment in New Jersey schools. In I. A. Hyman & J. H. Wise (Eds.), *Corporal punishment in American education: Readings in history, practice, and alternatives* (pp. 62–88). Philadelphia: Temple University Press.

Redfield, J. H. (1900). *Recollections of John Howard Redfield.* New York: Printed for the Author.

Schlossman, S. L. (1977). *Love and the American delinquent: The theory and practice of "progressive" juvenile justice, 1825–1920.* Chicago: University of Chicago Press.

Stanley, M. (1983a). The mystery of the commons: On the indispensability of civic rhetoric. *Social Research, 50*(4), 851–883.

Stanley, M. (1983b). How to think anew about civic education. *Journal of Teacher Education, 34*(6), 38–41.

Sullivan, W. M. (1981). *Reconstructing public philosophy.* Berkeley: University of California Press.

Ten Bensel, R. W. T., Rheinberger, M., & Radbill, S. X. (1997). Children in a world of violence: The roots of child maltreatment. In M. E. Helfer, R. S. Kempe, & R. Krugman (Eds.), *The battered child* (5th ed., pp. 3–29). Chicago: University of Chicago Press.

Trennert, R. A. (1989). Corporal punishment and the politics of Indian reform. *History of Education Quarterly, 29*(4), 595–619.

Tsuneyoshi, R. (1994). Small groups in Japanese elementary school classrooms: Comparisons with the United States. *Comparative Education, 30*(2), 113–127.

Vardin, P. A., & Brody, I. N. (Eds.). (1979). *Children's rights: Contemporary perspectives.* New York: Teachers College Press.

Weis, L., & Marusza, J. (1998). Living with violence: White working-class girls and women talk. In S. Books (Ed.), *Invisible children in the society and its schools* (pp. 23–47). Mahwah, NJ: Lawrence Erlbaum.

Wishy, B. (1968). *The child and the Republic: The dawn of American child nurture.* Philadelphia: University of Pennsylvania Press.

Wollons, R. (Ed.). (1988). *Children at risk in America.* Philadelphia: Temple University Press.

CHAPTER 2

Poverty and Environmentally Induced Damage to Children

SUE BOOKS

> On a corner of Clinton and Delancey [on the Lower East Side of Manhattan], up a narrow stairway between a pawnshop and a Dominican restaurant, Ana Nuñez and her three children live in a single, illegal [120-square-foot] room . . . a $350-a-month rectangle, with no sink and no toilet. . . . Ms. Nuñez's teenagers, Kenny and Wanda, split a bunk bed, while she squeezes onto a single bed with little Katarin, a pudgy 4-year-old with tight braids. . . . Last winter, tuberculosis traveled from Kenny to his mother and younger sisters in a chain of infection as inevitable as their bickering.
> —*The New York Times,* October 6, 1996

Poverty hurts children socially, emotionally, and physically. Poor children, especially poor children of color, are assigned to the very worst schools (Kozol, 1991). They suffer the consequences of stress and anxiety in disproportionate numbers. Their food, housing, and medical care are all inferior. Consequently, they get sick and die more often. According to one national study, poor children are at least 50% more likely to die during childhood than are other children (Sherman, 1997).

This is not just unfortunate; it is unjust and ought to be regarded as a form of systemic violence against children. In this chapter I focus on one aspect of that violence, environmentally induced damage. Much is now known about environmental threats to children's health. However, far too little has been said either about who bears the brunt of this threat or about

Updated and revised from "Environmentally Induced Damage to Children: A Call for Broadening the Critical Agenda," *Encounter: Education for Meaning and Social Justice* (Summer 1998), pp. 10–21. Adapted with permission.

its social etiology. Poor children do not just happen to get sick more often than others. They are *made* sick more often than others.

Although often ill-equipped to respond adequately, school nurses are seeing more and more children with asthma, allergies, and respiratory disease (Children's Defense Fund, 1997). "Every class she's been in says they have the highest number of asthma kids they ever had," the mother of an 8-year-old asthmatic girl told a reporter for *The Los Angeles Times*. "It makes me wonder. What is going on?" (Cone, 1996, p. A1). Reflecting on the time he spent in the Mott Haven area in the South Bronx, Jonathan Kozol (1995) remarked that he could not remember "ever being in another place in the United States in which so many children spoke of having difficulty breathing" (p. 170).

As a society, we now know enough about lead poisoning to eradicate it. Nevertheless, in some inner-city neighborhoods, one out of every two children risks permanent mental impairment due to lead exposure (Wilson, 1996). Noting the prevalence of lead poisoning as well as asthma among the poorest of the young, Kozol (1995) challenges "liberal intellectuals" to recognize the implication of schools and educational scholars themselves in the violence and injustice of environmentally induced damage:

> Many children in poor neighborhoods . . . have been neurologically impaired, some because of low-weight prematurity at birth, some because of drug ingestion while in utero, and many from lead poison in their homes and also, shockingly enough, within their schools. (p. 155)

However, although the links between environmental damage and learning are clear, Kozol points out that many scholars

> concerned with questions of unequal access to secondary schools tend to focus more on inequalities that may be caused by our selection systems than on those that are engendered by environmental forces that are neurological in nature. In human terms, it's understandable. . . . It is less painful to speak of an unfair test than of brain damage since a test can someday be revised and given to a child again, but childhood cannot. (pp. 156–157)

It is less painful to speak of biased testing than of brain damage but not only, I believe, because the damage is less consequential. It also is less painful because the cost of responding significantly to the problem is much less, because the delineation of responsibility both for causing and for correcting the problem is cleaner, and because the horror is less shameful. These are explanations, however, not justifications.

In response to Kozol's challenge, I have reviewed some of the recent medical research on tuberculosis, lead poisoning, and asthma—all preventable diseases or conditions engendered or exacerbated by environmental forces—as well as news reports that suggest how schools and the broader society generally have responded to the alarming increase in asthma, especially among children, to the widespread damage suffered by children exposed to lead, and to what the president of the American Lung Association has called the "time bomb" of tuberculosis (Dr. Alfred Munzer, quoted in Pinkney, 1994, p. 12).

Although environmentally induced damage could be explained in any number of ways, in the medical and popular literature of today it largely is framed as "an affliction of the poor." A review of national news reports suggests that what doctors in the Bronx note about the asthma "epidemic" pertains to environmentally induced damage in general: "The epidemic is a singularly quiet one. It has not spawned headlines, demonstrations, advocacy groups or loud calls for public action. One explanation: it is an affliction of the poor, those who have less voice" (Nossiter, 1995, p. B2).

True as this may be, recognizing the link between poverty and environmentally induced damage does not necessarily lead to questions any broader than the usual ones having to do with individual risk factors, with strategies to "protect" individuals against environmental risk, or with individual treatments to ameliorate the damage. Unless poverty is seen in relative terms (that is, in its relationship to a society's wealth), there is no need to raise broad social and moral questions about the *distribution* of adequate housing, good health care, clean air, or the overall material conditions conducive to the health and well-being of human beings, young and old alike.

Environmentally induced damage is also commonly framed as an issue of misfortune: the bad luck inherent in the statistical probability of affliction or of being born to parents unable or unwilling to offer protection. Cast as an affiliate of poverty or as an individual case of bad luck, environmentally induced damage appears not as a predictable consequence of social policies and inaction, and so not as an issue of social values and political priorities. Rather, it appears as an unfortunate consequence of, for example, bad parental decision making about where to live and as something the unfortunate must cope with on their own.

Going beyond this decontextualized and individualistic perspective to recognize the moral and social horror of environmentally induced damage to children obviously will not reverse the damage. However, failure to understand, and speak up about, the gravity of the situation in its social depth and moral urgency insures that societal responses will continue to be shortsighted and dangerously marred by the prevailing propensity to do little besides teach children to cope as best they can, point fingers at their socially devalued parents, and look on a social level for the cheapest way out.

TUBERCULOSIS

In recent years in the South Bronx and other parts of New York, levels of household crowding and rates of tuberculosis, a contagious but preventable disease, returned to the peak levels of the Great Depression. Between 1987 and 1993, cases of tuberculosis among preschoolers up to 4 years old (not recent immigrants) climbed more than 300%, and the increases were particularly significant among poor children of color (Drucker, 1993; Ruben, 1994).

The number of cases of tuberculosis in the United States overall dropped steadily from 1975 (the first year for which data comparable to that collected today is available) until 1985, then began to rise slowly at first and then sharply in the early 1990s. "People will argue about what the main contributor was, but everyone has the same list . . . the dismantling of TB programs, H.I.V., poverty," said Barron Lerner, a physician and medical historian at Columbia University (quoted in Belkin, 1999).

In 1996, the number of cases of tuberculosis rose in 20 states and "sporadic outbreaks" of alarming drug-resistant strains continued to occur across the nation (Goldstein & Suplee, 1997, p. A3). "I've worked in Africa where TB is endemic, and what we're seeing here isn't any different from what we're seeing in other parts of the world," said Dr. Barbara Watson of Children's Hospital of Philadelphia (quoted in Pinkney, 1994, pp. 11–12).

Children develop tuberculosis faster and more intensely than adults. They "can become very, very sick very, very fast," said Dr. Jeffrey Starke, director of the TB clinic at Baylor College of Medicine (quoted in Pinkney, 1994, p. 12). Unlike for adults, only some of whom are newly infected, every case in a child is a newly acquired infection. "It is an epidemiologic emergency from that point of view," said Dr. Laura Gutman of Duke University Medical Center (quoted in Pinkney, 1994, p. 12). Yet with adequate resources and decision-making, doctors believe, pediatric tuberculosis could be almost eliminated in a few years. In fact, the opposite has occurred: A survey of 26 large-city health departments found 11 had slashed their TB-control budgets between 1988 and 1992 (Pinkney, 1994).

Identifiable groups of children are bearing the brunt of these cuts. In this country, non-White children up to 5 years old (African Americans, Asian/Pacific Islanders, Hispanics, and American Indian/Alaskan Natives) are 10½ to 12 times more likely to have tuberculosis than their White counterparts. For 5- to 14-year-olds, the racial/ethnic differences are even larger: Non-White 5- to 14-year-olds are 19 to 32 times more likely to have tuberculosis (Centers for Disease Control and Prevention, 1996b).

"Unless we reinvent our badly deteriorated public health system," warns Dr. Richard Jacobs, a national authority on TB, "this thing is going to get nothing but worse" (quoted in Ruben, 1994, p. 23).

LEAD POISONING

Largely as a result of the regulatory ban on lead in gasoline and lead-soldered cans, exposure to lead in the United States has decreased dramatically in recent years (U.S. General Accounting Office, 1999). Nevertheless, in the early 1990s, lead poisoning remained "the No. 1 environmental threat to the health of children" in this country, according to the secretary of Health and Human Services at the time (L. Sullivan; quoted in Lively, 1994, p. 316). About two thirds of all homes with young children still have lead paint or dust hazards (U.S. Department of Housing and Urban Development estimates; cited in Goldman & Carra, 1994, p. 315). The California Department of Health Services found that 78% of the public elementary schools in that state contain potentially hazardous lead paint, 38% of these schools have paint in deteriorating conditions, and 18% have excessive lead in the drinking water (Smith, 1998).

As with tuberculosis, poor children of color, especially young children in inner cities, suffer disproportionately from the "entirely preventable" threat of lead poisoning (Goldman & Carra, 1994, p. 315). A 1994 study showed 36.7% of all African American children in the United States were suffering from lead poisoning, compared with 17% of Latino children and 6.1% of White children (Brody et al., 1994; cited in Rosen, 1995). Most vulnerable are children living in older homes with deteriorating lead-based paint (U.S. General Accounting Office, 1999). Every year more than 1,000 new children in some of the poorest neighborhoods in New York City are found to suffer from lead poisoning ("Get the Lead Out," 1999).

A 1999 study by the U.S. General Accounting Office shows that young children served by federal health care programs for low-income families, Medicaid and WIC (Special Supplemental Food Program for Women, Infants, and Children), remain at significant risk of lead poisoning. More than 8% of the 1- to 5-year-olds who rely on these programs have harmful blood-lead levels, a rate almost five times as great as that for children not served by these programs. Despite federal policies, most of the children served by the federal programs are not being screened for lead. For almost two thirds of the children with elevated lead levels, a screening conducted in conjunction with the study was their first ever.

The poorer the family and the younger the child, the greater the risk of lead poisoning. A study that looked at family income and lead poisoning among young urban White children 6 months to 5 years old found that 32.4% of the children in families with annual incomes of at least $15,000 had lead poisoning, compared with 50% in families with incomes of $6,000 to $14,999 and 68.2% in families with incomes of less than $6,000 (Rosen, 1995). Another study, conducted between 1988 and 1991, found that although 4.5% of the population had toxic blood-lead levels, 11.5% of children 1 to 2 years old had blood-lead levels in this range. The highest rates were among poor children of color, many of whom live in older, poor-quality homes where they are exposed to the single most concentrated source of lead: paint and dust (Brody et al., 1994; cited in Goldman & Carra, 1994).

Numerous studies have documented "the serious, sometimes irreversible, damage" to children exposed to lead. This includes cognitive and hearing impairment, convulsions, coma, and even death (Children's Defense Fund, 1997, p. 30). Studies dating back to 1929 have linked high lead exposure to retarded physical growth and development, brain damage, learning disabilities, hyperactivity, hearing impairments (Lively, 1994), and, most recently, tooth decay. According to the authors of a recent study, lead may be responsible for 11% of all pediatric cavities, which poor children in urban areas suffer in sharply disproportionate numbers (O'Neil, 1999).

Studies since 1943 have linked lead exposure with impaired psychometric intelligence. Even at low levels, lead exposure has been shown to impair children's IQ (Needleman & Gatsonis, 1990). Elevated lead levels have been linked with reading difficulties and general school failure and, recently, with attention problems, aggression, and delinquent behavior (Needleman, Riess, Tobin, Biesecker, and Greenhouse, 1996). A 1996 study found that boys (first grade through age 11) with relatively high bone-lead levels had more attention problems, were more aggressive, and suffered more anxiety and depression than their peers—this according to the judgments of parents, teachers, and the boys themselves. "If the findings . . . are found to extend to the population of U.S. children, the contribution of lead to delinquent behavior would be substantial," the authors of the study concluded. "Altered social behavior may be among the earliest expressions of lead toxicity" (Needleman et al., 1996, p. 369).

ASTHMA

Asthma is now the most common cause of hospitalization among children in the United States. The disease afflicts about 5 million children and young people in the United States and has reached epidemic proportions in the nation's largest urban areas (Noble, 1999). The number of acute asthma attacks among children has doubled in the past decade (Centers for Disease Control statistics; cited in Noble, 1999). Among 5- to 14-year-olds, asthma-related deaths more than doubled between 1979 and 1995 (National Institutes of Health, 1998).

The increases in asthma attacks, hospitalizations, and deaths have occurred despite the development of highly effective medications (Noble, 1999).

> Knowledge about how to treat asthma has vastly improved in the last 15 years. There are daily medications to calm the inflamed airways to prevent attacks. Pocket-sized inhalers for emergencies that can be tucked into a child's jeans. Lifesaving breathing machines that are carried in a shoulder pack. Support groups for parents. Asthma camps for kids. Curricula for schools. (Cone, 1996, p. A28)

Nevertheless, the numbers have gone up and up, especially among poor children of color in inner cities. In 1993 African American children under 4 years old were six times more likely to die of asthma than their white counterparts; African American children 5 to 14 years old were four times more likely to die of asthma; and African American children and young people up to 24 years old were 3.4 times more likely to be hospitalized (Centers for Disease Control and Prevention, 1996a, p. 351). Although asthma among Latino children has mirrored the rise among White children, doctors say that Latinos in major cities are starting to suffer the same "rampant severity" as African Americans (Cone, 1996, p. A28).

The asthma problem is worst in large cities. A recent study by the Children's Health Fund in New York City found rampant asthma among homeless children. At least 38% of children in New York City shelters have asthma. This is more than six times the national rate for all children (6.3%) and more than double the rate found in a 1996 study of some of New York City's poorest neighborhoods (Bernstein, 1999; Redlener, 1999). Another recent study found asthma hospitalization rates as much as 21 times higher in poor minority neighborhoods than in affluent areas in New York City.

> In [some] neighborhoods of lower East Harlem . . . the rate of hospitalization was 222.28 per 10,000 per year. In five high-income ZIP codes—in the Wall Street and Trinity sections of Manhattan, two in the Glen Oaks section of eastern Queens and one in the Rockaways— . . . no one was hospitalized over a period of one year. (Noble, 1999)

Not surprisingly, asthma is now the most prevalent health problem in many New York City schools, especially elementary schools in poor areas. Asthma is a leading cause of absences; serious attacks often keep children home for a week at a time. School nurses have had to call ambulances for some children, and teachers say the fatigue and breathing problems affect children's concentration and achievement.

In a 1994 survey of new students in elementary and junior high schools throughout New York City, almost 4% said they had asthma; in poor areas, the rate rose to 12% (Belluck, 1996). A fourth-grade teacher in the South Bronx said that 12 of his 30 students have asthma and that eight bring breathing pumps to class. The principal of another school in the South Bronx said that 40% of her school's prekindergarten to eighth-grade students have asthma (Nossiter, 1995).

"The reality of the new protocols for asthma treatment means . . . we should accept no missed school days because of asthma, no staying up all night and coughing, and no missed physical activities," said Dr. Irwin Redlener, president of the Children's Health Fund (Herbert, 1999, p. 31). Nevertheless, asthma accounts for more than 10 million missed school days each year (National Institutes of Health, 1998). It's not unusual for an asthmatic child to miss 20 to 40 days of school a year (Cone, 1996).

Why are poor children, especially poor children of color in inner-city neighborhoods, getting sick with asthma and dying from it so much more often than other children? Lack of preventive care, Kozol (1995) suggests, accounts for some of the difference:

> When you ride on the Number 6 train from East 59th Street to the racial cutoff point at 96th, you pass beneath an area in which 2,400 private doctors, most of them highly qualified, have their offices and in which the ratio of doctors to residents is approximately 60 to 1,000. When you leave the subway at Brook Avenue, you are in a neighborhood in which the ratio is two per 1,000. (pp. 172–173)

In line with these numbers, *The Los Angeles Times* reported that the school nurse at an elementary school in East Los Angeles discovered that none of the school's 30 asthmatic students was receiving preventive medication from a doctor (Cone, 1996).

Poor families often cannot afford inhalers, which cost $15 to $40 each and often last only a couple of weeks (Kozol, 1995). People living in dilapidated homes frequently have intermittent heat and so use gas ovens for warmth. Because these homes are often poorly ventilated, pollutants from stove exhaust build up and make asthma attacks more likely (Eggleston, 1995). A recent study found that living in a cockroach-infested home heightens a child's chances of suffering from asthma. David Rosenstreich, the main author of the study, attributes about 25% of all asthma in inner cities to roaches (Leary, 1997, p. A18). According to a health care provider in the South Bronx,

Some of it is environmental—housing infestation, pesticides, no heat in an apartment. But a great deal is emotional as well. Fear of violence can be a strong constrictive force. If you moved these families into a nice suburb, nine tenths of this feeling of constriction, I'm convinced, would be relieved. (Jesus Gilberto, quoted in Kozol, 1995, pp. 173–174)

RESPONSES: SCHOOLS AND SOCIETY

The numbers I have cited reflect immense suffering and injustice. Children literally are gasping for their lives, suffering irrevocable damage to their brains and nervous systems, dying painfully and young from the ravages of tuberculosis. Sadly, it is the same old story: Poor children of color, already suffering disproportionately in so many other ways, also are bearing the brunt of environmentally induced damage. "It is a hard truth that those with the highest risk of exposure also tend to be the most disadvantaged members of society with the fewest options for removing themselves from the risk" (Lively, 1994, p. 331).

As noted by several of the people I have quoted, the problem is not lack of information. As a society we know how to control asthma, know how to eradicate lead poisoning, and know how to prevent tuberculosis, and we are well aware of environmental racism.

Racial demographics have proved to be a critical determinant of environmental quality. . . . Private and governmental research has identified significant disparities in the placement of waste sites, enforcement of environmental laws, remedial action, location of clean-up efforts, and the quality of clean-up strategies. (Lively, 1994, p. 311)

Clearly, the problem is not due to lack of resources. By traditional measures, the economy is doing very well. Despite the economic boom of the mid-1990s, when the stock market hit an all-time high and the joblessness rate hit a 25-year low, almost one in every 5 children lived in poverty in 1997 (Children's Defense Fund, 1999, p. 3; *Kids Count*, 1999).

The number of children in working-poor families grew by almost a third between 1989 and 1997 (*Kids Count*, 1999). The number of working-poor families hit a record high in 1997, with 3.7 million families with children living in poverty despite being headed by a wage earner—the highest number in the 23 years these statistics have been collected. The number of children living in extreme poverty—that is, in families with incomes of less than half the poverty line ($6,401 for a family of 3) also increased to 44% in 1997 (Children's Defense Fund, 1999).

These figures, as revealing as they are, conceal significant racial/ethnic and geographic disparities: Whereas 16.1% of all White children lived in poverty in 1997, 37.2% of all Black children and 36.8% of all Hispanic children lived in poverty that year (Children's Defense Fund, 1999). In nine states, at least 25% of all children living in the state were poor in 1996. In the District of Columbia, the child poverty rate was 40% (*Kids Count,* 1999).

Given the society's knowledge base and the health of its economy, no child should be suffering the effects of environmentally induced damage. But many are. According to the American Lung Association (1996), "Critical gaps and barriers [remain] between patients and appropriate resources" (p. 4). Fewer than a third of the states have an initiative targeting asthma in their state health plans, and even fewer have actually implemented a program.

Meanwhile, the growing "asthma market" has unleashed a competitive race for new treatments (Begley, 1997; Gellene, 1996). In what may be a sign of what's to come, a Silicon Valley firm, Click Health, is marketing a Super Nintendo video game designed to train young asthmatics in self-care skills. While attempting "to keep Bronkie [the Bronchiasaurus] or his female counterpart, Trakie the Trachiosaurus, from coughing and wheezing in an environment riddled with allergens such as dust, smoke and pollen," game players are exposed to product plugs from drug and medical-device companies (Chase, 1998, p. B1).

The federal government in recent years has required all states to screen young children covered under Medicaid for lead. However, as the U.S. General Accounting Office (1999) report cited earlier found, this isn't happening—in part because compliance with federal policies is not being enforced or even monitored, in part because many children still do not receive adequate preventive health care, and in part because follow-up treatments can be expensive.

A plan developed and published by the Centers for Disease Control in 1991 calls for a shift in strategy from simply "finding and treating children with lead poisoning" to also "remov[ing] sources of lead in the child's environment before poisoning occurs" (p. ii). Years later, the plan is still not fully implemented (Nancy Tips, Lead Poisoning and Prevention Branch, Centers for Disease Control, personal communication, August 14, 1997). Rather, in a "ludicrous cycle," doctors still "find and treat lead-poisoned children, only to see them return to their contaminated environment" (Dr. Stephen Marcus; quoted in Kannapell, 1998, p. NJ6).

Importantly, the Centers for Disease Control plan has been stalled *not* because the cost of preventing lead poisoning cannot be rationalized. On the contrary,

the Plan estimates the costs for deleading homes and the benefits that accrue from reduced need for medical care, for special education and the increase in

> wages that goes with having a higher IQ. . . . The conclusion of the analysis,
> described as conservative by Centers for Disease Control, is that the net return
> to our society for deleading the housing stock in the United States would be
> $28 billion more than the costs of the abatement. . . . The numbers are clear;
> it makes unequivocal fiscal sense to make this investment in human capital.
> (Needleman & Jackson, 1992, p. 680)

Clearly, more is involved here than straightforward cost-benefit analysis.
Reluctance to respond directly to the problem of lead poisoning, and more
generally to environmentally induced damage, reflects judgments of worth
(whose health is worth protecting?) bound up in the social values and political struggles of our time.

As so often happens, the broader society has looked to its schools for
at least a token response to the problem of environmentally induced damage, and the schools are responding in characteristic ways—namely, by
helping individuals learn to cope better.

> To help children and parents learn how to function better with asthma,
> schools have begun to hold special asthma classes for children, organizing
> after-school asthma meetings, scheduling weekend asthma fairs and staging cer-
> emonies staring famous asthmatics, like Jackie Joyner-Kersee, the Olympic
> track star. Some are giving out picture books and coloring books like "The
> Asthma Adventure" and "Asthma Explorers Official Asthmatic Trigger Book"
> (Belluck, 1996, pp. A39).

Although clearly valuable, such coping-oriented responses are aligned with
a particular interpretation of environmentally induced disease—namely,
that this is a private matter for afflicted individuals and their families to
cope with on their own through treatment and education, and not fundamentally a social issue with a social etiology requiring a social response.

Continuing along this narrow interpretative path almost certainly will
lead to more lessons in how to cope, more treatment products, and more
pseudoeducational gimmicks, but not to public outrage or to a broad social
commitment to providing all children with what they need to be healthy,
grow, and learn. Efforts to teach kids to cope better, although helpful, do
not address the fundamental problem, which is that many, many children
who cannot simply "choose" to move are living in unsanitary, polluted,
hyperstressful environments.

QUESTIONS OF FRAMING AND INTERPRETATION

"Talk about people's needs," Fraser (1989) argues, "is an important species
of political discourse" (p. 161). What will be regarded as a matter of legiti-

mate political concern is an open question, subject to struggle and contesta-
tion. Needs once regarded as private matters sometimes become politicized
and vice versa. Fraser uses the example of wife battering—a phrase that
did not exist until about 25 years ago. Rather,

> when spoken of publicly at all, this phenomenon was called "wife beating"
> and was often treated comically, as in "Have you stopped beating your wife?"
> Linguistically, it was classed with the disciplining of children and servants as
> a "domestic"—as opposed to a "political" matter. (p. 175)

Feminists then changed the language and altered the perceptions of the
practice by arguing that

> battery was not a personal, domestic problem but a systemic, political one; its
> etiology was not to be traced to individual women's or men's emotional prob-
> lems but, rather, to the ways these problems refracted pervasive social rela-
> tions of male dominance and female subordination. (p. 175)

So it is with respect to environmentally induced damage and disease.
The damage ought to be linked not with individual risk factors, but rather
with social relationships shaped by an unequal distribution of power and
wealth, and by perceptions of dignity and worth. However, environmentally
induced damage generally is construed not as a reflection of a torn social
fabric, but rather as an affliction of "other people's children" (Delpit,
1995)—and, furthermore, as something for which these children's parents
largely are to blame.

Consider, for example, the assumptions implicit in these comments:
"These kids wind up, more often than not, managing their own asthma,
because the parents aren't around or the parents have asthma that they
themselves don't know how to manage," a public health administrator for
a school health program in East Harlem told a reporter for *The New York
Times* (Belluck, 1996, p. A41). A landlord in the Bronx was quoted in *The
New York Times* as saying,

> I'm very suspicious of where [children poisoned by lead] are getting the lead
> from. I've even thought that some parents might be feeding it to them just
> like there were parents who were throwing their kids out of the window so
> they could sue for kids falling out of the window. (Purdy, 1994, p. B3)

Public health issues, including environmentally induced damage, have
not always been construed as a private responsibility to be coped with,
individually, as best one can. Neither have public health issues always been
framed as problems to be managed primarily through treatment or educa-

tion of the afflicted children and their parents. During the early 1900s, child health was regarded as a social problem with a social etiology and as a matter of public responsibility, and not primarily therefore as an issue of personal misfortune or parental irresponsibility. "It was recognized that disease was a 'removable evil' and that the elimination of social problems, like crowded housing, poor nutrition, and limited sanitation, could improve children's health" (King, 1993, p. 121). This recognition led to a

> moral campaign against the problems that faced American children. . . . Physicians, social workers, psychologists, child advocates, and mothers worked side by side in local and national organizations . . . to further the health of American children. . . . Mothers and physicians alike were concerned with the care of individual children, but increasingly they addressed the social and political problems that confronted families and professionals across the nation. (pp. 121–122)

Not surprisingly, many health problems were solved, and fewer children died of preventable diseases and injuries during this time. It seems that such a perspective on environmentally induced damage and child health in general could be revived.

Yet these are very different times. Self-righteous victim-blaming and simplistic parent (usually mother) bashing stand in for serious social analysis, and a dangerous antipathy lurks just below the surface of much of our public talk about the poor. "We so desperately distrust and dislike lower-class adults that we are willing to let their children suffer as well," speculate Grubb and Lazerson (1982, p. 207). "I feel embarrassed by it all; ashamed," confesses a Catholic priest in Brooklyn's Southside neighborhood. "The politicians have decided to treat the poor people like cockroaches, as things to be squashed" (Msgr. Bryan Karvelis; quoted in Sexton, 1997, p. A27).

As a group, poor children of color have already been damaged in wildly disproportionate numbers, and are continuing to be—irrevocably, in many cases. This is a conclusion, I am well aware, that can be bent to frightening political ends. (Consider, for example, Herrnstein and Murray's [1994] argument for what they construe as a "humane social segregation" of the allegedly genetically inferior.) To speak of damage to children in a society such as ours that lacks any "public love" for them (Grubb & Lazerson, 1982, p. 44) is both necessary and in some ways risky. The public discourse on poverty, across most of the political spectrum, already construes the poor as figuratively diseased (Polakow, 1993). That this appears to be literally true to an unconscionable degree invites at least two very different responses.

One is to recognize the social etiology of environmental damage and disease and respond accordingly—by demanding, collectively, that the fundamental causes (unsanitary living conditions, dangerous and dilapidated housing, toxic pollution, unrelenting stress, and so on) be removed and the damage thereby prevented. Ernest Drucker's (1993) conclusions, based on his research on crowded living conditions and childhood tuberculosis in the South Bronx, are much to the point:

> The current tuberculosis epidemic may be associated with social decline and, in the United States, with public policies which congregate the very highest risk populations in jails, shelters for the homeless, and public hospitals and clinics—before sending them back to overcrowded housing. Although the historical linkage of tuberculosis to squalor and overcrowding is well established, what is startling is where this squalor is now located. In many areas of the developed world we are now recreating social and environmental conditions akin to those of the third world or the 19th century . . . a "fourth world" of marginalized populations prone to the spread of infectious agents, which do not necessarily respect conventional boundaries. (p. 818)

Consequently, Drucker (1993) warns, "Enhanced tuberculosis treatment and control measures, even aided by space-age technology, may . . . prove fruitless without a commitment to ending the extremes of social inequities which have always nurtured this ancient disease" (p. 818).

Based on his research on health inequities in developed countries, Richard Wilkinson (1996) makes the same point with respect to the relationship between overall public health and inequalities in levels of income: "The quality of the social life of a society is one of the most powerful determinants of health and . . . this, in turn is very closely related to the degree of income inequality" (p. 5). "What matters within countries is relative rather than absolute income levels" (p. 7). When income levels within developed countries differ significantly, public health declines, Wilkinson found, regardless of a society's overall wealth.

This broader moral and social perspective invites questions not only about the quality of housing available to people, like Ana Nuñez and her children, on the lowest rungs of the social ladder, but also about the social ladder itself—that is, about the distribution of adequate housing and other requisites of human beings' health and well being, including the economic means to acquire these things for one's self and family.

However, there is another possible response to the environmentally induced damage suffered so disproportionately by poor children of color: to resolve to see no more than absolutely necessary and to keep one's own distance if at all possible. I can imagine many people thinking: "Environmentally induced damage doesn't affect my child. Why should I worry about this? If *they* don't want to clean up their homes or take their asthmatic children to the doctor, what can I do about it? And if *their* lead-poisoned children can't learn or won't behave, why should my children suffer alongside them in the classroom?"

When environmentally induced damage is construed as an unintended consequence of self-perpetuated or inevitable poverty rather than as the predictable consequence of social injustice, the young minds and bodies bearing witness to this systemic violence evoke pity perhaps, but not the broad public outrage necessary to any serious response. In the absence of public outrage grounded in an understanding of the moral significance of, and broad societal implication in, environmentally induced damage to children, the facts and figures of this violence can easily be used to rationalize more disregard and indifference, not less. Trying to cultivate a consciousness of outrage in the face of such injustice is not easy in times such as ours. However, this work is now a matter of almost life-and-death urgency.

REFERENCES

American Lung Association. (1996). Focus: Asthma. In *Lung disease data, 1996* (pp. 3–5). Washington, DC: Author.

Begley, S. (1997, May 26). Yearning to breathe free. *Newsweek,* p. 62.

Belkin, L. (1999, May 30). A brutal cure. *The New York Times Magazine,* pp. 34–39.

Belluck, P. (1996, September 29). As asthma cases rise, tough choices and lessons. *The New York Times,* pp. A39, A41.

Bernstein, N. (1999, May 5). Thirty-eight percent asthma rate found in homeless children. *The New York Times,* p. B1, B3.

California school becomes notorious for epidemic of TB. (1994, July 18). *The New York Times,* p. A1.

Centers for Disease Control and Prevention. (1991, February). *Strategic plan for the elimination of childhood lead poisoning.* Washington, DC: U.S. Department of Health and Human Services.

Centers for Disease Control and Prevention. (1996a, May 3). Asthma mortality and hospitalization among children and young adults: United States, 1980–1993. *Morbidity and Mortality Weekly Report, 45*(17), 350–353.

Centers for Disease Control and Prevention. (1996b, August). *Reported tuberculosis in the United States, 1995,* pp. 5–6. Facsimile transmission from the National Center for HIV, STD, and TB Prevention, Atlanta, Georgia.

Chase, M. (1998, October 5). Can video dinosaurs help children manage illnesses like asthma? *The Wall Street Journal,* p. B1.

Children's Defense Fund. (1997, March). Special report: A healthy start. *CDF Reports, 18*(4), 5–9.

Children's Defense Fund. (1998). *The state of America's children: Yearbook 1998.* Washington, DC: Author.

Children's Defense Fund. (1999). *The state of America's children: Yearbook 1999.* Washington, DC: Author.

Cone, M. (1996, October 27). Leaving a generation gasping for breath. *Los Angeles Times,* pp. A1, A28, A30.

Delpit, L. (1995). *Other people's children: Cultural conflict in the classroom.* New York: New Press.

Drucker, E. (1993, October 2). Molecular epidemiology meets the fourth world. *The Lancet, 342*(8875), 817–818.

Eggleston, P. (1995, October 17). Doctors see increase of asthma in inner city kids [Interview]. National Public Radio.

Fraser, N. (1989). Struggle over needs: Outline of a socialist-feminist critical theory of late capitalist political culture. In N. Fraser (Ed.), *Unruly practices: Power, discourse, and gender in contemporary social theory* (pp. 161–187). Minneapolis: University of Minnesota Press.

Gellene, D. (1996, September 11). Making hay fever: As U.S. allergies grow, so does market for new products. *Los Angeles Times,* pp. D1, D5.

Get the lead dust out. (1999, June 21). [Editorial]. *The New York Times,* p. A14.

Goldman, L. R., & Carra, J. (1994, July 27). Childhood lead poisoning in 1994. *JAMA, 272*(4), 315.

Goldstein, A., & Suplee, C. (1997, March 25). District TB rate bucks downward trend. *The New York Times,* p. A3.

Grubb, W. N., & Lazerson, M. (1982). *Broken promises: How Americans fail their children.* New York: Basic Books.

Herbert, B. (1999, June 10). Children in crisis. *The New York Times,* p. A31.

Herrnstein, R., & Murray, C. (1994). *The bell curve: Intelligence and class structure in American life.* New York: Free Press.

Kannapell, A. (1998, March 1). Moving (too slowly for some) to fight lead poisoning. *The New York Times,* p. NJ6.

Kids count data book: State profiles of child well-being. (1999). Available from the Annie E. Casey Foundation, 701 St. Paul St., Baltimore, MD 21202; (410) 223-2890.

King, C. R. (1993). *Children's health in America.* New York: Twayne.

Kozol, J. (1991). *Savage inequalities: Children in America's schools.* New York: HarperCollins.

Kozol, J. (1995). *Amazing grace: The lives of children and the conscience of a nation.* New York: Crown.

Leary, W. E. (1997, May 8). Cockroaches cited as big cause of asthma. *The New York Times,* p. A18.

Lively, D. E. (1994). The diminishing relevance of rights: Racial disparities in the distribution of lead exposure risks. *Boston College Environmental Affairs Law Review, 21*(2), 309–334.

National Institutes of Health. (1998, December 11). Global plan launched to cut childhood asthma deaths by 50%. NIH News Release.

Needleman, H. L., & Gatsonis, C. A. (1990, February 2). Low-level lead exposure and the IQ of children. *JAMA, 263*(5), 673–678.

Needleman, H. L., & Jackson, R. J. (1992). Lead toxicity in the 21st century: Will we still be treating it? *Pediatrics, 89*(4), 678–680.

Needleman, H. L., Riess, J. A., Tobin, M. J., Biesecker, G. E., & Greenhouse, J. B. (1996, February 7). Bone lead levels and delinquent behavior. *JAMA, 275*(5), 363–369.

Noble, H. B. (1999, July 27). Study shows big asthma risk for children in poor areas. *The New York Times*, p. B1.

Nossiter, A. (1995, September 5). Asthma common and on rise in the crowded South Bronx. *The New York Times*, pp. A1, B2.

O'Neil, J. (1999, June 23). Study finds lead poisoning is tied to children's tooth decay. *The New York Times*, p. A15.

Pinkney, D. S. (1994, February 14). Our failure to stem the spread of TB is creating a new set of victims: children. *American Medical News, 37*(6), pp. 11–12.

Polakow, V. (1993). *Lives on the edge: Single mothers and their children in the other America*. Chicago: University of Chicago Press.

Purdy, M. (1994, August 25). Cost of lead cleanup puts more children at risk. *The New York Times*, pp. B1, B3.

Redlener, I. (1999). *Still in crisis: The health status of New York's homeless children*. New York: Children's Health Fund.

Rosen, J. F. (1995). Adverse health effects of lead at low exposure levels: Trends in the management of childhood lead poisoning. *Toxicology, 97*, 11–17.

Ruben, D. (1994, April). TB's toll on kids. *Parenting, 8*(4), 23.

Sexton, J. (1997, August 24). A priest faces up to some harsh realities. *The New York Times*, p. A27.

Sherman, A. (1997). *Poverty matters: The cost of child poverty in America*. Washington, DC: Children's Defense Fund.

Smith, D. (1998, April 18). Lead paint believed to be in most schools. *The Los Angeles Times*, p. A18.

Stevens, A. L. (1995, July). Lead poisoning: The plague of America's inner cities. *USA Today, 124*(2606), 88–89.

U.S. General Accounting Office. (1999). Lead poisoning: Federal health care programs are not effectively reaching at-risk children. GAO/HEHS-99-18.

Wilkinson, R. G. (1996). *Unhealthy societies: The afflictions of inequality*. New York: Routledge.

Wilson, R. A. (1996). Healthy habitats for children. *Early Childhood Education Journal, 23*(4), 235–238.

CHAPTER 3

Poverty and Youth Violence
Not All Risk Factors Are Created Equal

JOSEPH A. VORRASI AND JAMES GARBARINO

In the United States, poverty and youth violence share an intricate interrelationship that is difficult to tease apart. However, one thing is clear: The vast majority of youth who commit violent crimes in this country live in low-income, inner-city neighborhoods. In 1995, more than 25% of all known juvenile homicide perpetrators lived in five U.S. counties, primarily the inner-city areas of New York, Chicago, Houston, Detroit, and Los Angeles (Office of Juvenile Justice and Delinquency Prevention, 1997). The goal of this chapter is twofold: to document the parallel and interrelated trajectories of poverty and youth violence and to discuss the nature and directionality of this interrelationship.

EXAMINING POVERTY AND YOUTH VIOLENCE IN AMERICA

In recent decades, the child poverty rate has exploded, rising from 14.4% in 1973 to more than 20.5% in 1996. In fact, estimates suggest that 33% of American children will live below the poverty line at some point in their lives and that 25% of all children born in this country are born poor (Children's Defense Fund [CDF], 1998). Increased child poverty in the United States is partly attributable to the development of an economy characterized by sharply increased job insecurity and falling real wages in a context of growing social and economic inequality. The disappearance of work, particularly in inner-city neighborhoods, is related to the general decline of jobs available to semiskilled and unskilled workers in the context of globalization and automation. Decreased manufacturing in U.S. cities, the suburbanization of new industry, and continuing racial and gender discrimination in the labor market have thwarted the ability of low-income earners to lift their families from poverty (Wilson, 1996).

American society is also experiencing unprecedented levels of single motherhood, which is in and of itself a strong predictor of poverty in the American context (i.e., a market economy void of the social insurance policies that work to eliminate the association between single parenthood and poverty). For example, in Denmark and Sweden, social programs and policies such as universal health and child care, child allowances, and advance-maintenance child support enable single-parent families to avoid lives of poverty. According to the Children's Defense Fund (1998), the poverty rate for families headed by a single mother in America is double what it is for families headed by a single father, and almost five times higher than the poverty rate for families headed by a married couple. In the late 1950s, 95% of children were raised in two-parent families, but by the mid 1990s, the number had dropped to less than 60% (Bronfenbrenner, McClelland, Wetherington, Moen, & Ceci, 1996). In 1996, while the poverty rate for a two-parent family was 10.1%, the poverty rate was 22.8% among families headed by a single father and 49.3% among families headed by a single mother (CDF, 1998). Therefore, present American socioeconomics are such that being poor also means growing up under the supervision of only one parent.

During a similar time frame, as our children grew poorer and poorer, American society witnessed a major change in the way young people experienced childhood and adolescence. They became increasingly troubled, hostile, and violent—violent not only toward society, but also toward one another. Unfortunately, looking to official statistics representing the nation's overall violent crime index fosters only an incomplete understanding of the true magnitude and pervasiveness of youth violence. What national statistics tell us is that crime is on the decline, suggesting that our efforts to regain control of our streets have been successful. This take on youth violence, though partially accurate, is terribly misleading. The overall crime rate *has* stabilized in some regards—in fact, it has dropped in still others. However, the single biggest change in the way violence plays itself out in America is reflected in the ever growing youthfulness of today's victims and perpetrators of violent crime (Garbarino, 1999). The average age of perpetrators of homicide decreased from 33 to 27 years of age between 1965 and 1993 (Bronfenbrenner et al., 1996). Furthermore, while the overall homicide rate in the United States has remained relatively constant for more than 30 years, the rate of homicides by youths more than tripled between 1965 and 1990 (Bronfenbrenner et al., 1996). Not only are homicides involving a teenage perpetrator a bigger problem today than ever before, but homicides involving teenage victims are approaching an all-time high. In 1996, the number of homicide deaths per 1,000 adolescent males aged 15 to 19 was twice as high as it had been in 1979, rising from 15 to 30 homicide deaths per 1,000 teenage males (CDF, 1998).

While these more specific homicide statistics demonstrate the significance and magnitude of the youth violence epidemic currently sweeping our nation, they still tell an incomplete story. Casualty data focusing only on death provide an imprecise indicator of the overall problem. We must keep in mind the fact that behind each murder stand many nonlethal assaults. For example, in 1993, Chicago officials reported that the city's homicide rate, during an era characterized by rampant community violence and insecurity, was approximately the same as it was in 1973. What officials failed to report was that during that time the city experienced an increase in nonlethal assaults of more than 400% (Garbarino, Dubrow, Kostelny, & Pardo, 1992). Because advances in emergency medical technology prevent many assaults from becoming homicides, it is shortsighted to assume that a declining homicide rate is indicative of a less violent society or a "less toxic" social environment (Garbarino, 1995).

Social Toxicity

Social toxicity is a term used to represent the degree to which the social world has become poisonous to a person's well-being. The term was originally offered as a parallel to the environmental movement's analysis regarding *physical* toxicity as a threat to human well-being and survival. The nature of physical toxicity is well known. For example, we know that air quality is a major problem in many places, so much so that in some cities, just breathing "normally" is considered a health risk, and cancer rates reflect levels of physical toxicity.

In the past 10 years, some communities have improved the quality of their physical environment as enhanced public and professional awareness has led to changes. In the matter of recognizing, understanding, and reversing *social* toxicity, however, we lag far behind. But what are the social equivalents to lead and smoke in the air, PCBs in the water, and pesticides in the food chain? They include community violence, child abuse, domestic violence, family disruption, poverty, despair, depression, rejection, paranoia, alienation, and other social pollutants that demoralize families and divide communities. These forces contaminate the social environment of children and youth and are the primary elements of social toxicity.

No one is immune to the deleterious effects of potent social toxins, but vulnerability varies cross-sectionally. Children are most vulnerable to social toxicity, just as they are most vulnerable to physical toxicity. When air pollution reaches dangerous levels, children, especially those with asthma or some other respiratory condition, show the effects soonest and with the greatest intensity. Similarly, as the social environment becomes more and more toxic, it is our children—particularly the most vulnerable among them—who are affected first and most severely. But who are the most vulnerable among them? We refer to this subgroup's heightened vulnerability as a state of "psychological asthma" (Garbarino, 1995). Psychological asthmatics are those children and youth who already face an accumulated pattern of developmental risk factors. As we will see, it is the synergistic effect of multiple risk factors that gives rise to developmental dysfunction.

Accumulated Risk

It is no coincidence that the negative trajectories of poverty and youth violence exploded almost simultaneously, and there are a number of empirically validated explanations of why poverty and youth violence tend to co-occur. However, the relationship is an indirect one. That is, poverty alone does not cause youth violence any more than youth violence alone causes poverty. Large numbers of poor American children and teens are entirely nonviolent, and large numbers of today's violent youth will go on to lead productive and economically successful adult lives. The relationship between poverty and youth violence is not one-to-one, and no single risk factor is a necessary or sufficient condition to cause one or the other. Poverty and youth violence have complex etiologies marked by the convergence of multiple risk factors that give rise to either or both of these social ills.

  This idea follows what researchers and theorists have called an *accumulation of risk model* (Sameroff, Seifer, Barocas, Zax, & Greenspan, 1987). The accumulation of risk model is predicated on the idea that almost all children are capable of coping with low levels of risk until the accumulation exceeds a developmentally determined individual threshold. Once accumulated risk moves beyond this threshold, systems of strong compensatory forces (i.e., opportunity factors) are needed to prevent the precipitation of physical and psychological harm. Attempting to identify this threshold, Arnold Sameroff and his colleagues (1987) explored the impact of accumulated risk on the intellectual development of preschool children. Using a pool of eight risk factors, these researchers found that the presence of one or two major risk factors was associated with virtually no developmental damage (in this case, diminished IQ scores). However, the adaptive coping capacity of the children was exceeded with the accumulation of four or more risk factors, and as a result, maladaptive functioning actualized.

Because studies of resilience demonstrate that "at least average" intellectual ability is highly predictive of a child's ability to respond effectively to environmental stress, threat, and adversity (Losel & Bliesner, 1990), this example suggests that children and youth growing up within a context of accumulated risk are most vulnerable to the toxicity of today's social environment, hence the term psychological asthmatics.

Extending Sameroff's approach, Dunst and Trivette (1992) included in the developmental equation the counterpart opportunity measure for each of the original eight risk factors (e.g., a present and highly supportive father as the opportunity counterpart to an absent father). This simultaneous assessment of both risk and opportunity is crucial to our understanding of the long-term effects of early developmental experiences because it more accurately captures the reality of how children develop. Every child's life is filled with both risk and opportunity factors that need to be understood within their real-world context.

Dunst and Trivette's reconceptualization has important implications for research, policy, and practice because they document the validity of an "accumulation of *opportunity*" model. Such a model suggests that risk factors may be neutralized or at least partially offset by the introduction of opportunity factors into other realms of the child's life, even when patterns of risk are thought to be impervious to intervention. Additional evidence supporting this idea of opportunity counteracting risk is embedded in the finding that maltreated children who have regular contact with a highly involved nonparental adult figure show normative psychological and behavioral trajectories similar to those of their nonmaltreated counterparts (Cicchetti & Rizley, 1981).

It is only when poverty is part of a larger pattern of risk that it is associated with notably impaired functioning. To understand the stress of being a poor child in America, we must go beyond conventional single-variable studies to examine the complex contextual meaning of poverty in the lives of children. That is, we must continually ask ourselves what it means to be a poor child in America (Garbarino, 1998).

Poverty Represents Multiple Risk Factors

From many points of view, being poor means being at statistical risk—risk for a number of physical, social, and psychological pathologies. Poor children tend to live in environments filled with threats such as violence, racism, unstable care arrangements, economic deprivation, and community insecurity. Academic failure, child maltreatment, and learning disabilities increase in the face of these potent social toxins, and poverty is a central element of this social toxicity as well as one of its important correlates.

Poverty is increasingly part of an ecological conspiracy in which elements of social toxicity converge. There is a general pathologizing of poverty in that it has become increasingly associated with other developmental risks.

A study conducted in Chicago by Patrick Tolan (1995) offers insight into what happens when poverty begins to converge and interact with other salient developmental risk factors. Tolan asked, What proportion of kids living in the most abusive families in the most stressful neighborhoods can be said to be resilient when resilience is defined as a 15-year-old being neither more than one year behind in school nor in the clinical range of the Child Behavior Checklist? (This is defined as having an externalizing or internalizing behavior score that exceeds the point at which clinical consensus has determined that there is little or no doubt that professional mental health services are required to restore "normal" functioning [Achenbach & Edelbrock, 1983].) Tolan's answer? Zero percent. Not a single child in the study met these liberal criteria for resilience, highlighting the potential for dysfunction when poverty is experienced within the context of an abusive family in a stressful neighborhood. The synergistic effect of these three potent social toxins was universally debilitating.

A BOY NAMED MALCOLM: AN ILLUSTRATIVE CASE STUDY

Malcolm has been poor since he was 7 years old. That was when his father abandoned the family after Malcolm's mother called the police because of the beatings he was inflicting on her and her children. It was not uncommon for the beatings to result in a trip to the emergency room. As Malcolm recalls,

> Sometimes he'd hit us so hard we couldn't feel it anymore, and it was almost like he was hitting somebody else. It wasn't until I was older that I realized it wasn't supposed to be that way. When I was younger, I just assumed everybody got hit like that, but I was wrong.

Malcolm's dad was a construction worker for the city and earned an income that kept the family comfortably above the poverty line, even after the money he spent on sporadic drinking binges had come out of his paycheck. Financial stability was the only reason why Malcolm's mother put up with the abuse for as long as she did. At 16, pregnant with Malcolm, she dropped out of high school and became completely dependent upon Malcolm's father for money. Prior to the split-up, she worked for a cleaning service a few days per week to help her husband make ends meet.

When Malcolm's father left the family, his income left with him, and Malcolm saw neither again. So, as a single mother with no particularly marketable skills and three young children to care for, Malcolm's mother gave up her cleaning job and took a minimum wage job working at a nearby fast food restaurant. Unfortunately, most weeks offered only 30 hours of work, and the single-parent family soon became poor.

Malcolm's mom struggled to meet the many demands she faced, but the stress took its toll on her. She was often irritable and frequently lashed out verbally and physically at Malcolm and his younger sisters. Theirs was a grim childhood: "My family was poor—poor in every way," Malcolm recalls at age 17.

> We didn't have any money and it made everybody stressed out, especially my mom. She wanted me and my sisters to have stuff, but she couldn't get it for us because she really didn't make any money. She was realizing that she couldn't provide for us, and it really stressed her out. Sometimes she'd get frustrated and whack us up pretty good, but it was nothing like what my dad used to do to us.

When Malcolm was 12, his cousin Tyler offered a partial solution. He introduced Malcolm to Quinton, a crack cocaine dealer who controlled the street sales in Malcolm's neighborhood. Tyler told Malcolm how he was making $100 per week working as a lookout for Quinton and that Malcolm stood to make as much or more if he was good at it and willing to work nights. Quinton took an instant liking to Malcolm and gave the young boy his first paying job. Malcolm quickly moved up the ranks, next becoming a runner and holding packets of cocaine and vials of crack so the older dealers would not be caught in possession if the police showed up for an unexpected shakedown.

In the years that followed, Malcolm proved himself reliable, and Quinton soon gave him more responsibility and a higher salary. Malcolm used most of his money to help out at home—buying clothes and food for his mother and sisters. In his words, "I was making more in one day than my mom was making in a whole week. I hated seeing her work like a dog for some tiny little paycheck, and she really hated that job." By the time Malcolm was 15, he was using his drug money to pay the rent on the family's one-bedroom apartment. Malcolm's mother never asked where the money came from, and he took that to mean that "she didn't want to know." In less than a year, the family was able to trade in their one-bedroom apartment for a three-bedroom house just a few blocks away.

Malcolm had been lucky. He went more than 3 years without being stopped by the police or being robbed by the street hustlers who preyed on the younger members of Quinton's operation. That all ended one night when Malcolm was jumped at gunpoint on the street in front of his apartment building. Fortunately for Malcolm, he was not hurt and Quinton was understanding. He didn't punish Malcolm for losing the money and the drugs, but instead handed him a nine-millimeter semiautomatic pistol, telling him that a gun would protect him and keep other people's hands off of their money and drugs. Malcolm never went after the hustlers who jumped him, but from that day on, he never went anywhere without his "9."

For Malcolm's 16th birthday, Quinton gave him a corner of his own in appreciation of his loyalty, initiative, and productivity. This meant much more money for Malcolm (and by extension, his family). "I was sometimes earning seven, eight hundred dollars a day," he recalls.

> I was buying all kinds of stuff for my family and friends. We even had a car again—a nice car, nice clothes and everything. Other people was starting to get jealous of all the stuff we had. My mom even went down to half time and started spending more time at home with my sisters.

Less than 3 months later, Malcolm was in jail facing murder charges. He had shot and killed a 17-year-old crack dealer who, despite numerous warnings, continuously "sold rock" on Malcolm's corner. "I had to do what I had to do," said the now incarcerated Malcolm of the shooting.

> That dude was stealing my family's money—money we needed real bad, money we needed to survive. What was I suppose to do—watch my family starve? I couldn't have my mom going back to some job she hated just to barely put food on the table. I wanted us to be normal again and have my mom be able to be with my little sisters like she could before. I didn't know what else to do . . . I didn't see any other solution.

MEDIATORS OF THE RELATIONSHIP BETWEEN POVERTY AND YOUTH VIOLENCE

It is clear that a relationship between poverty and youth violence exists, but it is a relationship of an indirect nature. We contend that poverty influences patterns of youth violence through its effect on other processes known as *mediators*. Mediators provide a mechanistic explanation of why certain relationships exist by suggesting how certain variables affect each other. We propose three such mediators: perception of economic inequality, exposure to family violence, and participation in the illicit economy. Develop-

FIGURE 3.1 Explaining the relationship between poverty and youth violence with three primary mediators

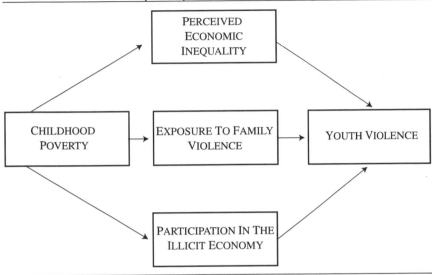

mental theory and research suggest that poverty puts children at risk for each of these three mediators, which in turn puts them at risk for becoming hostile, aggressive, and violent (see Figure 3.1).

Perception of Economic Inequality

Messner (1988) implicates perceived economic inequality as being the primary socioeconomic correlate of violence and aggression. The daughter of a colleague once wrote a school essay in which she referred to herself as "the poorest kid on her block" because she lived in the smallest house. She was right—she *did* live in the smallest house on the block, but it was a *seven-bedroom* house on a block of even larger mansions. Alternatively, there is Malcolm: "Before I was dealing drugs, there were times when my mom used to have to ask the neighbors for food because she didn't have enough money to feed us. I'd get real embarrassed whenever she'd do that, because it made me feel like we were the poorest family in the projects." Here we have two examples of children who identify with being "poor," yet only one of them meets our nation's official definition of "poverty-stricken." Given this apparent inconsistency, how do we assess what it means for a child to be poor if he or she uses such relative inclusion criteria where being poor means having less than others, no matter how much they have?

Take, for example, international comparisons of poverty rates and definitions. When most of the world's people live on incomes comparable to only a few hundred U.S. dollars per year, what does it mean when Americans define the poverty level at $13,500 per year for a family of three persons (CDF, 1999)? India defines poverty as having access to fewer than 2,100 calories per day in one's diet (Blanc, 1994), and using that yardstick suggests that only 20% of the population is poor in what we North Americans would consider a predominantly poor society. Interestingly, this 20% figure is roughly comparable to our overall poverty rate, but if poor children in other nations of the world are shoeless, how do we make sense of the fact that American "poor kids" can be seen wearing $150 running shoes? Analyzing the links between poverty and violence in the lives of children and youth is a difficult task largely because poverty is a contextual judgment rather than an absolute attribute. It surely is not a matter of simple accounting.

Poverty is an assessment of one's position in an overarching social order, and the underlying psychological meaning of poverty lies for the most part in *relative deprivation.* Poverty is not so much a matter of what a child or family has as it is what that child or family *does not have* in relation to other children and families. Karl Marx made note of the powerful distinction between absolute and relative poverty: "It's not living in a hovel that humiliates people, but living in a hovel next to a palace" (as cited in Gilligan, 1996). This sense of relative deprivation is related to important issues of self-esteem and shame, issues that are central to understanding violence.

Relative poverty leads to shame, because being poor is about being left out of what society tells people they can expect if they are included. This is a social proposition at its root, and thus one that plays an important role in generating stress. Recently, a child asked, "Dr. G., when you were growing up were you poor or regular?" The young boy's question captures perfectly the psychological implications of living in poverty—being poor is the opposite of being regular. Being poor means being inadequate, unworthy, not meeting the fundamental standards set by a larger society. The message is one of difference, one of exclusion, inferiority, and lowliness.

The United States suffers from many forms of injustice that spawn shame and ultimately social toxicity and violence. Racism and poverty are certainly at the top of the list. Racism and poverty create a dynamic of humiliation and power imbalance that is likely to be perceived as threatening. Working with murderers in the Massachusetts state prison system, James Gilligan (1996) found shame and humiliation to be potent precursors of lethal violence, because shame and humiliation create situations in which individuals—and sometimes groups—feel threatened by psychic annihilation. So threatened are these individuals and groups that they often respond with violence at even the slightest provocation. Violence gives them a sense of having what they often lack amid the exploitation and humiliation of their daily lives—power, control, and the respect of others. As Gilligan (1996) writes:

> Some people think armed robbers commit their crimes in order to get money. And of course, sometimes, that is the way they rationalize their behavior. But when you sit down and talk with people who repeatedly commit such crimes, what you hear is, "I never got so much respect before in my life as I did when I first pointed a gun at somebody," or, "You wouldn't believe how much respect you get when you have a gun pointed at some dude's face." For men who have lived a lifetime on a diet of contempt and disdain, the temptation to gain instant respect in this way can be worth far more than the cost of going to prison, or even dying. (p. 109)

Succinctly echoing Gilligan's analysis, one convicted murderer put it this way: "I'd rather be wanted for murder than not be wanted at all."

It is important to understand these issues, as they have significant implications for the dramatic wave of lethal youth violence that began shocking American society in the late 1990s. However, for cases in which suburban boys take their schools hostage with arsenals of assault rifles and pipe bombs, the core issue is not economic poverty, since many of these boys come from middle-class families, but emotional and psychological poverty. The lethality of the rage and shame of these socially marginalized boys reminds us of the need to deal with spiritual and psychological poverty. These "lost boys" may be rich in possessions, but they are undeniably poor in spirit and self-esteem (Garbarino, 1999). Fitting into trends similar to those reflective of economic poverty, these boys probably rank somewhere in the bottom 20% on factors such as social inclusion and peer acceptance—two strong predictors of youth violence and aggression (see Fraser, 1996, for a review). Often these friendless and self-loathing boys have been rejected and discarded by teenage society, and violence is their vehicle toward redemption. It becomes the primary means by which they combat their intense feelings of shame and humiliation. The "poor" label, almost universally, suggests that one is among the bottom 20% for whatever the relevant classifying criterion might be. Poverty means being inferior to the dominant culture, regardless of the scale, and to deal with the negative feelings associated with oppression and being devalued, troubled youth often respond with violence and aggression—the primary by-product of their pent-up frustration and rage.

Mahatma Ghandi said, "Poverty is the ultimate form of violence." This is an important quote because it suggests that poverty *is* violence. Ghandi understood that inequality is a principal defining feature of the human experience, although its physical concomitants are variable across cultures and societies. In some societies, poverty may mean shortened life expectancy and institutionalized violence. In still others, poverty means having a sense of relative deprivation, but the extent of this feeling varies universally as a function of the gap between the "rich" and "poor," however defined. Poverty represents a psychological assault against self-esteem and identity—a direct act of violence *in and of itself*.

Consider Malcolm. This boy's desire to provide a relatively comfortable lifestyle for his family exemplifies his need to meet the standards set by a judgmental and materialistic society. The American ideal is simple: Make as much money as you can while working as little as possible. Accordingly, because Malcolm internalized this ideal early in life, it pained him to see his mother "work like a dog" for minimum-wage compensation—so much so that he was ashamed of his family's destitute situation. He resented his father's leaving and saw drug dealing as an opportunity to provide his family with an involved mother, an apartment, a livable income, and a number of possessions that made Malcolm feel "normal" again. He, like most adolescents, wanted to fit in and wanted to feel adequate. In Malcolm's mind, the boy he killed was reduced to just one more obstacle impeding his lifelong plight for adequacy and normalcy, an obstacle he was compelled to eliminate.

Exposure to Family Violence

Social and economic stressors are positively related to family violence, and the severity and magnitude of family violence increase as a function of accumulated socioeconomic stress. Nationally representative data tell us that the nation's poorest, most socially isolated, and most economically frustrated parents are most likely to use family violence as a coping strategy (Wolfner & Gelles, 1993). These same data suggest that relative to their more affluent peers, poor children are more likely to be abused by their parents and run an increased risk of witnessing marital violence in their homes (Straus & Gelles, 1990). These findings have direct relevance to the present discussion, because living in poverty can mean being exposed to large amounts of family violence, and exposure to family violence is a primary risk factor for the development of aggressive and antisocial behavior.

Although some empirical research points to a link between experiencing abuse as a child and engaging in family violence as an adult, the primary emphasis in this area has been on linking child physical abuse to adolescent delinquency. An investigation of a sample of 97 incarcerated delinquents yielded the finding that 75% of violent delinquents and more than 33% of less violent delinquents had histories of severe child abuse (Lewis, Shanok,

Pincus, & Glaser, 1979). More recently, Scudder, Blount, Heide, and Silverman (1993) tested the validity of this relationship and concluded that delinquents experience higher levels of childhood victimization than nondelinquents and that abused children are more likely than nonabused children to become delinquent.

Many research efforts have focused on understanding the *intergenerational transmission of violence* (Curtis, 1963): the continuity and perpetuation of violence over time and across generations. This is the idea that violence is passed from one generation to the next through a combination of genetic similarity, mutual context, and associative conditioning. However, Huesmann, Eron, Lefkowitz, and Walder (1984) noted:

> Genetic, physiological, and other constitutional factors undoubtedly play a role in [producing aggression], but the presence of the "appropriate learning conditions" is probably more important in most cases. The appropriate learning conditions seem to be those in which the child has many opportunities to observe aggression, in which the child is reinforced for his or her own aggression, and in which the child is the object of aggression. (p. 1120)

Bandura (1973) used social learning theory to explain the link between childhood exposure to family violence and subsequent manifestations of violent behavior. Physically abused children raised in hostile home environments observe caregivers using violence to get their way. Through intimidation and the use of brute force, these parents coerce their children into conforming to demands, and according to social learning theory, these children come to believe that they too can get people to conform by using violence. Such a process legitimizes the use of aggression as a means to one's end and, in many ways, vicariously and directly reinforces its use.

The second part of the social learning explanation revolves around what is called *script-based knowledge*. Scripts, quite simply, are the conceptualizations we have of how the world works. Abused children and children exposed to family violence learn that violence is an acceptable way to confront anger and frustration, and they internalize this script because it follows what has been modeled to them by influential adult figures. Their repertoire of coping behaviors, skewed toward the aggressive end of the continuum, promotes a chronic and self-maintaining pattern of aggressive and hostile coping.

However, like most developmental relationships, the relationship between exposure to family violence and subsequent displays of violent behavior is not one-to-one. On the basis of the observation that large numbers of physically and sexually abused children never show any signs of violent or aggressive tendencies, developmental neurobiologists offered an alternative to the traditional social learning explanation. The work of Bruce Perry (1997, in press) exemplifies this approach.

Studying the impact of early stress and trauma on brain development, Perry documents that early experiences of this kind do affect brain development—a possibility that is pertinent to understanding the relationship between exposure to family violence and the subsequent expression of violent behavior. Briefly, the cortical and limbic regions of the brain regulate complex and abstract forms of expression and behavior (e.g., moral reasoning and impulse control), whereas the midbrain and brainstem modulate more primitive and reactive behaviors (e.g., aggression and impulsivity). The brain develops in a *use-dependent* fashion, whereby the areas receiving most stimulation develop most quickly and, in turn, get used most frequently. Children raised in characteristically stressful and violent family environments develop an overactive stress-response apparatus, located primarily in the midbrain and brainstem. Overstimulation in this area of the brain results in a predisposition to act impulsively, aggressively, and violently.

Malcolm's reflection on the murder he committed—"I didn't know what else to do. . . . I didn't see any other solution"—epitomizes the principles of the neurobiological and social learning perspectives simultaneously. Severely abused children and those exposed to chronic marital violence not only come to believe that violence is an *acceptable* way to cope with stress (what social learning theory predicts), but also that violence is the *only* way to cope with stress (what developmental neurobiology predicts). Accordingly, violence becomes their default coping strategy. Malcolm witnessed domestic violence and was physically abused throughout his childhood, and repeatedly saw his parents use violence to get their way. Given this, it comes as no surprise that Malcolm turned to violence when trying to cope with the rival drug dealer—Malcolm was both primed and taught to do just that.

Participation in the Illicit Economy

Drugs are repeatedly cited as causal agents, precipitating large amounts of violence in America. However, there is little evidence to support a psychopharmacological explanation of the relationship between drugs and violence. In fact, Elliott (1994) reports findings that suggest that the use of marijuana and opiate drugs actually decreases violent tendencies. A second widely held misconception about the relationship between drugs and violence is that addicts regularly commit violent crimes in order to support their addictions. This, however, is a rare phenomenon, occurring primarily within the context of severe withdrawal (Elliott, 1994). In fact, the most strongly documented connection between drugs and violence lies in the structure and nature of their distribution. That is, it is dealing drugs, not using them, that leads to violence.

Poverty and illicit economies go hand in hand. The isolated impoverished neighborhoods of the urban war zone provide the ideal conditions for illegal behavior and black markets. These communities tend to be those that have been written off and forgotten by the larger society. Interviews with youth from the poorest and most dangerous neighborhoods of Chicago and New York confirm this tendency (Garbarino, 1999). These youth report a sense of community isolation that extends from pizza delivery all the way to major medical and emergency services. As one boy put it,

> Pizza Hut won't come to our neighborhood. They ask if your order is for pickup or delivery, but when you give them the address they say they don't deliver or that they're understaffed that night. It's funny how they're understaffed every time I call. Even the people at 911 don't come when you call them. If you call after you see someone stabbed or shot in the street, 30 or 40 minutes will go by, but nothing happens—no cops, no ambulance, no nothing.

The message rings loud and clear: Nobody comes because nobody cares.

Although community isolation does, in fact, give rise to illicit economies, the relationship between community isolation and their emergence is not unidirectional. On the contrary, the relationship is both bidirectional and circular. When there is inadequate policing and a general unwillingness to stand up for the better good of an afflicted community, illicit economies flourish. And similarly, when illicit economies flourish, violence soon follows and the larger community tries to quarantine the "outbreak" by cutting off efforts to regulate and integrate the afflicted community. This triggers a vicious cycle of community isolation, drug dealing, and violence that is self-perpetuating and difficult to interrupt. But exactly how does drug dealing translate into youth violence?

Economically impoverished children and youth often turn to drug dealing as a way to make money—*lots* of money. Adolescent males living in the poorest housing developments of New York City report earning potentials from $100 to $800 per day. This has two important implications for the poverty-violence equation. First, many of these teen entrepreneurs use their street earnings to supplement their family's income. It is not uncommon for parents in poor communities to fail to meet the day-to-day physical needs of their families, and in many cases, drug dealing sons or close relatives help offset the cost of such things as food, shelter, and clothing. Second, money gives poor individuals a feeling of power and adequacy, even if only on a superficial level. Dealing drugs for just a few hours a day has the ability to make "haves" out of "have-nots" like no other profession or pseudoprofession. It should then come as no surprise that the "senseless" violence and killings we read and hear about in the urban war zone tend to center around drug-turf disputes. Territoriality, self-regulation, and defensiveness are inherent components of this industry, and the street money at stake plays such an immediate and meaningful role in the lives of the participants that they are often willing to go as far as to kill anyone who threatens its source.

Take, for example, Malcolm. He was able to restore his family's standard of living by dropping out of school and working in various sectors of the crack cocaine industry. At the peak of his involvement, he made in a single day what once took his mother almost a month to make as an honest fast-food worker. His earnings provided more than luxury. They provided the day-to-day staples needed to maintain his family—food, clothing, shelter, and transportation. The drug money meant more to Malcolm than a new jacket and a handful of gold chains. It meant that his mother could leave a job that made her miserable and that she could spend more time at home with him and his sisters. It meant that the family could have an apartment big enough for the four of them and that his mother could rest and begin to feel less inadequate. In short, the money represented the physical and psychological survival of his family, something for which Malcolm was willing to kill. Recall his words:

> That dude was stealing my family's money—money we needed real bad, money we needed to survive. What was I suppose to do—watch my family starve? I couldn't have my mom going back to some job she hated just to barely put food on the table. I wanted us to be normal again and have my mom be able to be with my little sisters like she could before. I didn't know what else to do. . . . I didn't see any other solution.

CONCLUSION

More than 90% of people who are arrested for violent crimes are either unemployed, underemployed, or living below the poverty line (Lang, 1994). The relationship between poverty and violence, however indirect, is undeniably strong. Although not every poor child grows up to commit a violent crime, poverty certainly puts them at significantly increased statistical and ecological risk.

Accumulation of risk models treat risk factors equally (e.g., Sameroff and his colleagues assigned equal weight to each of their original eight risk factors), but the fact of the matter is that not all risk factors are created equal. Important to keep in mind is the idea that poverty, by virtue of representing a conglomerate of developmental risk factors, reigns superior to most other individual risk factors with respect to having the ability to catalyze dysfunction. For example, when children live in poverty, they also run an increased risk of being raised by a single parent, being abused, and participating in the illicit economy. It is for these reasons that a single dichotomous "poverty variable" correlates so strongly with youth violence. When we talk about poverty, we are talking about a whole host of risks and social toxins.

As for our case study, what should be made of Malcolm and his crime? Was it his fault for pulling the trigger, or do we have his parents or society to blame for putting him in such a dreadful situation in the first place? While we do not intend to resolve that issue here, one thing is clear. Interpreted in context—amid the poverty and all the drug dealing, community isolation, economic inequality, domestic violence, and child abuse that come along with it—Malcolm's crime seems much less "senseless" than it probably did in a newspaper headline that read: "TEEN KILLS TEEN OVER SENSELESS DRUG TURF DISPUTE."

REFERENCES

Achenbach, T. M., & Edelbrock, C. (1983). *Manual for the child behavior checklist and revised behavior profile.* Burlington, VT: Queen City.

Bandura, A. (1973). *Aggression: A social learning analysis.* Englewood Cliffs, NJ: Prentice Hall.

Blanc, S. (1994). *Urban children in distress: Global predicaments and innovative strategies.* Langhorne, PA: Gordon and Breach.

Bronfenbrenner, U., McClelland, P., Wetherington, E., Moen, P., & Ceci, S. (1996). *The state of Americans.* New York: Free Press.

Children's Defense Fund. (1998). *The state of America's children: Yearbook.* Washington, DC: Author.

Children's Defense Fund. (1999). *The state of America's children: Yearbook.* Washington, DC: Author.

Cicchetti, D., & Rizley, R. (1981). Developmental perspectives on the etiology, intergenerational transmission, and sequelae of child maltreatment. *New Directions for Child Development, 11,* 31–55.

Curtis, G. C. (1963). Violence breeds violence—perhaps? *American Journal of Psychiatry, 120,* 386–397.

Dunst, C., & Trivette, C. (1992). *Risk and opportunity factors influence parent and child functioning.* Paper presented at the Ninth Annual Smoky Mountain Winter Institute, Ashville, NC.

Elliot, D. S. (March, 1994). *Youth violence: An overview.* Boulder: The Center for the Study and Prevention of Violence, University of Colorado.

Fraser, M. W. (1996). Aggressive behavior in childhood and early adolescence: An ecological-developmental perspective on youth violence. *Social Work, 41*(4), 347–361.

Garbarino, J. (1995). *Raising children in a socially toxic environment.* San Francisco, CA: Jossey-Bass.

Garbarino, J. (1998). The stress of being a poor child in America. *Child and Adolescent Psychiatric Clinics of North America, 7*(1), 105–119.

Garbarino, J. (1999). *Lost boys: Why our sons turn violent and how we can save them.* New York: Free Press.

Garbarino, J., Dubrow, N., Kostelny, K., & Pardo, C. (1992). *Children in danger: Coping with the consequences.* San Francisco: Jossey-Bass.

Gilligan, J. (1996). *Violence: Our deadly epidemic and its causes.* New York: Putnam.

Huesmann, L. R., Eron, L. D., Lefkowitz, M. M., & Walder, L. O. (1984). Stability of aggression over time and across generations. *Developmental Psychology, 20*(6), 1120–1134.

Lang, S. S. (1994). *Teen violence.* New York: Franklin Watts.

Lewis, D. O., Shanok, S. S., Pincus, J. H., & Glaser, G. H. (1979). Violent juvenile delinquents: Psychiatric, neurological, psychological, and abuse factors. *Journal of the American Academy of Child Psychiatry, 18,* 307–318.

Losel, F., & Bliesner, T. (1990). Resilience in adolescence: A study on the generalizability of protective factors. In K. Hurrelmann & F. Losel (Eds.), *Health Hazards in Adolescence.* Berlin, Germany: Walter de Gruyter.

Messner, S. F. (1988). Research on cultural and socioeconomic factors in criminal violence. *Psychiatric Clinics of North America, 11*(4), 511–525.

Office of Juvenile Justice and Delinquency Prevention. (1997). *Juvenile offenders and victims: Update on violence.* Pittsburgh, PA: National Center for Juvenile Justice.

Perry, B. (1997). Incubated in terror: Neurodevelopmental factors in the cycle of violence. In J. D. Osofsky (Ed.), *Children in a violent society* (pp. 124–149). New York: Guilford.

Perry, B. (in press). *Maltreated children: Experience, brain development, and the next generation.* New York: Norton.

Sameroff, A., Seifer, R., Barocas, R., Zax, M., & Greenspan, S. (1987). Intelligence quotient scores of 4-year-old children: Socio-environmental risk factors. *Pediatrics, 79,* 343–350.

Scudder, R. G., Blount, W. R., Heide, K. M., & Silverman, I. J. (1993). Important links between child abuse, neglect, and delinquency. *International Journal of Offender Therapy and Comparative Criminology, 37*(4), 315–323.

Straus, M., & Gelles, R. (1990). *Physical violence in American families.* New Brunswick, NJ: Transaction.

Tolan, P. (1995, August). The limits of resilience. Presentation to the annual meeting of the American Psychological Association, New York.

Wilson, W. J. (1996). *When work disappears: The world of the new urban poor.* New York: Knopf.

Wolfner, G. D., & Gelles, R. (1993). A profile of violence toward children: A national study. *Child Abuse and Neglect, 17,* 197–212.

CHAPTER 4

Framing Children in the News
The Face and Color of Youth Crime in America

LYNNELL HANCOCK

The case began with a numbing discovery: an 11-year-old girl's body found bludgeoned and mauled amid the rubble in one of Chicago's most crime-addled neighborhoods. Local newspapers gave the story the standard crime-scene treatment in July 1998—reporting what happened, where, when, and to whom. Police said the little girl was riding her bike near her grandmother's home during the day when she was struck in the head, dragged to a weed patch, sexually brutalized, and suffocated.

As horrifying as it was, the story did not fit the conventional page-1 formula for a Chicago blockbuster. If Ryan Harris were an affluent child, killed in one of the city's relatively safe sections, news attention would undoubtedly have been far more intense. But as it was, this bright girl's death in the all-minority streets of Englewood nearly disappeared in the clip morgue of violent tales of poor children in poor neighborhoods.

Then the story took a jolting turn from neglected paragraphs to national headlines. Three weeks after the little girl was found with her underwear stuffed in her mouth, and dead leaves jammed in her nose, Chicago police produced their suspects—two children, ages 7 and 8. Officials said the Englewood boys likely killed Ryan Harris for her Road Warrior bike. The scared, skinny kids were escorted before the press and the judge, their hands engulfed to the wrist in the court officer's palm. The spectacle brought home how far America's justice system has gone in treating children as adults, and how closely entangled the news media has become in the process. These second and third graders were the youngest ever in American history to be charged with first-degree murder.

The public gasped in dismay, but not disbelief. In the first weeks, it seemed plausible to most that such young children could kill, so violently, for so little. After all, the nation had been pummeled with the truly appalling stories of young kids in Arkansas, Mississippi, and Oregon gunning down their classmates in the hallowed halls and school playgrounds. A few months after the Englewood murder, two teens in Littleton, Colorado, went on a murder spree in their high school, killing 13 fellow students before turning their Tec-9 semiautomatic weapons on themselves (Bai, 1999).

These aberrant events tested the limits of common understandings about children's behavior. And yet they are, in fact, aberrations. And the question still haunts: How did the public reach the point where it could so readily believe that 7- and 8-year-olds can be so brutal? What has happened to our collective understanding of children and violence that we can describe such young children as "predators," as we do animals in the wild? Is it true that children are more savage today? Is it a myth born of media saturation and newsroom racial biases? Or is it the tragic truth found somewhere between?

In this chapter I examine the news media's role in shaping the public's fear of children—or more specifically, the fear of *other people's* children. How do reporters use statistics, context, sources, and the power of story choice? What role does race play in stories about kid criminals? How does the media's portrayal of youthful offenders influence legislators and the public debate about solutions? And finally, what happens when responsible journalists cover crime beyond police reports, bringing context to the crime and humanizing texture to the victims, the suspects, their families, their communities?

The overall picture poses a serious challenge to newsrooms in America. Most news organizations—television news most egregiously—still practice drive-by coverage of local juvenile courts, child protection services, foster care agencies, and correction facilities. Full-time reporters are rarely assigned to specialize in children's institutions the same way they would City Hall. Journalists almost never have sufficient training in child development, public health, or the art and ethics of interviewing kids. The day-to-day realities of childhood and teenage life are little covered and less understood. Therefore, when the anomalous violent act erupts—a foster care child commits suicide, a troubled teen is arrested for torturing a younger child, a pair of friends spray the school grounds with gunfire—general-assignment reporters swoop in with inadequate tools to probe for answers. The public is left with a glut of stories repeating myths about violent kids (the majority of whom are minority and male) and an anemic understanding of these children's lives and communities' responses to their needs.

The horrific spate of schoolyard slaughters from 1997 to 1999 jolted some news editors into the realization that timeworn news conventions and assumptions do not work when it comes to covering children and crime. Some papers are attempting to expand the crime beat into a more comprehensive violence beat, where reporters would routinely place juvenile arrests in a larger context, exploring not only the facts of the crime, but also the roots of violence and the impact on the community (Stevens, Dorfman, & Wallack, 1997). Others offer in-house workshops using experts in juvenile law and child development to help reporters understand that the world of children can be very different from the world of adults. If this kind of thoughtful press coverage becomes more prevalent, we may eventually see coverage that calms fears, points to salient solutions, and avoids the sad series of misunderstandings that seemed almost inevitable for the families in Chicago.

AMERICA'S LITTLEST MURDER SUSPECTS

The news that the two little Chicago boys were arrested for murder hit the newsstands on August 11, 1998. Police, reporters, editorial writers, readers—everyone except the residents of Englewood—expressed little more than resignation that the newest killers were so small they couldn't see over the judge's bench, let alone understand their Miranda rights to remain silent and request an attorney upon arrest. "We were all primed to believe this could happen," said Alex Kotlowitz, author of *There Are No Children Here* (1992), a groundbreaking account of children and violence in a Chicago housing project. After the arrests, Kotlowitz found himself on "CBS This Morning" earnestly calling on citizens to find ways to prevent any more Ryan Harrises in the future (A. Kotlowitz, personal communication, February 15, 1999).

The *Chicago Tribune* reporter Maurice Possley told me that his first instinct was to believe the police. "We all tend to give the benefit of the doubt to authorities," Possley said. "We need to believe them. They are in charge of public safety" (M. Possley, personal communication, February 11, 1999). Most Chicagoans remembered that some of the most alarming childhood crimes of this decade happened in their city. In 1994, two grade school children dropped five-year-old Eric Morse out of a 14th-floor window because the kindergartner refused to steal candy for them. Months later, 11-year-old Yummy Sandifer shot a 14-year-old girl, and then was himself gunned down days later by his own teenage gang members. "I'm continually amazed at the extent and scope of human cruelty I see all the time," said Possley, a 28-year Chicago crime reporter. "Anything's possible."

The first wave of coverage underscored this tendency to believe the worst. *The Los Angeles Times* announced "the end of innocence" in the headline of its first-day editorial. In the piece, the editor asked, "Why are children who used to only quarrel or push and shove now capable of murder?" ("End of Innocence," 1998, p. B6). The *Chicago Sun-Times* opined that "more and more we are seeing child play replaced with *predatory behavior* in children too young to comprehend fully the implications of what they have done" ("Lives Endangered," 1998, p. 37; emphasis added). *Time* magazine dropped a reckless line in its first story about the case, saying that "neighbors told *Time* that R. [the 7-year-old] is a gang-banger with the notorious Black Disciples," an outrageous accusation that was never corroborated (Stodghill, Cole, & Grace, 1998, p. 62).

The poignant punchline to this story is that these boys didn't kill Ryan Harris. Prosecutors dropped the murder charges a few weeks later. (Semen was found on the girl's clothing, a biological impossibility for boys so young.) Police faced public ridicule for their roughshod interrogating and sloppy investigating. An official rule has since been issued insuring that children have parents present and videotapes rolling when under police interrogation (Kotlowitz, 1999). The subsequent news reporting demonstrated the best and the worst of media coverage of kids and violence, depending on which newspaper you happened to read.

THE TALE OF TWO PAPERS

A closer look at the Englewood story demonstrates several aspects of the news media's influence when it comes to shaping public opinion on children and crime. One, as detailed above, is the press's potent prelude to this story, which helped solidify the public's firm belief that children these days are more savage than ever. Another is the power of seemingly innocuous, standard-fare crime reporting to subvert children's rights. This is done most effectively through handing over full control of the story to the sources—in this case, the police. A third is the potential power of the press, when used responsibly, with a special sensitivity to children, to subvert all of the above, and to protect children's rights in the courts.

By-the-book, cop-beat regulations dictate that reporters find out who is arrested for what crime, when, where, and why. Police are often the only source of information that a reporter can draw on and still meet tight deadlines for filing a story. Child suspects tend to be unprepared emotionally and cognitively to deal with police interrogations and legal proceedings.

They certainly have few resources with which to reach reporters and make sure their voices are heard. A daily police-blotter crime story does not allow for probing beyond the cop version to bring context and human focus to the suspects, the victim, the families, or the community. These questions are important when it comes to stories involving adults. They are imperative when the subjects are children. But most reporters do not consider the special circumstances of child suspects. When crime writers treat children's cases exactly as they would adults' (just as the legal system tends to do for violent crimes), children's rights are severely compromised.

On the other hand, other news organizations (notably *The Chicago Tribune*) demonstrated how hard work and child-sensitive journalism can actually protect children's rights. Some reporters at the paper challenged inconsistencies in the official story from the outset, questioning police interrogation methods and conclusions about children's mental and physical capabilities. They talked to the boys' families. They placed a template of the police version of events over a knowledge of child development. They asked questions such as, What are children really capable of at what ages? How would a child respond in certain circumstances to authorities? Is it really sensible to treat children as young as these as adults in the legal system, or in the press? One could argue that this kind of sensitive press attention coupled with strong legal representation helped to restore the boys' legal rights.

The day that police announced they were arresting two little boys, *The Chicago Tribune* decided this was a big story—big enough to send one of its most senior crime reporters. Possley had covered the Oklahoma City bombing case and the Unabomber trial. He had a clip morgue full of experience. Possley admitted that he went into this story with a set of assumptions culled from nearly 30 years as a newsman in Chicago (M. Possley, personal communication, February 11, 1999). He told me he expected to find, for instance, that the adults in these boys' lives were dysfunctional—"mother all strung out, father missing"—like so many poor, Black families whose kids end up in trouble with the law. He assumed that these children were cut out of the notorious Yummy Sandifer mold, having grown up in a world of gangs and fear. Neither stereotype turned out to be true.

The police held a hearing first, describing the brutal crime, including lots of "adult sex stuff," said Possley. Then the reporters filed over to juvenile court for the hearing. An audible gasp greeted the children as they were marched out to meet the judge. As Possley said,

> I think we were all expecting to see demon children—Damiens—based on the police description. Then these two little skinny kids come

out. They stand next to the bench that was built for kids to see over. And they can't see over it. I'm sitting there thinking of my deadline, trying to write the story in my head, and I thought—these little squirts? It just doesn't make sense.

The Dangers of Objectivity

Here is a sample of the first-day stories of Chicago's two main papers.

The Chicago Sun-Times published "just the facts, ma'am" standard fare on the first day, rarely straying from the police version of events:

> Two boys, age 7 and 8, accused of killing an 11-year-old girl, are the youngest suspects in memory to be linked with a murder here, Chicago police said Monday.
>
> Police believe Ryan Harris may have been killed last month for her bicycle.
>
> She died from a blow to the head, allegedly from a rock used by the 7 year old and from suffocation caused by clothing, grass and leaves stuffed into her mouth, police said. She was sexually molested with an object. (Carpenter & Lawrence, 1998, p. 1)

The dry recitation of the case illustrates the shortcoming of textbook Associated Press–style journalism. There is nothing overtly wrong with it. The police were treating the boys as adults. *The Chicago Sun-Times* was simply following suit. The facts are in order. There is no discernible opinion betrayed. But this dispassionate account reads more like a police-blotter report than a story. By objectifying the children, never challenging their special status as children, the story ends up dehumanizing them and giving unbalanced credence to the police's version of events. Readers are left with the impression that there is no more to it than the facts before them.

We read that the police describe the boys as of "average height and weight." The story does not describe them beyond this, even though the reporters have firsthand knowledge that they are skinny little boys. It does nothing to correct the assumption that these children must be remorseless thugs. Therefore, it's much easier for readers to believe the worst of cardboard criminals than of flesh-and-blood little boys.

At the end of the story, reporters balance this version by quoting Ryan's grandfather and the 8-year-old's attorney—both registering their disbelief that such small boys could have killed Ryan. It's significant that the reporter chose to bury this skepticism deep into the story.

Finally, the piece concludes with a mention of two other Chicago child-on-child murders: one last March, one 5 years ago. This is a common, and often misleading, way in which journalists try to contextualize a crime.

But simply listing similar crimes does not make for accurate context. It's a way of inventing a trend, leaving readers with the impression that an epidemic is afoot. The specific context for each individual crime is ignored. The most damaging result is that this list adds credence to the current crime, instead of a deepened understanding of its circumstances or consequences. In this case, the list was also completely misleading.

Reporting at the Child's Level

The Chicago Tribune's story began this way:

> The two slaying suspects, ages 7 and 8, sat patiently at the defense table, legs dangling above the floor Monday, as prosecutors accused them of fatally bludgeoning an 11-year-old girl to death last month in Chicago's Englewood neighborhood.
>
> Despite often-gruesome testimony, the boys, who are now among Chicago's youngest-ever slaying suspects, seemed mostly oblivious.
>
> The 7-year-old, with a pout on his face and his black hair braided neatly in cornrows ending in blue beads, sat hunched over a yellow legal pad, using a red pen to sketch a house with a smoking chimney below a sky filled with heart-shaped clouds.
>
> "Am I going to jail?" he whispered to Cathy Ferguson, one of his attorneys. In response, she handed him another sheet of drawing paper. (Possley, 1998b, p. 1)

The story goes on to describe the 8-year-old eating Skittles, smiling at his parents, before detailing the police case against them, and Englewood residents' disbelief.

Possley's story reflects his studied skepticism about the police version of events from the beginning. Readers see children, not demon seeds. The kids are calm (sitting patiently). They are small (dangly feet); they are not psychotic (sketching normal childlike pictures with houses and hearts, instead of the disconnected drawings of troubled children). And above all, they are not adults. They are grade school children, "oblivious" to the adult proceedings around them.

A few days later, reporters received the police records. Possley read them not through the standard view of the police, but through the eyes of the small boys involved. Detectives described holding the 7-year-old's hand, telling him that good boys tell the truth, insuring him that they were his friends. "The first thing a 7-year-old will want to do is to do is please the man, tell the man what he thinks he wants to hear," Possley told me. "It's hard to believe the child understood the implications of talking to these detectives."

Then there was the matter of the rocks the boys said they threw at Ryan. Police reports indicated that a medical examiner found that Ryan was struck by something much bigger and heavier than a rock. In fact, a bloody brick was found next to her body. The detectives decided that the boys were lying about the rocks, but not about other things. "There were too many inconsistencies to conclude so definitively that these boys killed her," said Possley. He dissected the reports, putting them in the context of Illinois law and juvenile justice practices, in a subsequent article (Possley, 1998a, p. 1).

Finally, in a powerful interview with the 7-year-old's mother, Possley dispels the commonly held myth that most poor children who encounter legal trouble live in homes headed by single parents who lack both education and a desire to work. Both boys lived with two parents who had college educations and full-time jobs (Possley & Puente, 1998, p. 1). Without the interview, the public stereotype would have prevailed. "It heightened the sensitivity about this case around here," Possley said.

The Chicago Tribune avoided the newsroom temptation to treat these suspects as adults, simply because the courts had charged them with an "adultlike" crime. This kind of perceptive treatment of children in the news goes a long way toward deflecting the public drumbeat of the coming wave of superpredators—male, Black, and young.

IF IT BLEEDS, IT LEADS, AND LEADS AND LEADS . . .

The Englewood debacle provides a good place to pause in the flurry of debate over kids and crime to examine news coverage of youth at millennium's end. Any honest reader will admit that human brutality makes for good reading. Any savvy editor will tell you that violence sells, whether we like it or not. "If it bleeds, it leads" is a timeless maxim in the newsroom. And since the advent of the penny press, a gory crime—particularly if the suspected perpetrator is baby-faced—is guaranteed front-page material. The trick for a responsible journalist is to cover these stories without falling into easy clichés and conclusions; to use these stories to inform, instead of entertain.

That trick has become a monumental hurdle in the 1990s, with the runaway proliferation of media outlets. Beyond the traditional newspapers and network television and radio news, the global audience now has access to hundreds of cable and satellite television stations, on-line media sites, and scores of entertainment talk shows, often confused by the public for news. Some are staffed by trained journalists, many only by trained technicians, and all have the rapid-fire capability of flooding airwaves and cyber-space with their own versions of the breaking stories of the hour.

When a huge story breaks, such as the schoolyard shootings in Jones-boro, Arkansas (where an 11- and 13-year-old trapped and fired at their classmates combat style), it hits the national and international airwaves in nanoseconds, and keeps coming and coming until the story runs its course. There is little time for reflection, no time to assess the impact of the ava-lanche of coverage on the lives of the children involved and the community they live in, or on the public's soured attitude toward all children. The damage is done instantly.

For weeks in the spring of 1997 audiences and readers were barraged by photos of the Arkansas suspects as toddlers dressed in combat fatigues, cradling rifles. *The New York Daily News* headline described them as demon-seed children who were "born to kill" (Williams, George, & Siemas-zko, 1998, cover). *Time* turned up the volume with "Armed & Dangerous" (Labi, 1998, cover). A *Newsweek* sidebar asked, "Why Do Kids Kill?" (Gegax, Adler, & Pederson, 1998, p. 45), instead of, Why did these particu-lar children kill? Even if some individual stories within these packages were balanced, the sheer volume of the coverage and the fear-mongering tone created by the editors who package the stories left a deadly impression. It takes a highly discriminating reader to avoid coming away from this flood of images and headlines without a gnawing fear that youth in general are more dangerous than ever.

The damage to children's rights by such unrelenting coverage was most obvious in the aftermath of the Littleton, Colorado, massacre. In the first few hours after the two teenagers gunned their way through Colum-bine High School on April 20, 1999, television and radio news shows were linking the pair to Nazi sympathizers and a "trench coat mafia" (O'Driscoll, 1999, p. 1A). School officials from Rhode Island to Japan began suspending children based on their dress, combing through their poems and homework for signs of violence. A siege mentality took hold on many campuses. Virtu-ally all schoolchildren became potential terrorist suspects. In the weeks that followed, the American Civil Liberties Union reported receiving dozens of complaints from students saying they were disciplined by school officials for a variety of issues, ranging from sporting blue hair to having nail clippers in their book bags (Mathis, 1999).

AMERICA'S CHILDREN: DEAD OR DIABOLICAL

Newsrooms run on the adrenaline of story-by-story deadlines, resisting the need to pay attention to the overall effect of their coverage. When it comes to the coverage of kids, violence overwhelmingly defines their image in the news, until recently. Children—predominantly minority kids—appeared as either dead or diabolical in the news far more often than just plain kids. A 1994 Children Now survey found that 40% of all print news involving kids was devoted to crime and violence. One quarter of the coverage involved education—the next largest category. The rest divided between public policy issues such as poverty, child care, protection services, and so on. Broadcast news was far more slanted toward the miscreants: 48% of its youth news coverage was about violence, and only 15% was devoted to education (Kunkel, 1994).

The picture four years later was more hopeful. The percentage of child violence stories dropped to 23% for newspapers, and 10% for television, according to the most recent Children Now study. One reason for the improvement was an overall media commitment to covering a broader range of kids' issues, such as culture, health, and education. Still, poverty, welfare, and other policy stories routinely ignore children (Children Now, 1999).

None of this is to say that childhood crime is not a concern and should not be covered. There is no question that arrests for teen homicides more than doubled overall between 1985 and 1995—a phenomenon that deserved rigorous public scrutiny (Sickmund, Snyder, & Poe-Yamagata, 1997). The danger comes when these crime stories are covered at the exclusion of others; when they ignore context, dehumanize the victims and suspects, and fail to search for answers that are neither easy nor stereotypical.

What sort of context is excluded? Juvenile crime is too often treated as if it happens in a bubble, disconnected from adult crime and social or family conditions. For instance, adults kill children at a far more astonishing rate than kids do, but the adult crimes are not always given equal column inches. Ninety percent of the murders of children under 12 and three fourths of the murders of 12- to 17-year-olds are committed by adults (Doi, 1998; Snyder, Sickmund, & Poe-Yamagata, 1996).

The press rarely supplies these kinds of comparisons. Author Mike Males points out in *Framing Youth: Ten Myths about the Next Generation* (1999) that the same day the Englewood boys were arrested, a suburban Los Angeles father gunned down his wife and three kids. The latter story was considered local, and received no national attention. The irony is that the phenomenon of adults killing children is not considered "unusual" enough to warrant news. We read it about it less and less, until it actually seems rare.

Other key questions, rarely asked, could help illuminate the root causes of violence: How many kids were abused or neglected during the same period in which the homicide rate shot up? The U.S. Justice Department reports that the abuse rate for children doubled between 1986 and 1993

(Sickmund et al., 1997). Experts have long known that kids who are abused are more at risk of behaving in dangerously aggressive ways (see chapter 3, this volume).

How many children were victims of violence? Federal statistics show that in 1994 alone, 12- to 17-year-olds were three times as likely as adults to be raped, mugged, or assaulted (Sickmund et al., 1997). If children learn from adults, then they learn violent behavior by experiencing it.

How many of the teen arrests for violent crimes involved guns? Franklin Zimring reports in his book *American Youth Violence* (1998) that the vast majority of the crimes committed by teens in the early 1990s involved firearms. Assaults involving fists and knives remained the same, suggesting that kids were not more innately savage in the 1990s, just better armed.

If reporters automatically asked these kinds of questions, their stories would be more informative, and the public could be inspired to call for longer term solutions: better child care, quality school counselors, decent housing and health facilities for kids, improved youth programs, effective gun control, more alternatives to jail. Instead, the steady drumbeat of slaughter and shock in the media distracts positive public discussion, leaving citizens numb. The cry becomes a focused crackdown on criminal kids. We fear them, so let's punish them. Rehabilitation is useless. The public believes that juvenile courts are too soft for this new, brutal breed apart. Adult criminal courts are the only answer (Zimring, 1998). A 1996 CBS News/*New York Times* poll found that 88% of those surveyed believed teen violence was a bigger problem now than in the past. Seventy percent believed that juvenile courts were too lenient with the youngsters (*False Images?,* 1997).

Fear Overwhelms the Facts

How did this happen? A quick look at the cover headlines of the nation's most respected news magazines over the decade hint at the media's contribution to this skewed fear of our children. Consider 1993, the cusp year for adolescent violence, when teenagers represented 18% of the arrests for violent crimes. *Newsweek* ran with "Teen Violence: Wild in the Streets," in August (Kantrowitz, 1993, p. 40). *U.S. News* published "Guns in the Schools: When Killers Come to Class—Even Suburban Parents Now Fear the Rising Tide of Violence" the next fall (Toch, 1993, p. 30). Adults committed 82% of the violent crimes that same year, but did not experience similar press treatment.

The following year, arrests among teens for violent crimes began to level off, along with crime in general (Fuentes, 1998). Still, the cover stories included "Killer Teens" in *U.S. News* (1994, p. 26), and in *Time,* "When

Kids Go Bad: America's Juvenile Justice System is Antiquated, Inadequate and No Longer Able to Cope with the Violence Wrought by Children Whom No One Would Call Innocents" (Lacayo, 1994, p. 60).

Not surprisingly, public perception did not catch up with the facts. In the following 3 years, juvenile arrests declined by 3%. Between 1995 and 1996 the rate dropped by 6%. A 1997 report by the National Center for Juvenile Justice concluded that delinquents today are not, in fact, much different from criminal kids of decades past. "Today's violent youth commits the same number of violent acts as his/her predecessor of 15 years ago," the authors wrote (Sickmund et al., 1997, p. 24). Still, news-magazine covers during those years continued to tinker with the fear barometer. *U.S. News* ran with "Teenage Time Bombs," in 1996 (Zoglin, 1996, p. 52). *People* magazine examined "Kids Without a Conscience" (Eftimiades, 1997, p. 46). (It's worth noting that seven out of the nine criminals focused on in *People* were over age 18 at the time of their arrests.)

The Coalition for Juvenile Justice argued that "this media firestorm has either created or reinforced a public impression that juvenile crime is rampant and a major threat to the safety of the community" (*False Images?*, 1997, p. 29).

The Teenagers Are Coming, the Teenagers Are Coming . . . or Are They?

News reporters are nothing without sources. The best will vary the ideological perspectives of their chosen spokesmeisters. But the bottom line is that whoever captures the media's attention with the newest theories and the snappiest quotes often takes the lead in shaping public opinion. From the mid-1980s to the mid-1990s, the news media helped three prominent academics, one more conservative than the other, dominate the child violence story: UCLA criminologist John Q. Wilson, Princeton political scientist John J. DiIulio, and Northeastern University demographer James Alan Fox. Their theories and statistics were provocative, their credentials impressive, their accessibility to the press free flowing. Whenever a child viciously murdered another, or a youth gang wreaked havoc somewhere, the press—especially the news magazines—turned to one in this triumverate to offer the "official" explanation. Perhaps this phenomenon, more than any other, explains how the public developed a conservative understanding of youth violence and an irrational fear of America's teens.

In November 1995, Princeton's DiIulio coined the most racially explosive word in the field to sum up his theories on urban crime. In a *Weekly Standard* article, the professor predicted the ominous "coming of the Super-Predator." This was a new breed of feral child, described by DiIulio as almost mythical in his savagery. The superpredator suffers from "moral poverty," and commits his "homicidal violence in 'wolf packs.'" He is raised in "chaotic, dysfunctional, fatherless, Godless and jobless settings where . . . self-respecting young men literally aspire to get away with murder." By the year 2010, the conservative moralist foresaw, 270,000 more such remorseless thugs—most of them Black, male, and urban—would be pouring into helpless communities (DiIulio, 1995, p. 23).

A respected demographer turned criminologist weighed in with some supporting and alarming arithmetic. Northeastern's Fox noted the expected rise in adolescent population over the next 15 years, linked it with recent juvenile violence arrests, and warned that more teens will mean more crime. That's because "teenagers," Fox told *Time* magazine, are "temporary sociopaths—impulsive and immature" (Zoglin, 1996, p. 52). UCLA's Wilson, a major influence on DiIulio and Fox, added that the new criminal is "remorseless . . . sullen—and very young" (Rodriguez, 1996, p. M1).

The Anatomy of the Superpredator Story

Embracing the theory's melodramatic undertones and its slave-era assumptions of Black male behavior, the press took these fear-mongering ideas and ran with them. Editors and reporters were primed to believe the new trend, since they had been relying on its theorists for years. Moreover, the theory was highly media friendly: simple, believable, and conducive to lively copy.

Newsweek pumped up the volume, asking if the current teen violence decline was actually "the lull before the storm." The writer then added, "Crime really is down, but teenagers are more violent than ever—and some cops and experts believe 1995 may turn out to be the good old days" (Morganthau, 1995, p. 40). That story was followed the next month by "Superpredators Arrive," which asked if Americans should consider *caging* "the new breed of vicious kids" (Annin, 1996, p. 57). *U.S. News* put together a "Crime Time Bomb" cover story in March of the same year (Gest & Pope, 1996, p. 28). Americans battened down.

Legislators helped provide the locks. Senator Orrin Hatch introduced legislation that would jail runaways with adult prisoners and expel kids from school for smoking cigarettes. Florida representative Bill McCollum warned Americans to "brace yourself for the coming generation of superpredators," to drum up support for his bill, The Violent Youth Predator Act of 1996 (Miller, 1998, p. 48).

Consequently, in 1999, more children are being sent to adult court for sentencing than in previous decades. Forty-seven states have tightened their juvenile justice laws, making punishment tougher. In a decade, the numbers of kids transferred to adult court nearly doubled (Sickmund et al., 1997).

In many ways, we are still seeing the aftershocks of this superpredator theory in Congressional acts. Post-Littleton, the House of Representatives passed a youth violence bill most noted for its provision allowing schools to post the Bible's Ten Commandments (a clause that will not likely withstand a constitutional challenge) (Fiore & Anderson, 1999). Less attention was paid to its provisions making it even easier for the courts to try children as young as 14 years old as adults, and to release their criminal records more readily to the public—reversing states' century-long practice of protecting the privacy of juveniles from the glare of public exposure (O'Rourke, 1999).

But there was one problem: The theory was dead wrong. Despite the media hype and the congressional endorsement, teenage wolf packs failed to materialize. The teen population continued to grow, but crime continued on its downward spiral. Experts note that this alarming prediction of waves of juvenile violence is based on fear, not science. Even the theory's conservative architects are now backing off, saying that other factors such as tougher crime prevention and the collapsing crack trade overshadowed demographic predictors. DiIulio has turned his attention to faith-based solutions in the inner city. He wrote most recently that jailing children with adults "will merely produce more street gladiators" (*Covering Criminal Justice,* 1999).

But the damage was done.

Black and Latino Boys Take the Rap

The superpredator concept—and all its dehumanizing connotations—still lives on, primarily in newscasts. And its most powerful message is race. It's a label reserved almost exclusively for Black and Latino males.

Certainly, a disproportionate number of young minority males are arrested for robbery and homicide, compared with Whites; the teen jail population is 63% minority, 37% White (Sickmund, 1997; Zimring, 1998). But even when White children are caught committing heinous crimes, they are rarely referred to as predators—super or otherwise—in the press. For example, coverage of the Jonesboro shooters from the beginning was sensitive to the community and to all the families. The public could sympathize with the anguish of the parents of the killers as well as of the killed. The California-based Freedom Forum (1998) organization praised the tone-setter for national coverage, *The Jonesboro Sun,* for neither demonizing nor glorifying the suspects or their victims.

"The Jonesboro suspects were given a certain sense of humanity in the coverage that Black, inner-city kids often do not get," said Alex Kotlowitz (personal communication, February 15, 1999). "There's little probing into the circumstances in their homes, their families, the financial and spiritual poverty in their communities."

Television news is the more blatant offender. A recent survey by the Berkeley Media Studies Group of more than 200 hours of local television news in California found that more than two thirds of the stories on violence involved youth. When Black children were interviewed for these stories, they were more often witnesses, victims, or perpetrators of violent crimes than White children were. White children were more often interviewed as victims of less threatening crimes, such as accidents (Woodruff, 1998).

"Right now, in the minds of the viewing public, youth crime is as much about race as it is about crime," concluded UCLA's political science professor Franklin Gilliam and Stanford professor of communication Shanto Iyengar (1998, p. 46). Gilliam and Iyengar tested their theory recently in a unique study that measured viewers' fear levels and racial attitudes in direct response to news stories. Viewers were chosen at random to watch a 15-minute newscast. A crime report was inserted midstream. Some viewers watched a "superpredator script" in which the alleged murderer was a young Black or Latino male. Other viewers watched the same segment with an Asian or White suspect. A third group saw the crime story, but was never shown the racial identity of the accused. Finally, the control group watched the newscast without the crime story.

The results were striking. Those who watched the minority youth arrested reported feeling more afraid of crime than those who did not. They also tended to support more get-tough crime policies. It's interesting to note that White and Asian viewers supported get-tough measures at a far higher rate than Black viewers. Most, though, believe society needs to be held somewhat responsible for these kids. Iyengar and Gilliam conclude that "body-bag journalism" is a concept that has lasted beyond its years. Newsrooms need to retool their coverage, or else continue to allow the small percentage of troubled youth in America to define the entire group (Gilliam & Iyengar, 1998, in press).

DEATH TO THE DEAD-BABY BEAT

Some call it body-bag journalism. Others call it the dead-baby beat. These are the facetious newsroom names for the spectacle of reporters swooping into courts, welfare offices, and foster care agencies when a huge story breaks—most often when a child's body is found. Some fine stories may be written in the meantime, sidebars about child abuse, the failures of the courts, or the negligence in the child welfare ranks. But after the story runs its course, reporters move on; the chance to provide sustained scrutiny of these institutions is lost.

Lost, too, are troves of stories culled from seasoned relationships between sources and journalists. The bureaucrats don't get a chance to develop a comfortable working relationship with the press. Journalists lose the opportunity to fully understand the agencies and the children they serve. And the public loses its power to scrutinize its government at work. When the next corpse is found, the process starts all over from scratch.

No one is pleased with this kind of drive-by reporting. Reporters loathe wolf-pack assignments as much as the public disdains the spectacle. One solution is to launch a full-time juvenile court beat. The case of the Englewood children might not have shocked the public quite so much if the Chicago press had had a history of covering youth courts. Possley said he recently asked the *Chicago Tribune* editors for that assignment, figuring files of untold stories would keep him busy for years. "They liked the idea," he told me. "But they don't feel they can spare the manpower" (M. Possley, personal communication, February 11, 1999).

This is a common response in resource-starved newspapers. In fact, only one U.S. paper dedicates a full-time reporter to the juvenile courts. "My phone rings off the hook with stories," said Jack Kresnak of the *Detroit Free Press.* "So many people are hungry for these stories to be told" (J. Kresnak, personal communication, February 21, 1999).

The juvenile court beat was born in 1988 after *The Free Press* ran a series on youth outlaws. Prodded by the coverage, the state legislature opened the doors and the documents of juvenile courts to more public scrutiny. The paper decided to cover it full time. "I showed up to court the first day it was open, and they kicked me out," Kresnak said. "They kept kicking me out, and I kept coming back. They really didn't know how to deal with the press at first."

Finally, a truce was called, and a rapport was built. Court officials realized that this persistent reporter was not going away. Kresnak learned about the workings of the court as well as the roots and risk factors involved in child violence and juvenile arrests. "As soon as they realized I was responsible, that I wasn't there to exploit children, access was never a problem again," he said.

But the experience at *The New York Daily News* is more typical. Several years ago, *Daily News* attorney Eve Burton, aided by the paper's editorial editor, pushed the state to open New York Family Court to more public scrutiny. The suit was successful. Judges were encouraged to open their doors. *The News* wrote one large exposé on the courts, and then virtually disappeared from its halls and hearing rooms. "It's hard to justify dedicating one reporter to family court, when the stories don't get in the paper that often," the managing editor told me (A. Brown, personal communication, April 11, 1998).

If one juvenile beat reporter is not a viable option for some papers, then the blended beat may be another solution. One way to integrate formerly distinct beats would be to form a children's beat. In this case, a youth reporter would be responsible for several children's agencies: juvenile court, child protection services, foster care, welfare. This journalist would make it her business to keep up with research in neuroscience, development, health, and the effects of poverty, in order to bring deeper understanding to her stories. The reporter would keep in touch with youth groups, community programs, places kids hang out. A smaller town, with a smaller budgeted paper, might consider folding child care and education into the children's beat.

Finally, consider another way to blend the beats: Mix crime with public health and science. Instead of a cop beat, why not a violence beat—one that places the arrest du jour in a larger context? Under this rubric, reporters would routinely ask questions such as, How common is this kind of crime in the community? Did unemployment play a role? How about alcohol, drugs, guns? What kind of guns? Where were they bought? What is the fallout of this crime to the families involved, to the community?

These are suggested questions posed by an innovative group of health experts and journalists at the Berkeley Media Studies Center Violence Project. The idea is to provide more information in every crime story, so the resulting coverage spawns a call for violence prevention instead of public fear. "Violence is preventable," said public health expert Lori Dorfman, co-director of the group. "And not just through the criminal justice system. Our goal is to help journalists find better tools to tell the violence story in a more meaningful way" (L. Dorfman, personal communication, March 13, 1999).

CONCLUSION

In the days following the Jonesboro shootings, I called up Howard Snyder at the Office of Juvenile Justice to discuss how quickly the media named the accused boys of five murders and attached photos to their stories. These were the youngest suspects—11 and 13—to be exposed so completely in the press. In a resigned aside, Mr. Snyder said, "Well, I was happy to see at least they were not Black and urban." They were in fact White boys, from a Southern town (Hancock, 1998, p. 18).

At first, I was startled by the comment. Certainly the shooting was an enormous tragedy that had nothing overtly to do with race. But I understood his point. The face of youth crime in America is by and large Black and Brown. It's an unexamined newsroom phenomenon that has fed the nation's overwrought fear of children—other people's poor and minority children. The proliferation of "wilding Black teen" stories helped fuel the punitive legislation now in place in most states. At least these two White, baby-faced Arkansas boys shook up the stereotype. These were not the children so often portrayed as expendable and hopeless offspring of the inner-city poor. It was harder for White middle class viewers to objectify them as demons, raised in "moral poverty."

We can only speculate what the coverage would have looked like had the boys been Black and from East L.A., spraying bullets in one of their own schoolyards. Would the press have leaped as far and deep into the story, double-teaming its coverage for weeks, even months? Would it have gone to such lengths to examine the pain not only of all those involved, but also of the neighborhood, and the nation as a whole? Would it have explored the myriad social and neurological roots of violence: culture, guns, abuse, brain damage? Or would the stories have just underscored perceived expectations—dismissing the impoverished boys as remorseless criminals with few connections to American society?

If the press has learned anything from the seemingly relentless spate of White children taking armed revenge on their classmates, it's that the issue of violence and children is enormously complicated. Most newsrooms are woefully unprepared to do it justice. The roots of the problem are as varied as the individuals involved, as the communities they come from. Children themselves, and the institutions that serve them, must be considered more worthy subjects of sophisticated and sustained coverage. Kids can no longer be treated as simply cute photo opportunities, or mindless, predictable thugs who should be treated as adults. Those who covered the Columbine shootings learned to shed such stereotypes instantly.

The problems emerged from these stories in bas-relief: The standard five-Ws approach (who, what, when, where, and why) to stories about crime is insufficient. By nature it objectifies the suspects, creating cryptic stories with cardboard suspects, dehumanizing them in the process. When it comes to children who are not emotionally equipped to wield their own power within the legal system and the press, the practice serves to strip them of their rights.

The pool of news sources for stories on kids and crime is too narrowly rooted in one ideology—in this case, conservative theories focusing on character flaws of minority urban youth. Mixing up a variety of viewpoints would allow readers a chance to consider a wider range of solutions, from improving schools to searching for alternatives to jail, instead of merely taking easy potshots at the perpetrators.

Finally, violence is treated as an isolated incident perpetrated by an aberrant child, without regard to his background, environment, social conditions, and weapon availability. When it's considered in a more inclusive context as a public health issue, one that's larger than the individuals involved, the public is left with a sense of potential for change, instead of fear and despair.

News editors tend to recognize these shortcomings and areas for improvement more often when nonminority children are involved. That's the final challenge: to develop a newsroom awareness of the press's role in fostering the public's fear of Black and Brown children. Perhaps then more cases of young children falsely accused—such as those of the young Black children in Chicago—could be averted.

REFERENCES

Annin, P. (1996, January 22). Superpredators arrive. *Newsweek,* p. 57.

Bai, M. (with Glick, D., Keene-Osborn, S., Gegax, T., Clemetson, L., Gordon, D., & Klaidman, D.). (1999, May 3). Anatomy of a Massacre. *Newsweek,* pp. 24–31.

Carpenter, J., & Lawrence, C. (1998, August 10). Boys linked to murder; girl, 11, may have been killed for bike. *The Chicago Sun-Times,* p. 1.

Children Now. (1999, July). *The news media's picture of children: A five-year update and a focus on diversity.* Oakland, CA: Kunkel, Dale.

Covering criminal justice: A resource guide. (1999). New York: The Center on Crime, Communities and Culture and *The Columbia Journalism Review.*

Covering violence: A report on a conference on violence and the young. (1994). College Park, MD: Casey Journalism Center for Children and Families.

DiIulio, J. J. (1995, November 27). The coming of the super-predator. *The Weekly Standard,* p. 23.

Doi, D. (1998, Winter). Media and juvenile violence: The connecting threads. Cambridge, MA: *Nieman Reports,* pp. 35–36.

Eftimiades, M. (with Goulding, S. C., Duignan-Cabrera, A., Campbell, D., & Podesta, J. S.). (1997, June 25). Heartbreaking crimes, kids without a conscience? Why are kids killing? *People Magazine,* p. 46.

The end of innocence. (1998, August 12). [Editorial]. *The Los Angeles Times,* p. B6.

False images? The news media and juvenile crime. (1997). Washington, DC: Coalition for Juvenile Justice.

Fiore, F., & Anderson, N. (1999, June 18). House blasts Hollywood but fails to act on violence. *The Los Angeles Times,* p. A1.

Freedom Forum. (1998). *Jonesboro: Were the media fair?* Arlington, VA: Author.

Fuentes, A. (1998, June 15–22). The crackdown on kids. *The Nation,* pp. 20–21.

Gegax, T. T., Adler, J., & Pedersen, D. (with Brauer, D., & McCormick, J.). (1998,

April 6). The schoolyard killers behind the Jonesboro tragedy. *Newsweek,* p. 45.

Gest, T., & Pope, V. (1996, March 25). Crime time bomb. *U.S. News & World Report,* p. 28.

Gilliam, F. D., & Iyengar, S. (1998, Winter). Superpredator script. Cambridge, MA: *Nieman Reports,* p. 46.

Gilliam, F. D., & Iyengar, S. (in press). Super-predators or wayward youth? Framing effects in crime news coverage. In N. Terkildsen & F. Schnell (Eds.), *The dynamics of issue framing: Elite discourse and the formation of public opinion.* New York: Cambridge University Press.

Hancock, L. (1998, July/August). Naming kid criminals: When should we protect them? *Columbia Journalism Review,* pp. 18–19.

Kantrowitz, B. (1993, August 2). Wild in the streets. *Newsweek,* p. 40.

Killer teens. (1994, January 27). *U.S. News & World Report,* p. 26.

Kotlowitz, A. (1992). *There are no children here: The story of two boys growing up in the other America.* New York: Doubleday.

Kotlowitz, A. (1999, February 8). The unprotected. *The New Yorker,* pp. 41–53.

Kunkel, D. (1994). *The news media's picture of children.* Oakland, CA: Children Now.

Labi, N. (with Monroe, S., Grace, J., Baker, J., Bland, E., & Cole, W.). (1998, April 6). The hunter and the choirboy. *Time,* pp. 28–37.

Lacayo, R. (with Behair, R., Burleigh, N., Norvell, S., & Willwerth, J.). (1994, September 19). When kids go bad. *Time,* p. 60.

Lives endangered. (1998, August 12). [Editorial]. *The Chicago Sun-Times,* p. 37.

Males, M. A. (1999). *Framing youth: Ten myths about the next generation.* Monroe, ME: Common Courage Press.

Mathis, D. (1999, June 14). When does school safety become oppression? *Gannett News Service,* p. ARC.

Miller, J. G. (1998, Winter). Riding the crime wave: Why words we use matter so much. Cambridge, MA: *Nieman Reports,* pp. 47–49.

Morganthau, T. (with Smith, V. E., Beals, G., Brant, M., & Annin, P.). (1995, December 4). Is it the lull before the storm? *Newsweek,* p. 40.

O'Driscoll, P. (1999, April 21). Killers leave gruesome crime scene. *USA Today,* p. 1A.

O'Rourke, L. M. (1999, May 10). Congress to tackle teen crime. *Sacramento Bee,* p. A1.

Possley, M. (1998a, August 30). How cops got boys to talk. *Chicago Tribune,* p. 1.

Possley, M. (with Puente, T., Poe, J., & Wilson, T.). (1998b, August 11). Police say suspects not too small to kill: Seven- and 8-year-olds accused in death of girl in Englewood. *The Chicago Tribune,* p. 1.

Possley, M., & Puente, T. (1998, August 13). Anguish grips mom of 7-year-old held in killing. *The Chicago Tribune,* p. 1.

Rodriguez, R. (1996, January 21). The coming mayhem. *The Los Angeles Times,* p. M1.

Sickmund, M., Snyder, H. N., & Poe-Yamagata, E. (1997). *Juvenile offenders and victims: 1997 update on violence.* Washington, DC: Office of Juvenile Justice and Delinquency Prevention, National Center for Juvenile Justice.

Snyder, H. N., Sickmund, M., & Poe-Yamagata, E. (1996). *Juvenile offenders and victims: 1996 update on violence.* Washington, DC: Office of Juvenile Justice and Delinquency Prevention, National Center for Juvenile Justice.

Stevens, J., Dorfman, L., & Wallack, L. (1997). *Reporting on violence: A handbook for journalists.* Berkeley, CA: Berkeley Media Studies Group.

Stodghill, R., II, Cole, W., & Grace, J. (1998, August 24). No more kid stuff: Is murder now child's play? Two boys ages seven and eight, are charged in the death of an 11 year old girl. *Time,* p. 62.

Toch, T. (with Gest, T., & Guttman, M.). (1993, November 8). Violence in schools: When killers come to class. *U.S. News & World Report,* p. 30.

Williams, K., George, T., & Siemaszko, C. (1998, March 26). Five slain in school ambush. *New York Daily News,* p. 1.

Woodruff, K. (1998, Winter). Youth and race on local TV News. Cambridge, MA: *Nieman Reports,* pp. 43–44.

Zimring, F. E. (1998). *American youth violence.* New York and Oxford: Oxford University Press.

Zoglin, R. (with Allis, S., & Kamlani, R.). (1996, March 25). Now for the bad news: A teenage time bomb. *U.S. News & World Report,* p. 52.

PART II

Schools, Violence, and Zero-Tolerance Policies

America's Least Wanted
Zero-Tolerance Policies and the Fate of Expelled Students

SASHA POLAKOW-SURANSKY

Dylan Klebold, Eric Harris, Kip Kinkel. They have become household names, and the stories of their crimes have dominated the front pages of major newspapers and journals, bringing school violence into the national media spotlight. And despite years of research on youth violence and escalating public concern about its dangers, violence in the schools continues to plague communities across the nation. Although Department of Education studies do not reveal a statistically significant rise in juvenile crime over the past two decades (Lewin, 1998), the shootings in Littleton, Colorado; Jonesboro, Arkansas; and Springfield, Oregon, have left the nation wondering why some students resort to such violent means to express their anger. In fact, the number of incidents involving guns has increased dramatically: Whereas only 74 gun-related murders were committed by 13- to 14-year-olds in 1980, the figure skyrocketed to 178 in 1995 (Fuentes, 1998), reinforcing the argument that increased access to firearms has contributed to today's crisis. Yet unlike Great Britain, which immediately passed legislation outlawing handguns following a school massacre in Scotland, the United States has yet to develop a similar legislative response (O'Brien, 1998).

Rather, in the United States, public opinion has led to calls for retribution and harsh sentencing against youths, who are increasingly seen as threats to the social order. Whereas a few decades ago academics and politicians struggled to understand where these children went wrong, today leg-

This chapter is a revised and updated version of *Access Denied: Mandatory Expulsion Requirements and the Erosion of Educational Opportunity in Michigan.* Ann Arbor, MI: Student Advocacy Center of Michigan (1999). Adapted with permission.

islators, such as Jim Pitts of Texas, are proposing extension of the death penalty to offenders as young as 11 (Fuentes, 1998). While Pitts's position represents the extreme of today's trend of punitive policy making, a shift of emphasis from the traditional model of juvenile rehabilitation to one of harsh punishment is visible throughout the nation (Dohrn, 1993).

THE RISE OF ZERO-TOLERANCE

Perhaps the most widespread manifestation of this policy shift is the almost universal use of "zero-tolerance" laws to punish and expel students who bring weapons, drugs, or anything deemed dangerous to school, no matter how vaguely defined. In school districts across the country students are being expelled under zero-tolerance policies for seemingly innocuous "offenses."

The most famous of these cases, known as the "Midol case," occurred in Fairborn, Ohio. Kimberly Smartt, an eighth grader, took two Midol tablets from the school nurse's office to relieve her menstrual cramps. She took one herself and gave the other to a friend who was also complaining of cramps. Kimberly was expelled from school for "transmitting" a drug. Her friend, charged with simple possession, was suspended for only 10 days. Kimberly's family filed suit, and the media took great interest in the case, but little coverage of the final verdict upholding the expulsion reached the newspapers (see Zirkel, 1997).

A similar case in Alexandria, Louisiana, reached the front page of *The New York Times*. There 8-year-old Kameryan Lueng became a victim of the Rapides Parish zero-tolerance policy after she brought a family heirloom, a pocket watch, to school. The pocket watch contained a one-inch knife that its owner had used to clean his fingernails. After school officials discovered the watch, Kameryan was promptly removed from school and placed in a "Redirection Academy." As *The New York Times* noted, most zero-tolerance policies

> leave principals little discretion in handling infractions. . . . [T]here is widespread agreement that strict punishments are appropriate in serious cases. But as zero-tolerance policies become more widespread there is growing debate about whether mandatory punishment makes sense in cases like Kameryan's . . . in which there was no intent to cause harm. (Lewin, 1997, p. A1)

According to Lueng's father, by adopting rigid zero-tolerance policies, "we have isolated our children and taught them that once they have gotten into trouble, they're doomed. We don't need zero-tolerance. We need to put our faith and trust and support in our principals" (Lewin, 1997, p. B7).

A few months later, a 10-year-old Seattle boy was expelled for bringing a one-inch plastic gun to school. His punishment was later reduced to a 3-day suspension after the board was ridiculed by newspapers across the country (Jones, 1997). In reference to the Seattle case, Mary Gannon, director of policy services for the Iowa School Boards Association, argued, "It's silly to expel a third grader for a year. . . . [They] probably have no understanding of the repercussions of their actions. . . . You're just going to ruin [a] child's life if he's out of school for a year" (Jones, 1997, p. 30).

Despite widespread criticism from civil rights advocates and the media, the vast majority of school districts continue to embrace zero-tolerance policies, often with minimal respect for students' rights. Although there is still considerable variation between states with respect to due process protections and alternative education, all states have now introduced some form of zero-tolerance legislation in order to comply with the federal Gun Free Schools Act of 1994 (GFSA).

The GFSA ushered in a new era of educational policy across the United States. Within one year of its enactment all 50 states had introduced zero-tolerance legislation, and mandatory expulsion became the rule rather than the exception in matters of school discipline. These laws gave school districts license to deprive certain children of educational services, ending a time-honored tradition of universal public education for all students. Zero-tolerance has been praised by many for its rigid approach to school discipline, but it has come under fire from many critics for its indiscriminate application, its limitation of local control, and its propensity for "quick-fix" remedies rather than long-term solutions. And for advocates of such harsh zero-tolerance measures, Michigan has been a primary testing ground.

In this study I analyze the impact of the Gun Free Schools Act and ensuing state zero-tolerance laws on students in Michigan. Their experiences mirror those of thousands of other students expelled across the country, and their cases have raised crucial civil rights questions and constitutional dilemmas at both the state and national level. In Illinois the recent intervention of Jesse Jackson drew nationwide attention to the relationship between race and expulsion policies. As the highly publicized Decatur, Illinois, case has shown us, the negative outcomes of zero-tolerance laws are by no means confined to a single state (Johnson, 1999; Wing & Keleher, 2000). Indeed the damaging impact of zero-tolerance has now received national visibility, and the Department of Education and the U.S. Civil Rights Commission have agreed to investigate allegations of racial bias and lack of due process (Webber, 1999). The state of Michigan, which has passed some of the most extreme measures, serves as a useful lens through which to view the impact of zero-tolerance legislation across the country.

ACCESS DENIED: A CASE STUDY OF MICHIGAN

Michigan's zero-tolerance law (Michigan Compiled Laws, 1988, sec. 380.1311) took effect on January 1, 1995. The law is considered by many analysts to be the harshest in the nation (Bogos, 1997), because of its permanent-expulsion mandate, the absence of due process guidelines, the lack of alternative education, and the failure to mandate data collection and reporting. Although certain districts have insisted on protecting their local authority to make discretionary decisions on disciplinary matters (see Olivet Community Schools, 1995, 1997), the majority of schools have followed the guidelines provided by the state, leaving them little latitude to exercise reasonable judgment before deciding to deprive students of an education. Although the law does include several exception clauses, which recognize a variety of mitigating circumstances, these provisions have been consistently ignored by many local school boards, much to the dismay of children's advocates and civil liberties lawyers across the state.

Furthermore, the state of Michigan has never developed a systematic monitoring mechanism to keep track of expelled students despite a federal mandate requiring that expulsions be reported (Gun Free Schools Act, 1994). Consequently, no one knows exactly how many children have been expelled, whether they have been readmitted, or where they have gone.

Due to the dearth of information following the law's passage, the minimal data collected by the State of Michigan's Family Independence Agency (FIA) and the Michigan Department of Education (MDE) emerged as the only available sources of expulsion information. Yet state officials have admitted that the MDE study is extremely limited and that their FIA data is far from complete, since many districts consistently fail to report. The FIA study includes only partial data from one third of Michigan school districts. In these approximately 180 districts the FIA study documented only 521 expulsions over the 27-month period from January 1995 to March 1997 (Family Independence Agency, 1997). In contrast the study described in this chapter documents as many as 582 expulsions in only 17 districts over an even shorter period of only 23 months, indicating the unreliability of state data. The data presented in this chapter indicate that expulsions are far more widespread, that many go unreported, and that the lack of documentation has served to eclipse the damaging consequences of mandatory expulsion requirements and shield zero-tolerance policies from public scrutiny.

This case study of the impact of zero-tolerance in Michigan reveals that a disproportionate number of African American students have been expelled in districts across the state, and in several districts the majority of the students expelled are under the age of 16, the cutoff for compulsory attendance in Michigan. Many of these students are expelled for petty offenses; they are not afforded proper due process procedures prior to expulsion; and local officials are given little discretion in making disciplinary decisions. Moreover, data indicate that most students are neither reinstated following expulsion (despite the fact that they are eligible), nor are they provided with any form of alternative education.

The current expulsion law has condemned hundreds of Michigan students to at least an entire year without any form of education, and drawn the ire of law enforcement officers who must deal with youths left with no place to go but the streets (Ceo, 1998). As we shall see, statistical studies of school discipline policies, legal analyses of mandatory expulsion requirements, and the horror stories of parents and students confirm that zero-tolerance laws are, at best, an ineffective short-term remedy for a serious long-term problem.

COLLECTION AND ANALYSIS OF DATA

This research study was undertaken as part of the continuing efforts of the Student Advocacy Center of Michigan to systematize and disseminate accurate information regarding discipline and exclusion policies in the Michigan public schools. The study is an attempt to fill in the gaps that remain as a result of inadequate documentation from the Michigan Department of Education, the Family Independence Agency, and nonresponsive school districts who fail to monitor the consequences of their own expulsion policies. The 100 school districts selected for analysis in this study were chosen according to geographic location, diversity of population, and annual rate of per-pupil spending in order to ensure a representative cross section of the state's 557 districts. Hence the sample ranges from the far reaches of northern Michigan to the industrial southeast. It includes districts such as Detroit and Benton Harbor with African American populations of more than 85%, and districts such as Cadillac and Traverse City where fewer than 5% of the enrolled students are minorities. Funding levels differ dramatically as well. For example, the East Lansing Public Schools operate on a budget of $7,891 per pupil per year, while Cadillac Schools spend only $4,797 annually on each student (Michigan Department of Education, 1997b).

Freedom of Information requests were sent to all 100 superintendents asking for expulsion data from the 1995–96 and 1996–97 school years disaggregated according to race, gender, special education status, free lunch eligibility, as well as information on students' placement following expulsion, such as referrals to state agencies, reinstatement, and alternative education placement. Few districts provided all of the requested information. Only 17 of the 64 respondents provided complete expulsion data. And even among these districts, there were many gaping holes in the data provided, particularly in regard to free lunch eligibility, the only available indicator of poverty among the student population. Nevertheless, the data presented here represent the most comprehensive and up-to-date expulsion information currently available in the state of Michigan. Among the most striking findings were those pertaining to race. Although many school districts claimed they did not keep disaggregated records, those who did keep such data revealed disturbing racial disparities in their expulsion patterns.

Racial Bias

Among districts supplying acceptable data on race, the average African American population was 39.8%, yet African American students accounted for 64% of the total expulsions. In the predominantly African American district of Benton Harbor (87%), African American students were still disproportionately expelled, making up 94% of the expulsions between 1995 and 1997. This trend is visible in other parts of the state as well. For example, in Port Huron, African Americans are a mere 7% of the student body but made up 18% of the expelled population in 1995–96. In East Lansing, where the African American population is 13%, 30% of the expelled students were African American during the 1996–97 school year. In the Lansing City School District, where African Americans account for only 34% of the population, they were expelled at twice that level, making up 67% of all expulsions. In Grand Rapids, where the student body is 42% African American, 70% of those expelled in 1995–96 were African American, dropping only slightly to 67% in 1996–97. And in Flint, where African Americans make up 69% of the population, they accounted for 96% of the expulsions during the 1995–96 school year (see Figure 5.1).

Legally Sanctioned Truancy?

Another significant finding emerging from Michigan expulsion data is the age of students expelled. Although the stereotypical perpetrator of school violence is an 18-year-old "thug with a gun" (Morain, 1995, p. 1), data show that the majority of students caught by the expulsion law are in fact between the ages of 12 and 15. In Benton Harbor, 73% of the students expelled during the 1995–96 school year were in grades 7–9, and in the following year 80% fell into this age bracket (see Figure 5.2). In Muskegon 22% of those expelled were elementary students, and 61% were 7th–9th graders, whereas only 17% were in 10th grade or above, indicating that the majority of students being expelled are under the age of 16, the legal dropout age in Michigan (Michigan Compiled Laws, 1998, sec. 380.1561) (see

FIGURE 5.1 African Americans: Percentage of school district population
     vs. percentage of expulsions by school district, 1995–1997

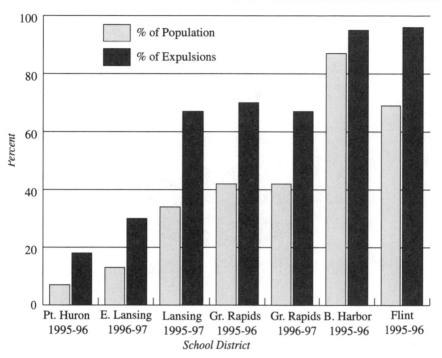

Figure 5.3). Since some of these students never return to school following expulsion and are not provided with alternative education, the state has created a situation that is tantamount to legally sanctioned truancy, whereby students not afforded the right to leave school are forcibly barred from attending, and are left with no educational opportunity whatsoever. Similar data in other districts confirm the prevalence of this trend. For example, 71% of students expelled in Bay City between 1995 and 1997 were under the age of 16 (see Figure 5.4).

The Struggle for Readmission

Perhaps the most disturbing data trend is the sheer number of expelled students who do not receive an education after being removed from school. Whereas most districts complied with state law and referred expelled stu-

FIGURE 5.2 Benton Harbor: Expulsions by grade for two school years

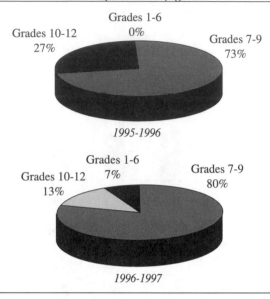

1995-1996

1996-1997

FIGURE 5.3 Muskegon: Expulsions by grade, 1995–1997

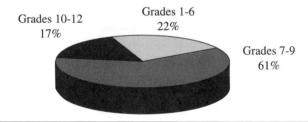

FIGURE 5.4 Bay City: Expulsions by grade, 1995–1997

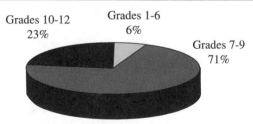

dents to the FIA or Community Mental Health, their record is much poorer when it comes to reinstatement rates and provision of alternative education. Most districts chose not to provide data or claimed they did not have any records. The paucity of information on this vitally important stage of the expulsion process is telling. As the Michigan Advisory Committee to the U.S. Commission on Civil Rights (1996) observed, "Without data there can be no analysis of the problem, no understanding, no corrective measures, and no improvement in the situation" (p. 75). Moreover, it is impossible to know what has happened to these students. Are they at home, in alternative schools, or on the streets? Until the state begins to take data collection seriously, Michigan citizens and law enforcement officers will be left in the dark with regard to these important questions, and expelled students will remain effectively invisible.

The only significant data on reinstatement came from the urban districts of Lansing, Flint, and East Lansing. In Lansing 64% petitioned for reinstatement; in Flint 50%; and in East Lansing, only 40% of those expelled actually petitioned. These figures can, in part, be attributed to the state policy that does not provide parents with any assistance in preparing petitions (see Michigan Compiled Laws, 1998, sec. 380.1311[5] [c]). This has created an added difficulty in the readmission process for families unfamiliar with legalistic paperwork and those who lack the resources to seek legal assistance. Of those petitioning in Lansing, no students were reinstated until after one year. At this point 54% were reinstated, while the remaining 46% were never readmitted to their schools. In Flint, during the 1995–96 school year, a mere 18% were reinstated in less than one year, 32% were reinstated after one year, and 50% were never reinstated. And in East Lansing 30% were reinstated in less than one year, 10% were reinstated after one year, and a majority (60%) never returned to school (see Figure 5.5).

Nowhere to Go: The Lack of Alternative Education

The record is even more dismal when it comes to alternative education. East Lansing and Lansing did not provide any information whatsoever about alternative placement. Flint indicated that 46% of its expelled students were provided with alternative education in 1995–96. Unfortunately these disquieting figures are corroborated in other national studies. Stone (1993) found that 52% of school districts nationwide provide alternative education programs to suspended students, but does not specify any figures for expelled students. And more sobering statistics on alternative education in Michigan are found in the Michigan Department of Education's (1997a) limited study of 35 districts. In these districts the MDE found that only 8.7% of expelled students received alternative education (see Figure 5.6). This chilling figure

FIGURE 5.5 Reinstatement of expelled students: Percentage of petitioning
students who were reinstated, by school district, 1995–1997

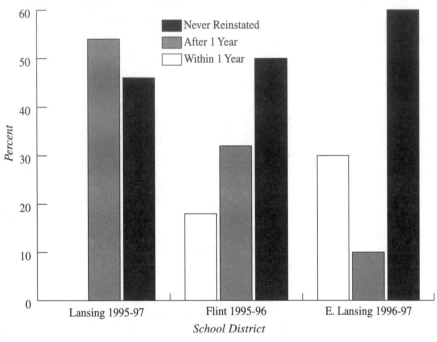

FIGURE 5.6 State of Michigan: Follow-up after expulsion, 1995–1996

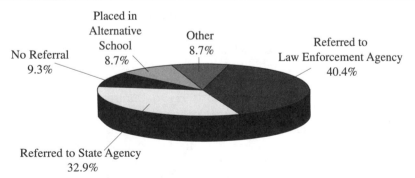

Source: Michigan Department of Education. (1997a). *Report on expulsions and suspensions in Michigan for the 1995–1996 school year.* Lansing: Author.

reveals just how few educational opportunities exist for a student once he or she has been expelled.

STORIES FROM THE MARGINS

In addition to the collection of quantitative data on school expulsions, I sought to gauge the impact of public policy on students' everyday lives. I conducted face-to-face interviews with expelled students and their families in southeastern Michigan school districts. The interviews covered students' disciplinary history, recounting of the expulsion process, impact of the expulsion on personal and family life, effects of the expulsion on educational aspirations and opportunities, as well as obstacles to reinstatement or alternative education. The regional specificity of the interview pool is due primarily to connections between members of the Student Advocacy Center staff and the interviewees based on prolonged casework. These relationships facilitated easier access to these students and their families. They cover different age groups, different races, different offenses, and different outcomes. All interviews were conducted in July 1998.

Their stories reveal disturbing truths about the state's zero-tolerance policy and suggest that it is often applied in an arbitrary and capricious manner by local school officials, with little or no provision of constitutionally protected due process rights. Often, the grounds for expulsion were nowhere to be found in the state law. Such was the case for a middle school student expelled for bringing a lighter to school, and a high school student expelled for cleaning his nails with a pocketknife.

Moreover, interviews reveal that exclusion from school leads to increased apathy, lowered self-esteem, family turmoil, and distrust of school officials, who were often cited as unfair and perceived as likely to abuse their power. All interviewees expressed dismay over their respective school districts' lack of commitment to providing alternative education for students once they had been expelled. Despite severely decreased motivation, most students interviewed claimed that they would prefer to be in school, but felt as if they were not wanted at their former school or in any school, thereby increasing their sense of marginalization.

The following narratives, based on interviews with students and their parents as well as case files from the Student Advocacy Center of Michigan archives, provide a portrait of the various expulsion experiences of Michigan students. However, all of these cases involved male students. This is due primarily to the disproportionate number of male students expelled in the state, and selective access to students and families through the Student Advocacy Center network. All names of students and school officials, as well as district affiliations, have been altered to protect confidentiality. It should also be noted that the cases cited here are unusual in that they involve lawyers and student advocates. The majority of expelled students and their families are left to fend for themselves while navigating through the bureaucratic maze of the expulsion process.

Kevin

Kevin is a soft-spoken 15-year-old White student from a small town in southeastern Michigan. In July 1998, I met Kevin and his mother in a park where his mother works as a playground supervisor. She also participated in the interview. Kevin was permanently expelled from the public schools in this almost exclusively White working-class community after he was allegedly caught selling LSD at school, an offense punishable by expulsion under the locally adopted school discipline policy. Another student told the physical education teacher that Kevin was selling drugs, and the teacher informed the principal. The school officials did not find any contraband on him, only a small amount of money, which they claimed he obtained from selling LSD to other students. Kevin was subsequently expelled permanently from the district and all other Michigan school districts under Section 1311 of the school code.

His mother did not realize that expulsion meant permanent exclusion from public schools. She had assumed that it meant one year at most. But Kevin still remained out of school 16 months after he was expelled, and he was not furnished with any alternative education whatsoever. The district's director of secondary education told the family that Kevin could "earn his way back." Therefore he was enrolled in a Catholic Social Services drug rehabilitation program despite the fact that he tested negative and maintains he has never used drugs, a claim confirmed by his mother. He and his mother also attended counseling. The following fall, his mother contacted the director about possible reinstatement. He instructed her to collect letters of recommendation from nonrelated acquaintances that could be submitted to the board. He did not provide them with a petition for reinstatement or any information about the procedure. Meetings were constantly scheduled and delayed for the next 6 months, prompting his mother to give up. She recounts her continuing frustration:

> I had pretty much given up [in spring 1998]. . . . at the time I was devastated. . . . I thought if I got all of these people to write letters of recommendation and if Kevin went to these drug classes then it would be OK. Right now Kevin is given too much freedom and that's not actually his fault. . . . he's worked when he could work, and I can't

afford home schooling. . . . I'm at poverty level. But my finances are none of their business. I shouldn't have to tell them those things. I don't want sympathy. I just want my kid to get a fair break here. His dad and I went before the director. . . . I thought we had done enough. I feel that in the year he's been out of school he's been punished enough. Right now at this point I don't think he should have to do anything else. I am so disenfranchised with those people, I told them when I went before them the first time that I didn't blame them for their policy because drugs are a scary thing and somebody could've gotten killed. If this was a solution to solve the drug problem then it would be different but it's not. I resent them and I'm hurt by them, and it makes me angry. . . . they're hurtin' my kid. It's like they don't think he's worth anything.

Meanwhile Kevin has worked hard since his expulsion and has constantly told district officials that he would like to return to school. He has had several different jobs in the year and 4 months since he was expelled, including babysitting the neighbor's 5-year-old daughter, working at a party store, completing side jobs for his dad, and blacktopping driveways. He says that he would prefer to attend the district's alternative school program because friends say that it is better than the regular high school. When asked how he feels about being expelled he replied angrily:

I hate it. . . . I could care less about [this school district] . . . all they've been doing ever since I got kicked out is jerkin' me around. They said they were gonna set up meetings and I haven't been to one yet. They don't really care that I care. I want to go back to school and I've been sayin' that since I got kicked out, but that don't seem to matter to them. . . . That's what they make me feel like.

Kevin's anger and his mother's frustration only worsened when the district began tempting them with false hopes of educational opportunities. Recently, the school district established an alternative program through which students such as Kevin can "earn their way back." The district will not allow him to attend the districtwide alternative program until he spends 6 months in this school for expelled students. But even this will not guarantee Kevin admission, because there are limited slots available. According to Kevin, "They keep everybody dangling." The district claims he must attend the program for expelled students because the districtwide alternative school is only for students over 16, and he is 15. He worries that if he waits until next school year to enroll in this program he will have been out of school for almost 3 years, an experience that one of his friends suffered through. His mother is also worried about the expelled-students program because it runs from 3 to 9 p.m., a schedule that would cause transportation difficulties, as the school district doesn't provide transportation for alternative programs.

Ruth Zweifler, executive director of the Student Advocacy Center of Michigan, argued that Kevin is eligible to be reinstated in the school of his choice and should not be required to attend a school for expelled students when he has already been out of school in excess of the required 180 days. She has since helped Kevin's mother secure pro bono legal assistance from a prominent Detroit law firm. According to Kevin's mother, Zweifler has been the only advocate for Kevin, and no one else has shown any concern. She noted that since getting a lawyer she has found the director to be much more responsive, even returning her phone calls, but only when she mentions her lawyer's name. Although the director apparently expressed his concern about Kevin's situation to the attorney, he did not follow up on oral agreements he made with her. The only suggestions he has offered the family are home schooling and correspondence courses, for which the family does not possess the necessary resources. At present, Kevin is still out of school, but his attorney has now threatened to take the district to court if Kevin is not reinstated into an acceptable educational program. Kevin's mother reflected:

> I know what it's like to live in futile situations, so I can relate to Kevin. . . . I've already had one son who didn't graduate from high school and I don't want to see that happen to my kids. . . . I'm still devastated in a lot of ways. . . . This has cost me my health because my blood pressure is sky high from worrying about this. . . . I don't believe 14-year-olds should be given a life sentence of no education. . . . it doesn't make sense to me.

Kevin's mother claims that many students have been expelled for similar offenses, and none have received legal help or alternative education. The school district that expelled Kevin did not provide any data for this study.

Martin

Martin is an 18-year-old African American student who was expelled from a southeastern Michigan school district for possession of a three-inch pocketknife in November of 1996. Martin was not a special education student and therefore was not eligible for alternative education under Section 504, a law prohibiting discrimination against disabled persons in any federally funded program, including the public schools (see Individuals with Disabilities in Education Act, 20 U.S. §1400 et seq.). Martin had been referred to the principal on several occasions for trivial violations of the no-coat rule and no-eating rule, and for remarks made to teachers. However, he had never engaged in any dangerous behavior nor been severely disciplined by the school.

On October 31, 1996, while in his auto repair class at a district-affiliated technical college, Martin was found picking his nails with a small knife. When his teacher inquired about the knife, Martin immediately handed it over to him. In a written statement to the board of education he explained, "I was sitting in the classroom alone going through my pocket when I pulled out my jersey. . . . the knife fell out and then I started scratching some black stuff that looked like tar or something off my fingers because it would not come off with soap and water" (Student Advocacy Center Files, 1996). The statements of two student witnesses who were passing in the hallway corroborated this statement. One wrote, "I saw Martin with the knife sitting in the corner scratching his hand and cleaning underneath his nails, but he wasn't using it in any threatening way towards anyone" (Student Advocacy Center Files, 1996).

In his summary report to the school board a district administrator wrote, "[The teacher] asked for the knife, Martin cooperatively gave the knife to him" (Student Advocacy Center Files, 1996). Nevertheless the school contacted the police regarding the incident. Due to the circumstances, the investigating officer opted to close the investigation after he concluded that "the incident should be handled as a school discipline incident. . . . There is not criminal intent shown" (Student Advocacy Center Files, 1996). Despite the principal's acknowledgement in a letter to the superintendent that Martin had done very well in his auto repair class, had excellent attendance and an above-average grade, and was a "cooperative, positive young man" (Student Advocacy Center Files, 1996), the principal still recommended expulsion. He went on to say, "Expulsion is mandatory unless the student can demonstrate one of the exceptions outlined in the law. . . . I believe Martin did not knowingly bring the knife to school, but when he discovered that he had it, he should have turned it in to the teacher" (Student Advocacy Center Files, 1996).

The exceptions referred to by the principal state that "a school board is not required to expel a pupil for possessing a weapon if . . . [t]he object or instrument possessed by the pupil was not possessed by the pupil for use as a weapon . . . [or the] weapon was not knowingly possessed by the pupil" (Michigan Compiled Laws, sec. 380.1311[2] [a] and [b]). Yet in spite of this crystal-clear statutory exception, Martin's clean record, and the fact that he willingly gave the knife to the teacher, the board of education voted to expel him. With the help of the Student Advocacy Center, Martin was able to enroll in classes at a local community college. He was recently readmitted to his old school, but the district has not agreed to allow the community college credits to be used as high school credit, contrary to an agreement made at the reinstatement hearing. Consequently, Martin's graduation has been held up. The school district that expelled Martin did not respond to the Freedom of Information request for data.

Shawn

I met with Shawn and his pro bono lawyer at his family's central Michigan home in July 1998. His mother was at work when the interview was conducted. In December 1996 when he was 16, Shawn and three fellow African American students were suspended from school for 10 days after they allegedly touched a 14-year-old girl inappropriately in the boys' locker room after school hours. The girl refused to provide the principal with any written statement or make any formal accusation, and the only evidence of the boys' misconduct came from a hall monitor who caught the girl coming out of the boys' locker room.

Shawn maintains that the touching was fully consensual and that the girl entered the locker room voluntarily. The school never informed his mother of the suspension and she therefore urged him to return to school. He returned to school three times and was told to leave on each occasion, and the school finally contacted his mother. On the 9th day of the suspension an expulsion hearing was held before the school board. Shawn and his friends never disputed the 10-day suspension but felt that the girl, who was also breaking school rules, should have received the same punishment. When he discovered that the locker room incident might result in expulsion, Shawn immediately tried to resolve the matter with the girl. He explained in his soft-spoken manner,

> At first I didn't know what was going on so I thought I'd go get the girl and talk to her. So I saw her walking in the hall and we went to the principal together. . . . She said "nothing happened, I went in there by myself." The principal said, "I'll take that into consideration," then she went back to class and I went back to class.

But the principal paid her statement no heed.

The expulsion hearing took place in December 1996 during the school's final exam period, from which the four boys were excluded. The school's case took 30 minutes to present and rested entirely on the story of the hall monitor, who was never inside the locker room. School officials asserted that the 14-year-old girl was too young to consent to touching and therefore the boys had committed statutory rape. Shawn's attorney corrected this legal error, proving that she could consent to touching under state law. The school board's attorney agreed. The charge was then changed to "sexual harassment" under district policy, and the board voted 4 to 2 to expel the students, despite the attorney's argument that they had not performed a thorough investigation and lacked any credible evidence, specifically a statement from the alleged victim.

At school many students boycotted Martin Luther King Jr. Day festivities to protest the decision, which they felt was excessive. Race was also an issue. A female student at the school complained, "The way they treat Black students, I don't think it's right and I don't think it's fair." Concerned parents brought up a similar case, in which two White students were caught having consensual sex in a car while on school property and were only suspended for 2 days.

Shawn's attorney appealed the expulsion on the grounds of poor evidence. After 10 minutes of review, the Circuit Court judge determined that the district had not abused its discretion. While Shawn's attorney was planning a second appeal to the appellate court, the superintendent of the district turned Shawn's case over to the police. The prosecutor threatened to authorize charges of first-degree criminal sexual conduct (CSC) unless the boys waived their right of appeal and plea-bargained for a lesser charge. Faced with a trial and potential prison sentence, the boys decided to accept the plea bargain. They were given probation and community service, and one served 7 days in jail.

Shawn had a difficult time finding alternative education, because unlike the other three boys, who were nearly 17, he was not eligible to enroll in a local community college. The expulsion cost him his entire junior year, because the district refused to let him take his first semester exams, and he was out of school in the second semester. But after he was denied admission to local private schools and charter schools, he signed up for correspondence courses, which helped him earn one semester of credit, although they were not free. He then applied to be reinstated in June of the following year. By this time the superintendent had been fired for misconduct, the board president had been voted out of office, and one incumbent board member had declined to run again. Hence, the climate had changed dramatically and the boys were reinstated. Looking back on his expulsion, Shawn describes the impact it had on him and his family:

> I got expelled and I looked down the road and I didn't see if I had a future. . . . I was scared too. I wasn't functioning normal. I'd wake up, cry, sit around the house. I was depressed and I wouldn't talk to anybody. Then I got sick with the chicken pox. . . . And it was stressful

for my mom because she had to deal with this and go to work and take care of my little brother. She'd go to work and do nothing but work on the case, calling people. She didn't know what to do, what to think, what to say. She didn't know where to turn. . . . All she could do was call our lawyer.

Since being reinstated, Shawn has successfully completed his senior year and will be attending a Michigan university on a football scholarship in the fall. But his attorney warns that this ending is not typical of expulsion cases:

These guys are very lucky. These are guys who were thinking about college anyway before this whole episode, and now that we were able to get them back in they'll get their fair shot. But it's been a long, hard, unnecessarily drawn-out battle. It should have never got out of hand the way it did. . . . If they didn't have the support behind them this never would have happened. The public was aware of this and a lot of people were sympathetic. But that's atypical. . . . For most students in these situations they show up—perhaps with their parents—they don't know what's going on, and it's all over in 30 minutes. And these kids are criminally expelled and many of them never get back into school again.

UNDERMINING DUE PROCESS AND LOCAL CONTROL

Despite widespread acceptance among legislators in certain states, zero-tolerance policies have damaged and disrupted the lives of students and parents across the nation as a result of their indiscriminate application and often blatant violations of due process rights.

Unfortunately, the current law has made cases such as these the rule rather than the exception in the Michigan public schools. The recent expulsion of two elementary students in the Muskegon public schools for bringing lighters to school (Karas, 1998) has raised questions about excessive punishment for minor, unspecified offenses. Although the state board of education has put on record that acceptable local discipline policy "defines the conditions under which students may be suspended or expelled" (see Michigan Advisory Committee, 1996, p. 104), and court decisions such as *Matter of P. J.* (1991) make clear that discipline must comport with explicitly outlined policies, school districts continue to expel students for nonstipulated offenses.

In Muskegon, Superintendent Joseph Schulze admitted that "possession of a lighter is not a crime" (Karas, 1998, p. 1A), but still recommended expulsion for two elementary school students accused of chasing each other with lighters during recess, despite the fact that district policy did not mandate expulsion for that offense. In Shawn's case, described earlier, administrators accused him and three other students of sexual misconduct while providing no substantive evidence to support the allegations. Nevertheless, the four students were still expelled, even after the school board admitted that it had no evidence of this charge. And in another case several students were expelled for allegedly "being in a stolen car on the way to school," and for "incorrigible behavior" (Student Advocacy Center Files, 1998).

These Michigan cases demonstrate the dangers of a policy that "refuses to distinguish between the hard-core offender and the child who simply happened to be in the wrong place at the wrong time" (Simmons, 1998, p. 2). Moreover, Michigan fails to outline procedural due process for students threatened with expulsion, thereby denying them their constitutional rights upheld by the Supreme Court in *Goss v. Lopez* (1975). While the due process rights guaranteed to suspended students in *Goss* are minimal (Jensen & Goffin, 1993), the court warned that "longer suspensions or expulsions for the remainder of the school term, or permanently, may require more formal procedures" (*Goss v. Lopez,* 1975, p. 584).

At present, the Michigan law contains no explicit reference to due process whatsoever, except in the case of special education students (Michigan Compiled Laws, 1998, sec. 380.1311[8]). Past and current bills in the Michigan legislature propose only minor additions and would leave local districts to adopt their own due process policies. But as Wendy Wagenheim (1998), legislative affairs director of the American Civil Liberties Union of Michigan, observes, such a policy will only exacerbate the already serious problem of disparate treatment in different districts. Furthermore by simply stating that "the school board . . . shall expel the pupil from the school district permanently" (Michigan Compiled Laws, 1998, sec. 380.1311[2]), current legislation effectively precludes any possibility of due process at a hearing, for it assumes that expulsion is the only possible outcome for students committing infractions involving weapons, arson, or criminal sexual conduct. Moreover, it violates the spirit of the 1961 Supreme Court decision that ruled: "The very nature of due process negates any concept of inflexible procedures universally applicable to every imaginable situation" (quoted in *Goss v. Lopez,* 1975, p. 578).

The dearth of due process language in the current law leads to the neglect of basic constitutional requirements. Furthermore, the law fails to outline detailed hearing procedures and decision-making processes, as is the case in California, Nebraska, and Indiana (see California Education Code, 1998, secs. 48918, 48918.5; Revised Statutes of Nebraska, 1997, secs. 79-

270 to 79-288; Burns Indiana Statutes, 1998, secs. 20-8.1-5-9 to 20-8.1-5-10). Instead, the Michigan law "mandates permanent expulsion in all cases, without regard to mitigating circumstances and without deference to the sound discretion of educators" (Simmons, 1998, p. 2).

By stripping local educational authorities of their discretion in expulsion cases, the law has created an adversarial relationship between school districts and the state legislature. In testimony to the House Education Subcommittee on Violence in the Schools, the Michigan Association of Secondary School Principals (1998) lamented their loss of authority:

> Principals had more flexibility in dealing with weapon carrying students before the recent legislative requirements. . . . The [current] policy presently does not allow districts to actively work with the expelled students in finding alternative education opportunities. (p. 1)

And the Superintendents of the 23rd House District (1998) in southeastern Michigan warned legislators:

> As educators . . . we want you to be fully aware that we are very cautious and sensitive to language that will *mandate consequences* for actions and which will *do away with our ability to govern*. Each of our school districts has worked very hard for a long time to ensure violence is not the norm but the rare exception. (p. 2)

Fortunately, a minority of Michigan school districts have resolutely asserted their right to local control in weapons cases that they did not believe warranted expulsion. One such district is the small central Michigan community of Olivet. The Olivet Community Schools (1995, 1997) respected students' constitutional due process rights by holding extensive school board hearings on expulsions. The board considered violations on a case-by-case basis and determined that the offenses did not warrant expulsion. Instead, this district utilized short suspensions, community service, and research projects on the dangers of school violence as ways to discipline offenders. Although Olivet's policy is exceptional in comparison to other districts, it nonetheless provides an excellent example of discretionary decision making accompanied by procedural due process, demonstrating that the two are not mutually exclusive. Allowing local districts discretion in each case ensures that school boards and principals are not forced to impose excessive punishment against their better judgment solely because the state mandates it. Likewise, statutory due process guidelines would protect students from arbitrary and capricious punishment by local school boards. Such a policy would enshrine in law the necessary due process requirements while protecting local authority.

THE NEED FOR ALTERNATIVE EDUCATION

The fact that quality alternative education programs are crucial to rehabilitating offenders has been documented in numerous federal and state studies (see Cortez, 1997; U.S. Department of Justice, 1997; Wolford and Koebel, 1995). Criticism of Michigan's lack of alternative education programs has been widespread since the expulsion law passed in 1995. To many it represents a false remedy, and at best it is a short-term solution:

> While the zero-tolerance policy aims to protect the safety and well-being of the faculty and students in school, at the same time, the law punishes society. . . . Without a provision guaranteeing an alternative educational program for those students expelled for a weapon violation, no productive structure is provided for those students who may be the most in need. (Bogos, 1997, p. 380)

This position was reiterated by students, educators, lawyers, psychologists, and law enforcement officers at House Education Committee hearings convened across the state of Michigan in early 1998. Nevertheless, the state has consistently failed to provide expelled students with such alternative education services. Ellen Ewing, superintendent of the Saline School District, observed, "You've only moved the problem. You're only treating the symptom. The root cause is left unattended" ("Weapons Law Gets Mixed Grades," 1996, p. C1).

Other educational organizations have expressed support for alternative education as well. The Michigan Association of Secondary School Principals (1998b) stated that expelled students must receive educational services. The National Association of State Boards of Education (1998) stressed the need for alternative education, stating, "Expulsion without alternatives is not a solution to youth violence. . . . At a minimum, alternative programs with strong academic and counseling components should be provided" (p. 2). Many critics of alternative education point out that the fiscal burden incurred by the new programs would be too much for local and state governments (Bogos, 1997). Although such programs are likely to cost approximately 25% per pupil more than average, the Michigan Federation of Teachers (MFT) (1998) noted that "the benefits returned to society by alternative placements make them a worthwhile investment" (p. 2). The MFT estimated the potential social benefits of alternative education to be $20,650 per year, taking into account learning time that would have been lost, reduced grade repetition, added tax revenue, reduced welfare costs, and reduced prison costs, while alternative education would only cost approximately $7,000.

In addition to educators, law enforcement officers have been among the most vocal proponents of alternative education programs. Ann Arbor

Deputy Chief of Police Jack Ceo (1998), who is also a trustee on the nearby Saline Board of Education, argued that "any bill calling for mandatory expulsion of a student for any reason needs to be accompanied by a reasoned method for insuring that the person continues to receive an education, and does not just put them out on the street to become a further problem for the police, and, ultimately, a burden on society" (p. 3). Law enforcement officers across the state share Ceo's position. The Michigan Police Legislative Coalition (1998), the Michigan Association of Chiefs of Police (1998), the Police Officers Association of Michigan (1998), and the Fraternal Order of Police (1998) all submitted statements in support of alternative education amendments to the House subcommittee.

While it is abundantly clear that alternative education is necessary, there is not consensus on how it should be brought about. Until now, legislators have remained content with vague language *allowing* students to enroll in alternative education programs, but not *mandating* them to do so. Even the most recent amendments do not mandate universal alternative education programs; instead, they merely provide detailed guidelines for districts who *wish* to establish "strict discipline academies" for expelled students (see Public Act 23, 1999). As a result, the problem of severely limited alternative educational opportunities remains.

But there is a solution. Michigan attorney general Frank Kelley concluded more than a decade ago that a school district expelling a nondisabled student is not required to provide that student with alternative education. However, Kelley noted that "the Legislature may, if it so desires, amend the School Code of 1976 to require alternative education programs for students that receive lengthy suspensions or expulsions" (Michigan Report of the Attorney General, 1985, p. 17). This opinion is elaborated upon in federal court decisions such as *Walter v. School Board of Indian River County* (1987) and *Matter of Jackson* (1987) that conclude that alternative education is necessary but that the courts may not order schools to provide such programs; instead legislation instructing schools to do so must be passed. Quite simply, alternative education for expelled students *cannot* become a reality absent a legislative mandate requiring schools to provide it.

Other states provide Michigan with a model for such legislation. California offers comprehensive legislation regarding alternative schools, including the establishment of community day schools, rehabilitation programs, and county plans for "providing education services to all expelled pupils in that county" (California Education Code, 1998, secs. 48662, 48916, 48926). Virginia provides extensive guidelines for alternative education programs while appropriating funds for their establishment (Code of Virginia, 1998, sec. 22.1-209.1:2[A]), as does the state of Texas (Vernon's Texas Education

Code, 1998, sec. 37.008). Even John Cole, president of the Texas Federation of Teachers and widely regarded as the father of zero-tolerance policies, insists that alternative education is a necessary component in any zero-tolerance legislation ("Teachers Union Wants to Expel," 1994, p. A13).

Several other states mandate continued educational services as well, although these services are not specifically defined as they are in the above laws. These states include Colorado, Maryland, Minnesota, Missouri, Nebraska, New Jersey, New York, Ohio, and Tennessee (see Code of Maryland, 1997, sec. 7305[3]; Colorado Revised Statutes, 1996, sec. 22-33-204[3]; McKinney's Consolidated Laws of New York, 1998, Title 16, sec. 3214[4] [D]; Minnesota Statutes, 1997, sec. 127.38; Vernon's Annotated Missouri Statutes, 1994, sec. 167.164; New Jersey Statutes, 1998, sec. 18A:37-9; Page's Ohio Revised Code, 1997, secs. 3301.121, 3313.64, 3313.662[3]; Revised Statutes of Nebraska, 1998, sec. 79-266; Tennessee Code, 1997, sec. 49-6-3402).

All of these states' laws are examples of legislative action designed to ensure that expelled students continue to receive an education. However, one must also be wary of laws that permit easy referrals to such programs, transforming them into easily accessible "dumping grounds" (American Federation of Teachers, 1997, p. 11). Research by the Intercultural Development Research Association shows that "there is the potential for overusing alternative education program referrals and for using this punitive measure disproportionately against certain groups of students" (Cortez, 1997, p. 1). Hence it is imperative that alternative programs are fairly administered and of the highest quality. The National Center for Education Statistics and the U.S. Department of Justice (1997) have offered models of quality programs. Some characteristics include: low student/staff ratio, strong leadership, highly trained staff, intensive counseling and mentoring, innovative curriculum and pedagogy, parental involvement, and collaboration with other agencies and schools. In addition, as the American Federation of Teachers (1997) has noted, accountability to state and local authorities is vital if such programs are to protect students' rights. This is particularly important in an era when for-profit alternative education programs have become a multibillion dollar industry, often behaving more like businesses than schools and sacrificing curriculum and academic standards in favor of efficiency and profitability (Bickerstaff, Leon, & Hudson, 1997).

Alternative education is an essential antidote to the debilitating effects of mandatory expulsion on students, their families, and society at large. Hence, Michigan's first task is to establish programs that are in accordance with the above guidelines. In so doing, the state of Michigan would take a gigantic step away from the current punitive policy with its short-sighted solutions toward the far more sensible goal of educating all of our children.

LEGISLATIVE RECOMMENDATIONS

It is doubtful that any child may reasonably be expected to succeed
in life if he is denied the opportunity of an education.
                    —*Brown v. Board of Education,* 347 U.S. 483 (1954)

Since its inception, Michigan's mandatory expulsion law has failed to
curb the problem of youth violence, while depriving hundreds of school-
age children of their right to an education. In reevaluating the current approach to combating school violence it is instructive to recall the testimony
of Professor Brent Simmons (1998) before the House Education Subcommittee on Violence in the Schools:

> How can it be that a State which is a leader in educating its citizenry is also
> a leader in expelling students—especially those students most in need of an
> education? It is my hope that this subcommittee will redirect the attention of
> the Michigan Legislature toward finding ways of keeping more children *in*
> school, rather than seeking out additional grounds for *mandating* their expul-
> sion. (p. 2)

In order to create more meaningful, lasting solutions it is imperative that
the Michigan legislature shift its focus from creating *more punitive* policy
to creating *more effective* policy. As is made clear in this chapter, current
legislation is lacking in many respects. The following is a list of recommendations for legislators attempting to create a more just and effective response to the problem of school violence and other disciplinary infractions.
Any such legislation must

- Protect the civil rights of all students, and safeguard against discrimi-
  natory discipline practices that lead to disproportionate expulsions
  of minority students.
- Maintain compulsory attendance requirements and create less stringent disciplinary measures for students under the age of 16, in order
  to ensure that these children are not left alone, unsupervised, and
  without educational services.
- Include state-mandated due process procedures designed to protect
  the constitutional rights of students going through the expulsion process.
- Clearly define and rigorously enforce reinstatement procedures, including assistance for families preparing petitions.
- Permit local administrators to use their own discretion in deciding
  whether to expel students based on the circumstances of each individual case.

- Mandate referrals of all expelled students to quality alternative education programs supervised by local officials and the state department of education. These programs should include high academic standards, counseling, and violence-prevention programs.
- Require extensive data collection and mandatory reporting requirements for each district.[1]
- Appropriate the necessary funds for all of the aforementioned programs.

These recommendations are applicable to all states where such legislation does not already exist. Indeed, all states have now adopted rigid mandatory expulsion requirements, and although they are not as harsh as Michigan's, many states do not outline due process procedures, nor do they guarantee alternative education.

Colorado currently has one of the most progressive school-discipline laws in the nation, declaring in statute that "expulsion should be the last step taken after several attempts to deal with a student who has discipline problems" (Colorado Revised Statutes, sec. 22-33-201). But in the wake of the catastrophe at Columbine High, forces in that state and across the country are already mobilizing to tighten expulsion laws amid a rising tide of hysteria. Seen in this light, it is vital that educational policy become proactive rather than reactionary, for as mandatory expulsion laws have shown, policy produced in reaction to crisis has countless pitfalls and, in the end, only creates a greater burden for society (Daniel & Coriell, 1992).

CONCLUSION

In formulating policy alternatives it is instructive to recall that the old common-law doctrine of *parens patriae*, or the state as parent, provides the legal foundation for America's public education system. Premised on the belief that the state should protect the welfare of its citizens, public schools and compulsory attendance laws have been established in all 50 states. Out of *parens patriae* grew the concept of *in loco parentis*, the belief that the state should act in the place of the parent. Historically, in loco parentis has been invoked by those favoring unfettered school authority to describe the ideal relationship of schools to their students.

The same concept of rigidly maintained discipline undergirds the philosophy of zero-tolerance. Yet strangely, the proponents of mandatory expulsion have failed to recognize the logical and moral contradictions inherent in such a position. For in constructing the school as parent, we assume not only that it should discipline its children but care for them as well. Yet

in adopting zero-tolerance policies with no provision of alternative education we have effectively forsaken our responsibility to care for *all* children,
and with it the common-law foundations of our nation's public education
system. Such is the sad irony of a society in which we condemn those
parents who abandon their children but condone those schools who abandon theirs.

But the most damning critique of mandatory expulsion requirements
comes from expelled students themselves, from the victims of a policy that
refuses to distinguish between violent offenses and foolish mistakes, and
places greater emphasis on keeping kids out of school rather than getting
them back in. Their silenced voices make the most compelling case for
reform. Listen to Kevin, who has been out of school for nearly 2 years:

> I want to go back to school and I've been sayin' that since I got kicked
> out, but that don't seem to matter to them. . . . I feel as though they
> think I'm a puppet or something. They say "do this, do this" but it's
> not helpin' me none. I don't see why they put me through it if it's not
> helpin' me none, and it's not helpin' towards gettin' back to school
> . . . it's like they're just tryin' to make me *dance . . . dance*.

Kevin's words are a wake-up call to all of us who care about the fate of
our children. As this study makes clear, the perils of zero-tolerance policies
are numerous. Students in Michigan and across the country desperately
need legislation that ensures equity, mandates compulsory attendance,
allows eligible students to be reinstated, and guarantees alternative education without limiting local control or denying due process rights. In addition, any such laws must require rigorous data collection in order to monitor their effects. Until such legislation is passed students like Kevin will
remain America's least wanted citizens: powerless puppets trapped in the
tangled strings of misguided policy and legislative neglect.

NOTE

1. The information collected by the state department of education should include number of expulsions, grounds for expulsion, state agency referral after expulsion, and alternative education provided. The states of Massachusetts (1998) and
California (1998, sec. 48916.1 [a–f]) provide excellent models for such data collection. It is also imperative that all of this information be disaggregated according to
race, gender, age, special education status, and free lunch eligibility in order to
determine whether certain groups of students are being expelled in disproportionate numbers.

REFERENCES

American Federation of Teachers. (1997). *National campaign for standards of conduct, standards of achievement.* Washington, DC: Author.

Bai, M. (1999, May 3). Anatomy of a massacre. *Newsweek,* pp. 27-31.

Bickerstaff, S., Leon, S. H., & Hudson, J. G. (1997). Preserving the opportunity for education: Texas' alternative education programs for disruptive youth. *Journal for Law and Education, 26*(4), 16-19.

Blank, J., & Cohen, W. (1997, December 15). Prayer circle murders. *U.S. News and World Report,* p. 25.

Bogos, P. M. (1997). "Expelled. No excuses. No exceptions"—Michigan's zero-tolerance policy in response to school violence: M.C.L.A. 380.1311. *University of Detroit Mercy Law Review, 74,* 357-387.

Brown v. Board of Education, 347 U.S. 483 (1954).

Burns Indiana Statutes, Annotated. (1998). Charlottesville, VA: Michie.

Cafeteria Workers v. McElroy, 367 U.S. 886 (1961) as quoted in Goss v. Lopez 419 U.S., at 568.

California Education Code, Annotated. (1998). St. Paul, MN: West.

Ceo, J. (1998). Testimony presented to the House Education Committee's Subcommittee on Violence in the Schools. Whitmore Lake, MI, p. 3.

Code of Maryland, Annotated. (1997). Charlottesville, VA: Michie.

Code of Virginia. (1998). Charlottesville, VA: Michie.

Colorado Revised Statutes, Annotated. (1996). St. Paul, MN: West.

Cortez, A. (1997, November-December). Alternative education programs: Resolution or exclusion? *Intercultural Development Research Association Newsletter, 24,* p. 1.

Cowley, G. (1998, April 6). Why children turn violent. *Newsweek,* pp. 24-26.

Daniel, P. T. K., & Coriell, K. B. (1992). Suspension and expulsion in America's schools: Has unfairness resulted from a narrowing of due process? *Hamline Journal of Law and Public Policy, 13*(1), 36.

Dohrn, B. (1993, Summer). Children and the law. *Criminal Justice, 8*(2), 9-10.

Egan, T. (1998, June 14). From adolescent angst to school killings. *The New York Times,* p. A1.

Family Independence Agency. (1997, July 25). *Weapons in schools (act no. 328, public act of 1994), final report of referrals received.* Lansing, MI: Author.

Fraternal Order of Police. (1998, May 6). Letter submitted to the House Education Committee's Subcommittee on Violence in the Schools.

Fuentes, A. (1998, June 15-22). The crackdown on kids. *The Nation,* p. 20.

Goss v. Lopez, 419 U.S. 565 (1975).

Gun Free Schools Act of 1994, 20 U.S.C. §8921(e).

Individuals with Disabilities in Education Act, 20 U.S.C. §1400 *et seq.,* or 34 C.F.R. sec 104.35.

Jensen, M. A., & Goffin, S. G. (Eds.). (1993). *Visions of entitlement: The care and education of America's children.* Albany: State University of New York Press.

Johnson, D. (1999, November 17). Jackson arrested in protest over expulsions of students. *The New York Times,* p. A16.

Jones, R. (1997, October). Absolute zero: Do zero-tolerance policies go too far? *American School Board Journal, 184*(10), 29–30.

Karas, J. (1998, June 17). Muskegon schools expels [*sic*] 7 students. *Muskegon Chronicle,* p. A1.

Lewin, T. (1998, March 25). Study finds no big rise in school crime. *The New York Times,* p. A20.

Lewin, Y. (1997, March 12). School codes without mercy snare pupils without malice. *The New York Times,* p. A1, B7.

Massachusetts Department of Education. (1998). *Student exclusions in Massachusetts public schools 1996–97.* Malden, MA: Author.

Matter of Jackson, 352 S.E. 2d 449, (1987).

Matter of P. J., 575 N.E. 2d 22, (1991).

Mayes, M. (1997, January 21). Protesters call expulsions biased. *Lansing State Journal,* p. B1.

McKinney's Consolidated Laws of New York, Annotated. (1998). St. Paul, MN: West.

Michigan Advisory Committee to the U.S. Commission on Civil Rights. (1996). *Discipline in Michigan public schools and government enforcement of equal education opportunity.* Chicago: U.S. Commission on Civil Rights.

Michigan Association of Chiefs of Police. (1998, May 5). Letter submitted to the House Education Committee's Subcommittee on Violence in the Schools.

Michigan Association of Secondary School Principals. (1998). A statement from the Michigan association of secondary school principals regarding violence in the schools. *The Bulletin, 39*(7), 1.

Michigan Compiled Laws, Annotated. (1998). Section 380.1311. St. Paul, MN: West.

Michigan Department of Education. (1997a). *Report on expulsions and suspensions in Michigan for the 1995–1996 school year.* Lansing, MI: Author.

Michigan Department of Education. (1997b). *Selected financial data, 1995–1996, bulletin 1014.* Lansing, MI: Author.

Michigan Federation of Teachers. (1998). Safe schools a requirement for learning. *Forum, 57*(3), 2.

Michigan Police Legislative Coalition. (1998, May 1). Letter submitted to the House Education Committee's Subcommittee on Violence in the Schools.

Michigan Report of the Attorney General. (1985). Opinion no. 6271, pp. 16–17.

Michigan Superintendents of the 23rd House District. (1998, February 19). Testimony presented to the House Education Committee's Subcommittee on Violence in the Schools.

Minnesota Statutes. (1997). St. Paul: Revisor of Statutes.

Morain, D. (1995, October 17). Wilson signs school safety, testing bills. *Los Angeles Times,* p. 1.

National Association of State Boards of Education. (1998). *Policy Update, 6*(10), 2.

New Jersey Statutes, Annotated. (1998). St. Paul, MN: West.

O'Brien, E. (1998, May 31). Guns and rage: Can we stop troubled teens who are mad enough to kill? *Ann Arbor News,* p. A3.

Olivet Community Schools. (1995, May 8). *School Board Minutes.*

Olivet Community Schools. (1997, February 26). *School Board Minutes.*

Page's Ohio Revised Code, Annotated. (1997). Cincinnati: W. H. Anderson.

Pedersen, D., & Van Boven, S. (1997, December 15). Tragedy in a small place. *Newsweek,* p. 30.

Polakow-Suransky, S. (1999, February). *Access denied: Mandatory expulsion requirements and the erosion of educational opportunity in Michigan.* Ann Arbor, MI: Student Advocacy Center of Michigan.

Police Officers Association of Michigan. (1998, May 6). Letter submitted to the House Education Committee's Subcommittee on Violence in the Schools.

Public Act 23. (1999, May 12). Lansing: Michigan Legislature.

Revised Stautes of Nebraska. (1997). Lincoln: Statute Commission.

Simmons, B. (1998). Testimony presented to the House Education Committee's Subcommittee on Violence in the Schools. Lansing, MI, p. 2.

Stone, D. H. (1993). Crime and punishment in American schools: An empirical study of disciplinary proceedings. *American Journal of Trial Advocacy, 17,* 351–366.

Student Advocacy Center files. (1996-1998). *Board Packet, Expulsion Hearing for* _____. Ann Arbor, MI: Author.

Superintendents of the 23rd House District. (1998). Testimony presented to the House Education Committee's Subcommittee on Violence in the Schools. Trenton, MI, p. 2.

Teachers' union wants to expel kids who carry guns. (1994, July 19). *The New York Times,* p. A13.

Tennessee Code, Annotated. (1997). Charlottesville, VA: Michie.

United States Department of Justice, Office of Juvenile Justice and Delinquency Prevention. (1997, February). *Juvenile Justice Bulletin.* Washington, DC: Author.

Vernon's Annotated Missouri Statutes. (1994). Kansas City, MO: Vernon Law Book.

Vernon's Texas Education Code, Annotated. (1998). St. Paul, MN: West.

Wagenheim, W. (1998). Testimony presented to the House Education Committee's Subcommittee on Violence in the Schools. Lansing, MI, p. 1.

Walter v. School Board of Indian River County, 518 So. 2d 1331, (1987).

Weapons law gets mixed grades. (1996, August 30). *Ann Arbor News,* p. C1.

Webber, T. (1999, December 10). Civil Rights Commission to examine impact of zero tolerance policies. Associated Press Wire.

Wing, B., & Keleher, T. (Spring 2000). Zero tolerance: An interview with Jesse Jackson on race and school discipline. *Colorlines.*

Wolford, B. I., & Koebel, L. L. (1995, Winter). Reform education to reduce juvenile delinquency. *Criminal Justice, 10*(4), 56.

Zirkel, P. (1997, June). The Midol case. *Phi Delta Kappan, 78*(10), 803-804.

CHAPTER 6

Listen First

How Student Perspectives on Violence Can Be Used to Create Safer Schools

PEDRO A. NOGUERA

Responses to the shootings at Columbine High School in Littleton, Colorado, tell us a great deal about attitudes and perceptions toward violence in American society. First, there was the intense media coverage during and immediately after the incident. In vivid detail, the public was provided around-the-clock coverage that included live footage from the school, on-the-scene interviews with students and police officers, and multiple reports on every possible aspect of the violent rampage. For a public seeking to understand what had happened, such coverage was at first illuminating, but as the days wore on, the reporting gradually changed from news to a perverse kind of entertainment. Within a relatively short period of time, the tragedy at Columbine High School became yet another hyped-up media spectacle, which, like so many other recent national media events, at times seemed cheesy and exploitative of the victims.

A similar transformation occurred in the statements made by politicians who quickly stepped forward to comment on the incident. At first their words seemed genuinely empathetic toward the victims and their families. However, as time passed, their comments became more ideological, calculating, and partisan. With the increased attention given to the issues related to the incident—regulation of firearms, school safety, youth culture, and so forth—politicians began to stake out strategic positions ever mindful of how their public stances would be interpreted by key constituents and financial contributors. At every public event—press conferences, funerals, and memorial services—the occasion became an opportunity for politicians to position themselves in ways they hoped would maximize their political advantages and minimize their losses.

Though no connection was made in the media, it seemed relevant to me that the incident occurred while the nation was engaged in an undeclared war against Yugoslavia; a war in which casualties inflicted upon civilians were rationalized as "collateral" damage incurred during what was proclaimed to be a "humanitarian" military mission. Interestingly, none of the media commentators or politicians ever explored whether there might be a connection between state-sponsored violence that was officially condoned and even applauded, and the actions of these troubled teenagers. Although many were quick to suggest a possible link between the tragedy at Columbine and the pervasive violence present in the media, on the Internet, and in popular music, few drew any connection at all to the government's use of violence in a foreign land. The unstated message was that state-sanctioned violence was "good" violence, and therefore would not be questioned.

Finally, the shootings at Columbine High School produced a rash of copycat incidents at schools across the country, with numerous school districts reporting bomb threats and students appearing in trench coats at their schools (Bell, 1999). Such incidents may be the most telling response of all. The outbreak of threats, real and imagined, at schools across the country in the days that followed reinforced the fear that what happened in Littleton could happen anywhere. It also added to an even deeper concern and recognition: that something is profoundly wrong with American culture if our schools and our youth are indeed this vulnerable to violence.

When considered in combination with and relation to one another, these responses are indicative of the contradictions in our society's attitudes and perceptions toward violence and toward children generally. First, they tell us that although violence of this kind may be repulsive and frightening it is also on another level intriguing, and perhaps even in some morbid sense entertaining. The media consistently defends its sensationalized coverage of such events by arguing that they merely provide what the public wants and that the public's appetite for graphic depictions of violence is at times insatiable. Second, the responses suggest that though violence is prohibited in school, its use in other contexts can be rationalized as legitimate if the perpetrator is the state. Even if the targets of violence are alleged to be mentally impaired, such as in the recent execution of Duane Babbit in California and the pending execution of Larry Keith Robinson in Texas

(Yardley, 1999), or noncombatant civilians in places such as Iraq, Serbia, or the Sudan, state-sponsored violence in defense of what are construed as national interests is permissible.

Violence is an integral part of American history and culture, and though there is a deeply felt fear of violence in many communities across the country, it is apparently not sufficient to lead to a decisive break from our societal obsession. We fear violence, but Americans own more firearms than any other people on the face of the earth (Larson, 1993). Politicians criticize filmmakers who produce films with gratuitous depictions of violence, yet such films tend to be tremendously successful at the box office (Barry, 1993). We deplore violence on the streets, but we applaud it on the playing fields. The search for strategies to reduce the threat of violence continues despite these contradictions. It may well be the case that without a complete purging of our societal fixation with violence, a more pervasive feeling of safety and social peace will remain out of reach. In the meantime, the search continues.

In our nation's schools, the search for safety has now reached the point of desperation. Although the available data and evidence suggest that the incidence of violence in schools is not rising and that violent acts are not becoming more prevalent (Glassner, 1999), among the general public there is a growing perception that schools are more violent and dangerous than ever before. In polls and surveys, students, teachers, and parents all report a greater degree of fear of violent assault at school, and greater concern about safety and student discipline generally than they did 10 years ago (Pollack, 1999).

In response to these concerns, several states and school districts have undertaken a variety of highly visible measures intended to provide some reassurance to the public that schools can be made safe (Shogren, 1994). This has included the adoption of security measures such as metal detectors and high-tech surveillance cameras, as well as an increasing reliance on armed security guards and police officers to address the security needs of school sites. At many inner-city schools, such measures are not new. Concerns about safety and discipline at schools in impoverished urban areas have been common for many years. However, the recent wave of shootings at predominantly White, middle-class suburban schools in Mississippi, Kentucky, Arkansas, Oregon, Colorado, and Georgia have shown quite clearly that violence is no longer limited to inner-city schools. Though there is no clear pattern linking the more recent violent incidents, in the national media these incidents have been portrayed as part of a dangerous national trend afflicting the nation's schools.

Given the strong reaction that an issue such as school violence evokes, it is not surprising that even if statistical evidence on the incidence of violence in schools suggests that no significant increase has occurred, policy on this issue at federal, state, and local levels will likely be driven more by public fears than by data. On such volatile and emotional issues, the facts don't speak for themselves. Even without clear and convincing documentation on the extent of the problem, policy makers and school officials feel compelled to take action. They feel compelled to adopt a variety of measures, some of which are quite costly, so that they at least appear to be doing "something" to assure a frightened public that order in schools can be maintained. Charged with the responsibility of managing our nation's schools, educational leaders, and increasingly politicians, feel compelled to take tough action, lest they be accused of being unresponsive to the public's concerns (Bell, 1999).

However, in the rush to act, policies are adopted and actions are taken too often without the benefit of careful dispassionate analysis. As a consequence, much of what is done may not only fail in reducing the likelihood of violence, but may even inadvertently contribute to its occurrence. For example, shortly after the Richmond public schools installed metal detectors at all of the high schools in the district, two students were shot at one of the schools by an individual who found a way to avoid the newly installed security system (Asimov, 1994a). It may well be the case that the metal detector created an illusion of security that led to a slackening of other forms of security (e.g., adult supervision in hallways) at the school.

Many of the "get tough" measures are premised on the notion that violence in school can be reduced and controlled by identifying, apprehending, and excluding violent or potentially violent individuals (Toby, 1993/1994). Such an approach generally treats violence as a form of individual deviance that can be rooted out through punitive and exclusionary measures. However, left unconsidered, and therefore unaddressed, are the social and environmental factors, which a significant body of public health research on violence cite as being central to the underlying causes of youth violence (Jenkins & Bell, 1992; Spivak, 1998). Finally, and perhaps most important, there is the failure throughout much of American society to recognize the connection between the deplorable social conditions under which large numbers of children live and the increased likelihood that these same children will become victims or perpetrators of violence as they grow older (Edelman, 1989).

It is even more problematic that research on youth attitudes and perceptions toward violence has had very little influence on the policies and measures that have been enacted to promote safety. In this chapter I will present an analysis of how a variety of social factors, specifically race, class, and neighborhood context, influence student perceptions toward violence in school and attitudes toward violent behavior. Using an analysis of interviews carried out at two middle schools in northern California, I will demonstrate the importance of incorporating student perspectives and concerns into the effort to curtail violence in school. I will argue that because students are the primary victims and perpetrators of violence in school, the perceptions, attitudes, and fears of students must be analyzed and taken into account if the strategies utilized to prevent violence are to succeed at making schools safe. My goal is to show how an understanding of student perspectives on violence can be incorporated into school violence prevention efforts and thereby increase the likelihood that schools will become safer places for both children and the adults who work in them.

THE CONTEXTUAL REALITY OF VIOLENCE

In many school districts, the pressure to create schools that are perceived as safe often becomes reduced to a numbers game. To reassure the public that actions are being taken to increase security, school officials point to statistics related to the number of weapons confiscated and the number of students suspended, expelled, or arrested as evidence that something is being done about the problem (Asimov, 1994b). Such reporting can be especially important when those responsible for security are competing for scarce resources. In order to secure funding for security, reports on the incidence of violence can be used to demonstrate that although valiant efforts are being made to reduce violence, the problem persists, and therefore the fight and the funding must continue. Statistics on violence prevention are also instrumental in framing public discourse about violence; even without making teachers and students feel safer, administrators can claim to be doing something by pointing to quantifiable data that show that results are being obtained.

Yet for parents, teachers, and students who live with the reality of violence and who must contend with the threat of physical harm on a daily basis, reports on the number of weapons confiscated or the number of students who have been expelled are unlikely to allay their fears. When engaging in ordinary activities such as walking to school or playing at the park generates so much fear and anxiety that many kids feel unable to participate in them, news that arrests or suspensions have increased is unlikely to provide the assurance of safety that many desperately seek.

Still, within the context of the fight against violence, symbolic actions take on great significance, even though they may have little bearing upon the actual occurrence of violence or its perception. Metal detectors, barbed wire fences, armed guards and policemen, and principals wielding baseball bats as they patrol the halls are all symbols of tough action. Even if most students realize that it is possible to bring a weapon into a school building without being discovered by a metal detector, and that it is highly unlikely that a principal will actually hit a student with a baseball bat, the symbols persist. They persist because without them the unstated truth would be known: Those responsible for preventing violence really don't have a clue about what to do to make schools safer places.

Part of the failure of traditional approaches is rooted in their inability to address the contextual factors that influence the incidence of violence and reactions to it. Expressions of violence are certainly not limited to schools, so it may be unrealistic to fashion remedies that respond to the issue without consideration of neighborhood and other contextual factors. For example, in developing a response to the threat of violence it may be important to understand the circumstances under which violence as a learned form of social behavior may be construed as legitimate or even appropriate by young people. Similarly, as pointed out earlier, we might also consider what role portrayals of violence in the media, sports, and officially sanctioned forms of state-sponsored violence (i.e., war or police actions) play in shaping attitudes toward violence.

Finally, given the persistence of certain characteristics and patterns with respect to the perpetrators and victims of violence, namely the disproportionate number of African American and Latino males found in both categories (Wilson-Brewer & Jacklin, 1990), it may be important to consider how the racialization of violence has shaped popular attitudes toward the issue. Orlando Patterson (1999), a sociologist at Harvard University, asked this question in a *New York Times* editorial: "What if the killers at Columbine High School had been Black?" (p. A24). This is not merely a rhetorical question, for prior to the recent wave of shootings at suburban schools, the media's portrayal of youth violence had been linked almost exclusively to Black and Latino youth (Silver, 1993). To the extent that violence is now widely recognized as more than just a minority issue, there may be greater willingness to explore the underlying social and cultural factors that contribute to its expression.

Additionally, as the shootings at Columbine High School have shown, it is important that we consider how peer groups and the social climate of a school may influence attitudes toward violence. Research suggests that kids who have been socially ostracized, bullied, teased, or mistreated, by school officials or other students, may be at greater risk of engaging in violent behavior (Coleman, 1978). An unwillingness to confront the implications of the connections between violence and social status may prevent us from seeing how expressions of violence may be linked to broader patterns of success and failure at school. It is significant that those most likely to receive punishment for disciplinary infractions in school also tend to be more likely to have been placed in special education or remedial classes (Meier, Stewart, & England, 1989).

In schools where teachers are afraid of students, where Black and Latino students are criminalized and uniformly treated as potentially violent gang members, and where responsibility for managing school safety has been relegated to poorly paid security guards, the potential for violence is great. Instead of providing a safe venue for teaching and learning, such schools come to reflect the violence present within the surrounding community. Within such a context, understanding the perceptions of those most at risk of violence becomes even more important for finding ways to reduce its occurrence.

UNDERSTANDING STUDENT PERSPECTIVES ON SCHOOL VIOLENCE

To begin to understand how students perceived the threat of violence within the context of their everyday experiences at school, I undertook a study of student attitudes utilizing the grounded theory approach developed by Glaser and Strauss (1967). As is typical for most researchers presenting inquiries that are premised on grounded theory, I had a great deal of prior knowledge about the subject matter, having worked and engaged in research with schools for many years. However, despite my familiarity with the subject, I had no compelling hypothesis or causal explanation for the questions that motivated the inquiry.

I wanted to understand how students perceived the threat of violence in their environment and how this perception might influence their attitudes toward violent behavior. I was also interested in understanding the ethical judgments they made regarding particular manifestations of violence that they observed, experienced, or both within their daily routines. Specifically, I wanted to know if there were circumstances in which students might regard violent behavior as legitimate or appropriate, and if so, what connection, if any, this had to their personal stance toward violence.

To find answers to these questions, I surveyed and conducted interviews with 48 students at two middle schools in northern California during the 1992–93 school year. I chose the two schools because they provided a striking contrast along the dimensions of race, class, and environmental context. I surmised that such a contrast would illuminate the ways in which social context—the community, neighborhood economy, and physical environment—influenced the attitudes and perceptions of young people toward violence. Additionally, I suspected that although students at the two schools seem to exist in completely separate worlds, a closer examination might reveal ways in which students' perceptions were similar as a result of their exposure to television and other media and the more diffuse influences of popular youth culture. Understanding how these factors—the cultural and the environmental—influenced the attitudes and perceptions of students toward violence was a primary goal of this inquiry.

In order to protect the identities of those associated with the two schools, I shall refer to them in this chapter as Schools A and B. School A is a relatively small middle school—347 students, 18 teachers, a principal, an assistant principal, and two guidance counselors. It is located in an industrial area in an economically depressed and socially isolated community; a neighborhood with a reputation for its dangerous streets, its dense housing projects, and the illegal dumping that occurs on its streets. The school, like the community, has a diverse non-White student population, made up predominantly of African Americans, but with significant numbers of students who are recent immigrants from Mexico, Southeast Asia, Africa, and the Middle East.

School B is a medium-size middle school—812 students, 36 teachers, a principal, two assistant principals, and three counselors. It is located in a parklike setting on 12 acres of land, with large athletic fields, a swimming pool, and tennis courts. It is surrounded by the homes of middle-class families, the average value of which exceeds $300,000, in a predominantly White, middle-class, suburban community. The community is made up largely of college-educated professionals, though there is a working-class side of town where most non-White families live (see Table 6.1).

TABLE 6.1 Characteristics of middle schools

	School A	School B
Student Population	347	812
Gifted	3%	17%
Compensatory Education	64%	16%
Below Grade Level		
Reading	60%	18%
Math	52%	12%
Eligible for Free/Reduced Lunch	95%	15%
Weapons Confiscated	14	2
Disciplinary Measures		
Expulsions	8	4
Suspensions	76	36

Note: All data are based upon official district reports from the 1992–1993 academic year.

Even though the actual distance between the two schools is less than 10 miles, in existential terms the schools feel as though they were thousands of miles apart. The contrast is most readily apparent in the physical aspects of the two schools. The hallways in School A are dark, and the play areas are covered with asphalt. The hallways in School B are bright with natural illumination entering through skylights, and grass and trees cover the campus.

Similarly, the way these schools relate to the surrounding community is also a telling feature of comparison. While School A is surrounded by a fence approximately 15 feet in height that borders the perimeter of the campus, School B and its facilities—pool, playing fields, tennis and basketball courts—are easily accessible to its neighbors and the general public. The design of the two schools suggests that whereas School A regards its community with suspicion and fear, School B perceives the community as an ally and its facilities are regarded by residents as a public resource and asset.

My access to both schools was made possible by prior relationships with the faculty and administration. In years past I had been involved in professional development workshops for teachers and had spoken to groups of parents and students at both schools. To obtain their participation in this study I approached each principal with an offer to assist them in devising a violence prevention strategy for their schools that would be informed by concrete knowledge about the views and perceptions of students. Like many principals, both were faced with growing concerns from parents and teachers related to the threats of violence. Though neither school had experienced any major incidents of violence in the past few years, heightened awareness about violence at other schools throughout the country prompted both principals to readily agree to participate in the study and welcome my offer of assistance.

The design called for surveys and interviews with students to be conducted in eighth-grade social studies classes with the support and cooperation of the classroom teachers. Twenty-two students were surveyed and interviewed at School A, and 28 students were surveyed and interviewed at School B. In both classes the study was introduced as part of a unit on violence prevention, which I taught as a guest teacher over a 2-week period. The unit began with a lecture/presentation on the forms of violence in American society—violent crime, interpersonal and domestic violence, police and military violence, and violent acts carried out by hate and terror groups. This was followed by a discussion of how these forms of violence are represented in the media. Following a brief interactive discussion to clarify the focus of the study and definition of terms, a survey was administered which consisted of 10 true/false statements and four multiple-choice and one open-ended question (see Table 6.2). Once the surveys were completed and collected, a discussion of the responses was facilitated with the whole group in an effort to understand why individuals responded as they did to the questions. This enabled me to get a better understanding of the logic behind the responses and also provided an opportunity for an open discussion of related issues.

Following completion of the survey, I conducted individual interviews with the students over the course of the week, using four multiple-choice questions and one open-ended question from the survey as the basis for our conversation. Each interview lasted approximately 25 minutes. All of the questions were designed to solicit the students' views and perceptions of violence and to ascertain the extent to which they perceived a threat of violence within the school environment. The following week I presented a unit on violence in the media for the purpose of investigating how students interpreted and responded to violent images in film. The results of that portion of the study will not be reported here, though its findings have indirect relevance to the issue of violence in schools.

In what follows I present an analysis of the responses of the students to the surveys and interviews conducted at the two schools.

School A

Of the 22 students who participated in the study at School A, 14 were African American (seven boys, seven girls), five were Asian American (three girls, two boys), and three were Latino (two girls, one boy). Among the entire student population only 3% of the students were designated gifted and talented based on their tests scores on the California Test of Basic Skills (CTBS). In contrast, 24% of the students at School A were designated as eligible for some form of special education, and 64% were qualified for compensatory education based on test scores that on average fell below the 38th percentile on the CTBS. More than 60% of the seventh graders at School A tested below grade level in reading, and 52% were ranked below grade level in math.

Compared with most schools serving middle-class children, the academic offerings at School A were quite sparse. Science courses were offered to 7th and 8th graders, but there was no modern equipment in the science labs. There was a school library, but according to the school librarian, no new books had been ordered or received in the past 10 years. Algebra was offered at the school to eighth graders, but only 15 students were considered sufficiently prepared to take the course at the time of this study. There was also a computer laboratory, but access was limited to students enrolled in the computer course. The only other elective course available was Span-

TABLE 6.2 Survey of student experiences with and perceptions of violence

	School A		School B	
True/False Statements	True	False	True	False
1. In the last year, someone that I know was a victim of violence and was either hurt or killed.	18	4	6	22
2. I sometimes carry a weapon for protection.	8	14	4	24
3. I have been in a fight in the last month.	9	13	4	24
4. I have been in a fight in the last two months.	13	9	4	24
5. I hardly ever fight if I can avoid it.	21	1	24	4
6. Using violence to get what you want is never the right thing to do.	7	15	16	12
7. I enjoy watching violent movies.	18	4	23	5
8. I often worry about being hurt by someone when I am at school.	19	3	3	25
9. I often worry about being hurt by someone when I am at home or in my neighborhood.	19	3	2	26
10. I respect and look up to people who know how to fight well.	11	11	2	26

Multiple-Choice Questions

11. *If you know that someone wants to fight with you, the best thing to do is:*

a. Tell an adult.	3	21
b. Tell your friends or family members so that you have some back-up.	15	3
c. Carry a weapon with you just in case you get jumped.	3	0
d. Try to talk to the person to resolve the conflict peacefully.	0	2
e. Other _____	1	2

TABLE 6.2 Continued.

	School A	School B
12. *If you knew that another student brought a weapon to school you would:*		
a. Tell a teacher or the principal.	0	15
b. Mind your own business and not tell anyone.	16	7
c. Talk to the person to find out what was going on.	2	1
d. Talk to your friends about it.	4	5
13. *If you know that two people are going to fight after school the best thing to do is:*		
a. Watch the fight.	16	17
b. Help the person that is losing.	0	0
c. Tell an adult.	2	7
d. Go home and mind your own business.	4	4
14. *Which of the following is a legitimate reason for fighting:*		
a. Someone looks at you the wrong way or says something bad about you.	6	2
b. Someone threatens you, a family member, or a friend.	15	12
c. Someone hits you, a family member, or a friend.	19	21
d. Someone says something bad about your mother.	9	7
e. Other	8	5
15. *Are there any occasions when violence may be appropriate? (Open-ended)*		

ish, which was limited to eighth graders, though a variety of ESL (English as a Second Language), special education, and remedial reading classes were also offered.

School A is located in a community with high concentrations of poverty, and the effects of poverty are manifest within the school in a variety of ways. In 1993, 95% of the students qualified, on the basis of parental income, for free or reduced lunch. Through a conversation with the school nurse I learned that 43% of the students were identified as asthmatic or having some other form of chronic respiratory condition; a condition that she attributed to the freeways and heavy industry pervading the community. Finally, and most surprising to me, 68% of the students at school A lived with an adult who is someone other than one of their biological parents (i.e., lived with grandparents or other relatives, or were in foster care).

From this description of the characteristics and conditions present at School A one might draw the conclusion that this is a school where concerns about the threat of violence were high. This was indeed the case during the time I was carrying out research at the school, but as will be shown later, a heightened sense of awareness about the threat of violence is increasingly common even at schools in communities that seem safer. In interviews with teachers and administrators, concerns about safety came up frequently, though most often outsiders and the surrounding neighborhood were perceived as the primary source of danger to the school.

During the 1992–93 school year, 14 weapons were confiscated from students at School A (one toy gun, five knives, three baseball bats, and five sticks or clubs). Within the school district of which it is a part, School A ranked 10th among 32 middle schools for the number of weapons confiscated. During the same period, eight students were expelled for violent behavior (mostly fighting) at school, 76 were suspended, and the police were called to campus on 21 separate occasions to respond to violent incidents involving students or outsiders. Many teachers admitted that the increase in police presence was attributable to a greater tendency to involve law enforcement in matters that previously would have been handled by the school administration.

The school principal attributed most of the problems related to violence to outsiders and a small number of difficult and disruptive students, who "lack sufficient guidance at home and act out at school in an effort to get attention" (interview 3/16/93). Though there had been only one instance of a student striking a teacher in the past 3 years, several teachers expressed concern for their personal safety because of what they perceived as an increase in violent behavior from students. This fear was expressed in the following statement from a veteran teacher at School A:

> In the past the kids would respect you just because you were the teacher. You were a person in authority and they knew they had to do as you said. Nowadays the kids are different. They have their own rules, and just because you're a teacher it doesn't mean that they're going to treat you any different than anybody else. On the wrong day, any of us could be the victim of an attack. (interview, 3/18/93)

School B

The contrasts between School A and B were striking. Test scores at School B revealed that 17% of students were identified as gifted and talented, and

16% had scores low enough to be eligible for compensatory education. At School B, 18% of the students entered the eighth grade below grade level in reading, with a corresponding 12% in math. Finally, fewer than 5% of the students at School B were identified as being in need of some form of special education.

Of the 28 students who participated in the study at School B, 17 were White (eight boys and nine girls), four were Asian American (three girls and one boy), and five were African American students (two boys and three girls). The students had access to a variety of elective courses that were offered at School B, including Spanish, French, computers, art, music, dance, and health education. Four sections of algebra and one class of honors geometry were offered to students who were deemed qualified. Only 15% of the students at School B were qualified to receive free or reduced lunch, and according to the principal, the PTSA (Parent, Teacher, Student Association) raised more than $100,000 during the previous year to support field trips and other educational activities at the school.

Despite the relative affluence of the school, the families it serves, and the community in which it is located, concerns about the threat of violence were high. In interviews with teachers and administrators, several expressed concerns and uncertainty about what they described as a "climate of violence." While the source of this threat was difficult to pin down, the sentiments expressed by this eighth-grade English teacher captured some of the anxiety that was conveyed to me:

> The attitudes of the children have changed. They use harsher language with each other when they argue, and when they fight, you'd think they wanted to kill each other. It's not a place where kids are carrying guns or anything, but something's different about kids today, and to me it's a lot more scary. (interview, 4/7/93)

Mirroring the national trends previously described, the teachers' concerns about violence were not matched by empirical evidence. Only two weapons (one knife and one club) were confiscated from students at School B over a 3-year period. During the 1992–93 school year 36 students were suspended and four students were expelled. The police were called to the school on two occasions for violent incidents at the school during the same period (both incidents involved students from other schools). There were five security guards at School B, an additional guard having been hired in the 1991–92 school year in response to heightened concerns about security. Interestingly, all five of the security guards were African American males, and they were the only African American males other than the custodian who were employed at the school.

LEARNING FROM STUDENTS' EXPERIENCES
WITH AND PERCEPTIONS OF VIOLENCE

Among the students at the two schools, the responses to both the survey and the interviews revealed dramatic differences, and some unexpected similarities. This was seen both in response to the true/false statements, in the discussion of the survey that followed, and in the individual interviews. For example, whereas 18 of the 22 students at School A responded "true" to statement 1, "In the last year someone that I know was a victim of violence and was either killed or hurt," only 6 of the 28 students at School B responded affirmatively (see Table 6.2). Similarly, in response to statements 8 and 9, "I often worry about being hurt by someone when I am at school [or at home, or in the neighborhood]," the vast majority of students at School A (19 of the 22) selected "true," while at School B only 3 students chose "true."

Other items revealed similar patterns of difference. In response to statement 2, "I sometimes carry a weapon for protection," students at School A were twice as likely to respond affirmatively (8 of 22) as students at School B (4 of 28). Similarly, students at School A were far more likely to respond "true" to statements 3 and 4, "I have been in a fight in the last month;" "in the last two months." Nine of the students at School A responded affirmatively to statement 3, and 13 to statement 4, compared with 4 students at School B who answered "true" to both. Though the vast majority of students at both schools responded "true" to statement 5, "I hardly ever fight if I can avoid it" (21 at School A, 24 at School B), more students at School A responded "true" to statement 10, "I respect and look up to people who know how to fight well" (11 at School A, 2 at School B).

Differences in the attitudes and perceptions of these two groups of students were even more dramatic in the interviews and whole-group discussions of the survey. For example, in response to question 11, the majority of students (15) at School A chose response 11.b—"Tell your friends or family members so that you have some back-up." In contrast, the overwhelming majority of students at School B (21) chose response 11.a, "Tell an adult," as the preferred method for handling a threat from another student.

In the discussions that followed their responses to this question, students at School A clearly felt that telling an adult if a person wants to fight with you is not a viable option because it can only provide temporary relief. According to one female student:

> If you tell a teacher that somebody wants to fight with you it's not like they're gonna walk you home. The most they can do is get the person

sent to the office, but if the fight didn't happen yet, the person ain't even gonna get in trouble.

For these students, telling a friend or family member was a better solution because it might enable the student to avoid the fight altogether, in that a show of force could neutralize the threat of violence. Another explained the logic behind such a response in this way:

> When they see that you got back-up, if your partners are with you, they know it ain't gonna be like they can just beat you down. Somebody is gonna get hurt and it ain't gonna just be on one side. Then they know they better just leave you unless they want some real action to jump off.

In contrast, the majority of students at School B considered telling an adult to be the most reasonable and effective way of handling a threat from another student. For these students there was no doubt that once such a matter was brought to the attention of a responsible adult, a violent conflict could be avoided. Adults at the school site were perceived as capable of protecting and supervising students, and these students believed that any individual threatening to use violence against a peer was likely to be punished severely. This certainty was conveyed by a male student at School B who asserted:

> The campus monitors at our school are really tough. If anyone wants to fight somebody they usually get caught right away by one of these guys. And they are really big. You'd have to be crazy to think that you could get away with fighting at this school, and if you tried to get someone after school, the principal or somebody will get you the next day, and kids who fight usually get suspended. You can't get away with any fighting around here, not even play fighting.

It is significant that at both schools in the study, conflict resolution programs have been in place for several years, and many students, including some who participated in the study (four students at School A, three students at School B), have been trained to serve as mediators at their school. However, despite this training, it is particularly noteworthy that none of the students at either of the schools chose response 11.d, "Try to talk to the person to resolve the conflict peacefully." In each interview, after discussing the student's responses to question 11, I also probed to find out why they had not chosen the other possible responses. At both schools, the most consistent explanation given by students for not attempting to resolve a conflict peacefully was that students perceived such an approach to be unrealistic and impractical. To varying degrees, all of the students were aware of the conflict resolution programs that operated at their schools, and several of the students stated that they had received training on how to use these methods. However, when confronted with the prospect of an actual fight with another student, this option was not seen as viable. The following quotes from students at Schools A and B provide some insight into their reasoning:

> When someone wants to fight you, they usually don't give you a chance to do any talking. That stuff (conflict resolution) only works if the principal or somebody is around. If it's just you and the other person, you got to let your fists do the talking otherwise you could get hurt. I usually try to get the first punch in. That usually works better than trying to talk about it. (Male student from School A)
>
> Conflict resolution is OK if you're in class, or PE or even during recess at lunch time. If you know that adults are around, it's smarter to try to talk it out than to fight. I don't fight anyway, but I was one of the people that was trained to be a school mediator, and I know that it only works during school, not after. (Female student from School B)

While it is difficult to discern whether or not students were being completely honest in their responses, it is important to point out that only three of the students at either school chose response 11.c, "Carry a weapon with you just in case you get jumped." Most of the students expressed the view that introducing weapons into a conflict increased the likelihood of escalation, and increased the penalties that might be imposed upon those who are caught. In the view of one female student from School A:

> If you bring a knife or something then the other kid is gonna probably bring something, then it just gets too crazy. It's better to fight and get your butt kicked than to make it worse by bringing a weapon. Somebody could get killed.

For the three male students from School A who felt that bringing a weapon might be an appropriate way to handle a confrontation, all stated that the use of a weapon was the best way to neutralize and prevent violence from a group of people who intended to do them harm. They also explained that acquiring a weapon, including a handgun, would not be very difficult given that they each knew friends and family members who possessed firearms.

Similar patterns were revealed in the responses of students to question 12, "If you knew that another student brought a weapon to school you would . . . " Students at School A were far more likely to choose response 12.b—"Mind your own business and not tell anyone about it" (16 of 22 students), whereas students at School B were more likely to choose response 12.a—"Tell a teacher or the principal" (15 of 26 students). Two female students from School A said that they would attempt to talk to the person about why he or she was carrying a weapon if they knew the individual (response 12.c). Four students at School A and five students at School B said that they would warn their friends that a student was in possession of a weapon so that they could avoid the individual (response 12.d). However, none of these students stated that they would tell an adult about the matter, either because they feared there might be retaliation at some point in the future from the student with the weapon, or because they felt this was the best way to avoid trouble.

Once again, the reasons for the differences in the students' responses to this question were rooted in their perceptions of security within and outside of school. Repeatedly, students at School A described feeling afraid that any attempt to report an armed student to school authorities would make it more likely that they would become a target of aggression. These students had no confidence in the ability of school administrators to provide them with protection. Moreover, several of the students expressed an unwillingness to violate school and community norms related to "snitching." This sentiment was summed up aptly by the following female student:

Why would you report someone for carrying a weapon in school? They probably need it for protection on their way home from school 'cause usually people don't use no weapons at school. Anyone who rats out somebody to the principal or the police deserves to get hurt. If they don't like it, they should mind their own business. That's the best way to stay out of trouble.

Such views were in stark contrast to those articulated by many of the students at School B. For these students, reporting another student to an adult was the most responsible way to respond to a student in possession of a weapon. These students had no doubt that school authorities would be able to protect them, and few even mentioned the possibility of reprisals from the reported student. Some of these students even expressed the view that by telling an adult about an armed peer, they were actually helping the armed individual because their actions could prevent the student from hurting him- or herself or someone else. According to one female student: "I would let one of the security guards know because they know how to deal with kids that have problems, and any kid who brings a weapon to school has problems."

In the interviews, students were also asked what they would do if they knew that two people were going to fight after school (question 13). Again, similarities emerged with respect to their interest in serving as spectators to fights among their peers. At School A, 16 of the students said that they would want to watch the fight, and at School B, 17 students said they would watch (response 13.a). At both schools students expressed some pleasure in watching other students fight, describing it as "fun," "exciting," "good action," and "hecka cool." What is interesting about this reaction is that it shows an important contradiction related to student and, I believe, societal attitudes toward violence: Although many are afraid of becoming victims of violence, they (we) may still derive vicarious pleasure from observing others engaging in it.

Perhaps the most striking contrast between students at the two schools concerned their perception of safety in their neighborhood (statement 9). Whereas only three students at School A said they felt safe when walking in their neighborhood, nearly all (26) of the students at School B reported feeling safe. In fact, students at School A said repeatedly that they felt safer at school than anywhere else in their neighborhoods. There was no similar split in the perception of students at School B with respect to school and neighborhood safety. Students at School B consistently reported feeling unafraid to walk home from school, or to play in parks or on the streets in their neighborhoods. Hence, while both groups of students may find some aspects of violence entertaining, the perception of the threat it posed to them varied significantly.

An examination of student attitudes and perceptions toward violence in school provides insight into how environmental factors influence their sense of vulnerability and safety. In this study, students at both schools— the middle-class, suburban school and the low-income, inner-city school— shared important similarities with respect to their attitudes toward violence. For example, the majority of students at both schools thought of fights between students as exciting and entertaining. Similarly, conflict resolution was not perceived by students at either school as an effective means of preventing fights when adults were not present.

Differences were evident with respect to the taboo against snitching among students at the two schools. Although most of the students seemed reluctant to report classmates who broke school rules, students at School B were much more willing to report an armed student to an adult than were students at School A, who said they were more likely to mind their own business. The unwillingness to communicate with adults about a matter so important to the well-being and safety of students at School A is very significant. It suggests two things: (1) that the pressure not to report another student who may pose a danger to others or him or herself is powerful; and (2) that the inability of the school to insure the safety of its students makes it unlikely that students will risk reporting their peers. Given the threat posed by the increased accessibility of weapons, the continuation of a taboo against snitching among young people adds considerably to the dangers that schools and students face.

This difference in attitudes among students at the two schools is also directly related to their perception of the threat they face within the school and the environmental context. Students who believe that adults can and will protect them if they are threatened are much more likely to call upon adults to intervene and to prevent conflicts. They have a certainty that fights can be avoided and their safety assured by adults who are charged with securing the school environment. In contrast, if students feel vulnerable outside of school, they are likely to feel afraid within school as well because they may believe that there is no way for adults at school to protect them once they leave, and therefore no way to avoid the threat of violence. The most significant evidence of the inevitability of violence among students at School A came from the fact that none of the students regarded telling an adult as a viable strategy for avoiding a fight. This was true among both boys and girls, and even among children who were seen by adults as nonaggressive and nonviolent.

RESPONDING TO THE THREAT OF SCHOOL VIOLENCE

How can we use information related to students' perceptions of violence to promote safety in schools? The first step is to recognize that what students think and feel about this issue matters and must be taken into account when policies are being adopted and implemented. Their perspectives matter because most reports indicate that students are more vulnerable to the threat of violence than is any other constituency—teachers, administrators, or others (Toby, 1993/1994). Consulting with students increases the likelihood that the policies enacted to insure safety actually address their fears and concerns about violence. Moreover, because the social reality of adolescents—their values, norms, and ethical standards—is generally very different from that of adults (Erickson, 1968), it is not uncommon for adults to be totally unaware of incidents, threats, brewing conflicts, or the circumstances under which students feel most threatened. Incorporating their perspectives on security issues will increase the possibility that their concerns are addressed and that policies are relevant to the real dangers they face.

When the perceptions and experiences of students are not taken into account, the policies adopted to help young people often miss the mark and may even generate greater polarization and antipathy toward authority figures. The question is not whether action should be taken to prevent violence, but rather what form of action will be most prudent and effective. Elsewhere I have argued that the preoccupation with controlling student behavior has inadvertently weakened the school's ability to insure safety (Noguera, 1995). This occurs because the fight against school violence has turned some schools into prisonlike facilities without responding adequately to the basis of fears felt by teachers and students. Just as closer connections between neighbors have been shown to be more effective in reducing crime than adoption of individual security measures (Currie, 1994), solutions to violence in schools may also come from greater connections between adults and students rather than from increased security.

John Devine (1996), in his study on school violence in New York City, takes a different approach. Borrowing from Foucault (1979), he characterizes the current climate or approach to safety in some of the worst schools as the "anti-panopticon": environments where the effort to construct the disciplined individual have been abandoned. He describes such schools as places where "teachers have lost all authority to discipline students; hallways and cafeterias have become sites where violent assaults occur regularly unless actively patrolled by guards; and the most disruptive and violent students freely intimidate their peers and their teachers" (Devine, 1996, p. 98).

Although such schools certainly exist, I believe that they have come to be that way because the desire to control student behavior is all that is left of the educational mission in some schools. In many of the schools located in the poorest inner-city neighborhoods, the need to create an atmosphere where teaching and learning are central to the operation of schools has been replaced by a fixation on security and order. Standards of behavior, like academic standards, have been lowered, and the authority of teachers has been undermined by policies and practices that have removed them from the disciplinary process (Devine, 1996). The focus on order and control remains, even if it is now delegated to administrators, security guards, and increasingly the police. This can be seen most clearly in budgetary expenditures that prioritize the hiring of more security guards over the hiring of teachers and librarians. In some districts, the acquisition of new metal detectors and surveillance cameras has taken precedence over the purchasing of books, computers, and lab equipment (Applebome, 1995).

I concur with those such as Devine who decry the response to the threat of violence in schools as weak and ineffective. However, I do not believe that this is because schools have given up on their mission of social control. Instead, I believe that the response to school violence has failed because it does not address the source of teacher and student fears. Schools, especially those in economically depressed urban areas, have become less safe because they have ignored the need to promote supportive relationships among students and adults in nurturing environments. The schools I have visited that are described by students and teachers as safe don't rely upon guards and metal detectors to prevent violence. Instead, they pursue strategies that insure that all students are known by adults and feel supported. Advocates of school reform have called for similar changes in an effort to increase student achievement (Sizer, 1992). Such schools construct systems that allow teachers, counselors, and administrators to have a high degree of personal contact with their students, and they promote security by encouraging a sense of collective responsibility for the school environment rather than relying upon intimidation and coercion (Meier, 1995).

Because of the importance of the quality of human relationships in producing safe environments, it is critical that schools recruit and retain personnel who command the respect and admiration of students, not because they are physically intimidating, but because they possess what Durkheim (1977) has called "moral authority." The authority of such individuals is rooted in the values and norms of a community. Those who possess moral authority can exert authority with young people without relying upon formal titles or coercion. They are deferred to as leaders because of what they represent to students socially, culturally, and historically (see also Ladson-Billings, 1994).

Such an individual was hired to work as a security guard at School A after my study was completed. One of my recommendations to the principal was that she attempt to recruit individuals who resided in the surrounding neighborhood to work at the school so that they could serve as a social bridge between the students, parents, and teachers. Shortly thereafter, an elderly woman who had previously served on the school's site committee was hired as a security guard. Unlike the other guards, this grandmother did not rely upon physical intimidation to deal with disruptive students. As a person familiar with the experience of the students outside of school, she was able to draw on her knowledge of the students and their culture to discipline, counsel, and console students without relying upon threats or intimidation. Within a short period of time, she was recognized as a valuable member of the school community, someone who could be counted on to maintain peace, order, and safety within the school environment.

I believe that this is precisely the kind of approach that schools must take if they are to succeed in making schools safer. If there is not a willingness to reconsider traditional approaches to school safety, to critically examine why our schools are now more vulnerable to violence, and to listen to the perspectives of students, it is unlikely that we will find answers to the problem of violence in schools. It is only through dialogue about the problem and all of its complexities that students and adults can work together in conceptualizing new possibilities for eliminating the threat of violence, and new strategies can be envisioned and created.

REFERENCES

Applebome, P. (1995, September 20). For the ultimate safe school, official eyes turn to Dallas. *The New York Times,* p. A26.

Asimov, N. (1994a, July 11). High schoolers surrounded by guns, violence. *San Francisco Chronicle,* p. 5.

Asimov, N. (1994b, July 16). Improved schools called key to curbing violence. *San Francisco Chronicle,* p. 11.

Barry, D. (1993). Growing up violent. *Media & Values, 62,* 2.

Bell, E. (1999, September 1). Sounding the alarm. *San Francisco Chronicle,* p. 7.

Brookover, W., & Erickson, E. (1975). *The sociology of education.* Homewood, IL: Dorsey Press.

Coleman, J. (1978, Summer). Deviant subcultures and the schools. *Journal of Research and Development in Education,* 26–37.

Currie, E. (1994, January 31). What's wrong with the Clinton crime bill. *The Nation,* pp. 13–14.

Devine, J. (1996). *Maximum security.* New York: New York University Press.

Durkheim, E. (1977). *Moral education* (E. K. Wilson & H. Schnurer, Trans.). New York: Free Press.

Edelman, M. W. (1989). Children at risk. *Proceedings of the Academy of Political Science, 37*(2), 79–102.

Erickson, E. (1968). *Identity: Youth and crisis.* New York: W. W. Norton.

Foucault, M. (1979). *Discipline and punish.* New York: Vintage Books.

Glassner, B. (1999, August 13). School violence: The fears, the facts. *The New York Times,* p. A28.

Glaser, B., & Strauss, A. (1967). *The discovery of grounded theory: Strategies for qualitative research.* New York: Aldine.

Jenkins, E., & Bell, C. (1992). Adolescent violence: Can it be curbed? *Adolescent Medicine, 3*(1), 6–8.

Ladson-Billings, G. (1994). *The dreamkeepers.* San Francisco: Jossey-Bass.

Larson, E. (1993, January). The story of a gun. *Atlantic Monthly,* pp. 16–28.

Meier, D. (1995). *The power of their ideas.* Boston: Beacon Press.

Meier, K., Stewart, J., & England, R. (1989). *Race, class and education: The politics of second generation discrimination.* Madison: University of Wisconsin Press.

Noguera, P. (1995, Summer). Preventing and producing school violence: A critical analysis. *Harvard Educational Review,* pp. 45–82.

Patterson, O. (1999, June 2). What if the killers at Columbine High School had been Black? *The New York Times,* p. A24.

Pollack, M. (1999, August 18). Changing student attitudes. *The New York Times,* p. A14.

Shogren, E. (1994, January 6). Violence on the rise in schools. *San Francisco Chronicle,* p. 5.

Silver, R. (1993). Challenging the myths of media violence. *Media & Values, 63,* 5.

Sizer, T. (1992). *Horace's compromise: The dilemma of the American high school.* Boston: Houghton Mifflin.

Spivak, H. (1998). Dying is no accident. *Children at Risk, 35*(6), 21–39.

Toby, J. (1993/1994, Winter). Everyday school violence: How disorder fuels it. *American Educator,* 11–18.

Wilson-Brewer, R., & Jacklin, B. (1990, December). *Violence prevention strategies targeted at the general population of minority youth.* Paper presented at the meeting of the Centers for Disease Control, Atlanta, GA.

Yardley, J. (1999, August 18). Texas court halts a death to determine competency. *The New York Times,* p. A17.

PART III

Juvenile Injustice

"Look Out, Kid, It's Something You Did"

The Criminalization of Children

BERNADINE DOHRN

A seismic change has taken place. Youngsters are to be feared. Our worst enemy is among us. Children must be punished, held accountable, expelled. We have developed zero-tolerance for children.

The tragedy at Columbine further escalated the decade-long process of criminalizing the behavior of children, recasting an additional icon to accompany the fearful, racially coded language describing *some* youth in trouble with the law as "superpredators" (Canada, 1995; DiIulio, 1995). The newly sensationalized school shootings of 1997–1999 involved suburban or small-town religious White boys with guns, killing their fellow students, spawning a White, upper-middle-class discourse of violent youth based on alienation and isolation (Schiraldi, 1998). School shootings have become a trope—an inspiration for politicians, funding streams, educational pandemonium, and law enforcement expansion. Yet perhaps more significantly, beneath the rarely occurring but dominant focus on youth homicides, normal youth behavior and misbehavior became further criminalized, all in the name of safety. Children bore the brunt of the national soul-searching into the conditions of childhood in America at the end of the twentieth century.

No one can ignore the shocking fact that in the decade of 1985–1994, 25,000 children were murdered in the United States (Sickmund, Snyder, & Poe-Yamagata, 1997). In fact, there is the equivalent of a Columbine virtually every day in America. The proliferation of lethal handguns in the possession of children that resulted in children killing children (83% of victims aged 12–18 were killed by handguns) (Zimring, 1998; Sickmund et al.,

1997); the syndication of youth gangs into illegal-drug cartels (Blumstein, 1995); the flourishing of youth violence reported on local TV news stations (Schiraldi, Donahue, & Ziedenberg, 1998; Zimring, 1998); the resulting public fear and pandering of politicians and law enforcement officials (Males, 1996); and the popularization of youth demonization by noted academics (Steinberg, 1999; Zimring, 1996)—these are the tangled elements that reinforce and strengthen one another, spiraling into an overlapping system of causes and consequences and qualitative changes in how society perceives, and even thinks about, its adolescents.

Today, behaviors that were once punished or sanctioned by the school vice-principal, family members, a neighbor, or a coach are more likely to lead to an adolescent being arrested, referred to juvenile or criminal court, formally adjudicated, incarcerated in a detention center, waived or transferred to adult criminal court for trial, sentenced under mandatory sentencing guidelines, and incarcerated with adults (Sickmund et al., 1997). The increase in discretion ceded to prosecutors and police has transformed the decision of what to charge for a given offense: Yesterday's battery may be inflated into assault, simple assault into aggravated assault, a schoolyard fight into multiple felony charges. The arrest of multiple juvenile defendants for each incident further escalates youth crime statistics.

This massive shift toward criminalizing youngsters is evident in the increasing numbers of court cases, detained and incarcerated youth in overcrowded facilities, and legislative crackdowns on juvenile crime (Lubow, 1999; Puritz & Scali, 1998). In the past decade, the number of formally processed delinquency cases increased 78% (Office of Juvenile Justice and Delinquency Prevention [OJJDP] Fact Sheet #104; Sickmund et al., 1997; Stahl, 1999).

Within this climate, a less visible, less sensational shift has quietly been executed. This change profoundly impacts millions of children, their classmates and families, and our common future.

This decade of relentless reconditioning of how citizens think about children—on the part of law enforcement, legislators, professionals, academics, the media, and frightened neighborhood residents—has shifted the paradigm. Through the catalyst of changes in criminal and juvenile law, much of adolescent behavior has been criminalized and youngsters themselves demonized. Casting children as frightening makes full use of racial, ethnic, and gender stereotyping, resulting in both disproportionate impact (Bell, 1998; Chesney-Lind, 1999; Sickmund et al., 1997) as well as generalizations impacting all youth (Drizin, 1999b). This transformation in how we think about ourselves thinking about children has taken an incalculable toll on adults and children alike. The daily discourse about children has shifted from innocence to guilt, from possibility to punishment, from protection to fear (Ayers, 1997). This sinister criminalization of childhood now permeates basic life: the schools, the parks and neighborhoods, child protection, and health care.

In the 1990s, fiscal priorities shifted from education, child protection, and scholarships to prison construction, law enforcement growth, and expanded mechanisms for the social control and exile of sectors of youth. Correctional spending nationally now exceeds $40 billion per year, to pay for a 500% rise in the prison population since 1972 (Mauer, 1999). In two short decades, budgets for prisons grew twice as fast as for education; prison spending increased 823% between 1988 and 1995, while education expenditures grew only 374%. More sobering, the vast majority of the states now spend at least one and a half times as much on prisons as they do on education (Phinney, 1999; see also Ambosia & Schiraldi, 1997).

In the past decade, New York State spent more than $700 million on prisons, while slashing the state and city college budgets by $600 million, with one result being that the number of people of color enrolled in New York's state colleges and universities is substantially lower than the number currently incarcerated there (Gangi, Schiraldi, & Ziedenberg, 1998; see also Macallair, Taqi-Eddin, & Schiraldi, 1998). Not only are more children currently seeing the inside of prison walls rather than classrooms, there is a new movement to place more, and younger, children into the adult criminal system.

One hundred years ago in Chicago, the world's first juvenile court for children was premised on the removal of children from adult jails and adult poorhouses (Rosenheim, 1976; Tanenhaus, 1998/1999). At the centennial of the juvenile court, children are being reincarcerated with adults, tried as adults in adult criminal court (Coalition for Juvenile Justice, 1998; Sickmund, Snyder, & Poe-Yamagata, 1997), and subject to imputation of adult *mens rea* with mandatory-sentencing statutes that reject rehabilitation as a goal (Coalition for Juvenile Justice, 1998; Geraghty, 1999; Sickmund et al., 1997).

THE CONFLICTING NATURE OF CHILDHOOD AND LEGAL ANARCHY

The age of legal childhood is a state of anarchy; it confounds reason. The 50 states have made hundreds of different determinations for the appropriate age of responsibility, reason, and judgment for drinking, driving, voting, marrying, consenting to medical treatment, serving in the military, withdrawing from public education, watching rated movies, eligibility for child protective services, juvenile court jurisdiction, trial as criminal adults, capital punishment, and entering into enforceable contracts. In fact, the only age on which all 50 states agree is the commercial determination that children under 18 cannot enter into binding contracts.

This legal chaos and popular confusion about childhood are conse-quences of centuries during which children were treated, like women, as the property of adult men, subject to the exclusive economic, patriarchal, and legal authority of fathers and state power. Their inferior status, despite the recent recognition that children have constitutional (*In re Gault,* 1967) and human rights (Convention on the Rights of the Child, 1989) persists in many forms today. Childhood itself is, in part, a socially and historically defined entity, not a timeless essence above culture, class, and religion (Po-lakow, 1992, 1993). Many accounts of childhood point to the frequent loss of life during birth and infancy as an explanation for the apparent devaluing of children's pain and vulnerability throughout history. The commonplace nature of infanticide, deformity and abandonment, child prostitution, and child labor historically and today, among a wide array of different cultures, suggests that childhood has not generally been seen as a distinct and sympa-thetic phase of human development (Ariès, 1962; Oberman, 1994). Fre-quently, children and women occupied the same adult world without pri-vacy, subject to force and domination (Polakow, 1993).

Law, if not practice, has recently settled that children are persons. It has been 30 years since Supreme Court Justice Fortas acknowledged the maltreatment of children within the juvenile justice system and the need to safeguard children's rights by appointed counsel (*In re Gault,* 1967; Pur-itz, 1995). In reality children are a special kind of person, dependent on caretaking adults for their development, education, and socialization. Simul-taneously, childhood is a time of being and becoming, a developmental stage of personhood on the way to adult rights and responsibilities (Dohrn, 1999). Children's voices are rarely heard about fundamental issues affecting their lives. Except in their ubiquitous role as consumers, children are so-cially invisible. Their human yearnings and basic needs for survival, for car-ing relationships, for growth and intellectual challenge, and for productive, meaningful futures are a major part of the human drive for fulfillment.

The contradictory, unsettled, and contending notions of children as small adults, as fully human, as needing protection, or as requiring disci-pline continues in the debates over children, violence and crime, innocence and evil, development and punishment. These underlying paradoxes feed the public and private conflict over how to respond to child misbehavior, malfeasance, and illegal actions, as well as how to respond to child victim-ization, abuse, abandonment, and need.

CRIMINALIZING YOUTH BEHAVIORS

A major consequence of the tidal wave of fear, violence, and terror associ-ated with children has been adult legislative and policy decisions to criminalize vast sectors of youth behavior. In part, this tendency is fueled by an organized drive on the part of certain political forces to "get tough on youth violence"; in part the changes have resulted from an accumulation of legislative reactions to a particular sensationalized case, the hackneyed mantra to "do something."

The sum total of a decade's *legal* responses is the transformation of the social landscape that children inhabit. Schools have become military fortresses. Hanging out becomes illegal. Fewer systems want to work with adolescents in need. Youngsters who have themselves been neglected or abused by adults pose too many challenges and have too many problems to be addressed. Health care and mental health services are rarely organized for adolescents. Schools want to get rid of the troublemakers and the kids who bring down the test scores. Minor offenses are no longer dealt with by retail stores, school disciplinarians, parents, or youth workers, but rather the police are called, arrests are made, petitions are filed.

Six of seven juvenile arrests are for a nonviolent offense. Of the 2.7 million arrests of young people under 18 years of age, property offenses (particularly larceny/theft), drug offenses, disorderly conduct, runaways, curfew and loitering, and liquor law violations account for the vast majority of the arrests (Sickmund et al., 1997). Ironically, if all male children aged 10–18 were incarcerated until their 25th birthday, eliminating youth crime tomorrow, there would still be 90% of violent crime: the adult offenders (Snyder & Sickmund, 1995). The intense focus on a youth crime epidemic thus is a social choice rather than a strategic response to the facts about crime and public safety.

The criminalizing of adolescent behavior takes place in multiple ways. Major social institutions for youth have constricted eligibility and eased methods for expulsion. Schools, child welfare systems, probation, and health services have all made it easier to violate, terminate, exclude, and expel youngsters. Where these youth go for survival, help, socialization development, care, and attention is unclear. One door that always remains open is the gateway to juvenile and criminal justice. Overcrowded juvenile correctional institutions, deficient youth facilities, and disproportionate minority confinement are among the consequences (Puritz & Scali, 1998).

Policing the Schools

> I would there were no age between ten and three- and twenty, or
> that youth would sleep out the rest; for there is nothing in the be-
> tween but getting wenches with child, wronging the ancieantry,
> stealing, fighting.
>   —Shakespeare, *The Winter's Tale*, act III, scene III, ll. 61–66

Schools have become a major feeder of children into juvenile and adult criminal courts; simultaneously, schools themselves are becoming more prisonlike. Closed campuses, locker searches, contraband, interrogations and informers, heavily armed tactical police patrols, uniforms (M. M. Harrigan, personal communication, 1998)—these are elements of public and even private high school life today. It is paradoxical but fundamental that a handful of high-profile school shootings masks a broader and deeper criminalization of school life, accompanied by the policing of schools, which has transformed public schools across America into a principal referral source for juvenile-justice prosecution.

Two policies contribute to this dramatic new role for schools: first, the increased policing of schools, leading to a significant increase in school-based arrests and the simultaneous abdication of educators; and second, the substantial increase in school exclusions, including suspensions/expulsions of students, propelled initially by the legislative green light that mandated "zero-tolerance" policies for gun possession as a condition of federal funding. That limited definition of zero-tolerance rapidly exploded, in practice, to include misdeeds of all sorts, both in school and outside of school. Rather than insisting on the teaching potential in adolescent misbehavior for both the miscreant and the other students, rather than seizing the "teachable moment," rather than keeping an educational perspective on sanctioning and social accountability, principals and teachers—admittedly under pressure from frightened parents—have ceded their authority to law enforcement personnel, particularly to police and prosecutors, and willingly participated in excluding troublemakers, difficult kids, disabled youth, and children in trouble from the very education that is their primary hope. These so-called zero-tolerance and security policies were escalating before the high-profile school shootings of 1997–98 and the 1999 Columbine High School tragedy. Since then, the policies, the dollars, and the hardware for policing and militarizing schools have mushroomed, and the trend is likely to continue into the next decade.

School-Based Arrests. How grave is the school crime problem? In 1997, there were more than 180,000 school fights leading to arrests, almost 120,000 thefts in schools leading to arrests, nearly 110,000 incidents of school vandalism leading to arrests, and fewer than 20,000 violent crimes (National Center for Education Statistics, 1998). Serious violent crime is extremely rare within schools and constitutes a small percentage of the total amount of school offending (U.S. Department of Education, 1998). Ninety percent of principals surveyed reported no major serious, violent crime in their schools (National Center for Education Statistics, 1998). In fact, victim self-reports indicate that actual school crime numbers have not changed significantly during the past 20 years (U.S. Department of Education, 1998).

The first three categories (some 400,000 arrests) are noteworthy. Most school crime is theft, some 62% (U.S. Department of Education, 1998). School-based incidents such as fighting, theft, and vandalism have traditionally been handled within a school disciplinary system. Forty years ago, an offender would be sent to the office of the vice-principal, a parent might be called, detention hall (remaining for an hour after school) might be mandated, a letter of apology might be required. It would have been difficult to imagine police being called, arrests and handcuffs employed, court filings and incarceration being options.

In today's Chicago public schools, and increasingly in suburban and rural school districts, police are routinely employed by schools. Some schools employ police officers in their teacher salary lines, and encourage police in uniforms, armed, tactical-unit police, and plainclothes police to patrol their schools. Police officers may make half again their salary by moonlighting with the public schools outside their regular duty hours. School-assigned police may be evaluated based on their numbers of arrests. Police may be under no obligation to consult with the school principal about how to respond to a particular youth's misbehavior or to a particular incident. In certain locations, police fail to inform principals or school officials that a student has been arrested during school hours, on school grounds. One authority has replaced another.

At Paul Robeson High School in Chicago, for example, local police precinct data indicate that 158 students were arrested at Robeson in 1996–97. The breakdown of those arrest charges, from a major urban high school, is revealing: 61 arrests for pager possession, 21 for disorderly conduct, 14 for mob action, 16 for (nonfirearms) weapon possession. In 1998, after the school adopted a strategy of small-school reform—breaking the massive high school into smaller units where no youth slips through the cracks—arrests plummeted to 28, 22 of those for pager violations! (Chicago Police Department Statistics, 1996–1997/1998; Klonsky, 1998).

Massive locker searches began in 1994–95 in Chicago schools, resulting in numerous student arrests during a single day's lockdown: 40 students at Westinghouse High School, 46 at Kenwood High School, 50 at Roosevelt High School, and 57 at Lincoln High School. In each case, the substantial majority of teens were charged with possession of beepers ("Fifty Teens," 1994; "Kenwood Reaps," 1994; "Lincoln Park," 1999; "Search Ends," 1995). Possession of pagers appears to be an offense that is both a status offense (for which adults would not be arrested) and an expansion of drug laws by labeling pagers as "drug paraphernalia" or contraband: transforming a technological convenience into a crime. School-based arrests for possession of pagers is a classic example of the criminalization of youth.

Additional school-based arrests include offense charges such as disorderly conduct or mob action, discretionary decisions that could be based on incidents involving significant disruptions or merely minor occurrences. Decisions to call a shouting match, a no-harm tussle, or locker graffiti a crime, to arrest rather than see a teachable moment, to prosecute rather than resolve disputes—these practices are turning schools into policed territory. Researchers suggest that the expectation of school crime in fact creates it (Devine, 1996).

This pattern of accelerating school incidents into delinquency offenses or criminal acts further heightens disproportionate minority arrests and confinement in juvenile justice. To date, it is the large, public, urban high schools that have become sites of substantial police presence, that are under pressure to control youth misbehavior, and that are without influential parents with resources to buffer their children from the juvenile justice system. Since Jonesboro and Littleton, suburban and rural high schools are also becoming fortresses, and arrests and mandatory expulsions are escalating. This bleeding of urban responses into middle-class life has its own dynamic and momentum, focusing more, perhaps, on drugs, tobacco, dress, and behavior toward authority, with more private institutionalization of youth as a consequence (Chesney-Lind, 1999).

The increasing regimentation of school time results in few breaks, little time for lunch, less physical education, an attrition of music, art, and humanities classes, and closed campuses in high schools. Closed campuses result from neighborhood residents' and parents' complaints about the mobile presence of children during the school day. Teachers monitor student lunch periods and move their own lunch time to the end of the day, shortening the school day. In fact, schools are increasingly simulating prisons, as if preparing their students for a likely future: locked in, regimented, searched, uniformed, pressured to become informers, and observed with suspicion (Pardo, 1999).

Search and seizure of student lockers, backpacks, and persons is legitimized (Wylie, Scheft, & Abramson, 1993). A culture of informing on fellow students is encouraged and mandated by school officials, without exploration of ethical considerations and conflicting values involved. The blurring of school discipline and delinquency accelerates (Pressman, 1995).

When school sanctioning is handed over to law enforcement *in the first instance* for the vast majority of minor school infractions, not only do the offender and the victim fail to learn from the incident, and not only is the consequence more likely to be crushing rather than illuminating, but the entire community fails to take hold of the problem as a school-community matter.

The failure to place serious reliance on peer juries, teen courts, or community-justice alternatives and to rely instead on armed police for school safety has startling and profound consequences. It is an abdication of adult responsibility and engagement with youngsters (Hart, 1998). It creates a juvenile delinquency record for vast numbers of youth who might otherwise not be in trouble with the law. Having any delinquency or criminal record has increasing consequences for scholarships, higher education, job eligibility, and escalated sanctions if there is a subsequent police investigation or arrest.

School Exclusion: Suspensions and Expulsions. Suspensions and expulsions from schools have simultaneously exploded as a new national trend, exemplified by the struggle over the expulsion of six Decatur, Illinois, high school students and their subsequent arrests (Ayers & Dohrn, 1999; see also chapter 5, this volume). Fueled by federal legislation in 1994 mandating a one-year "exclusion" for possession of a firearm on school property (Gun Free Schools Act, 1994), new legislation was passed in every state within a 5-month period to maintain federal-funding eligibility. One year later, the Safe School Act (1994) revised and expanded the prohibition to "dangerous weapon" rather than "firearm"; and "dangerous weapon" was defined, in the amended language, as "a weapon, device, instrument, material, or substance, animate or inanimate, that is used for, *or is readily capable of,* causing death or serious bodily injury." This opened the door for a stampede—and for wide discretionary expansion of the new exclusion policy by school personnel that is applied disproportionately to African American and Latino students. In Decatur, for example, 82% of all expulsions of students for over 3 years involved African American youth, although they constitute only 46% of school enrollment ("Judge Upholds," 1999). These youth are frequently left with dubious alternative education, leading to dropping out or incarceration, or with no educational resources or supports (see chapter 5, this volume).

In Massachusetts, for example, the number of school expulsions or exclusions under state law rose to more than 1,500 in 1996–97, with a disproportionate racial impact. Statewide, although African American students made up 8.4% of the school population, in 1996–97 they suffered 23% of the expulsions; Latinos, who were 10% of the school population, constituted 33.8% of the expelled students (Massachusetts Department of Education, 1996–97). This pattern is doubly troubling in states such as Massachusetts where there is no mandatory alternative education (Mulligan, 1997; see also Chapter 5, this volume). Further, it is rare to find students with legal representation at the administrative expulsion hearings (Children's Law Center of Massachusetts, 1998). In Chicago, approximately 20 hearings per day are scheduled on expulsion of Chicago public school students. All but a handful of students are expelled, according to the law students who sit as administrative hearing officers.

This synergistic relationship of police and principals goes further in Chicago, where law permits schools to suspend or expel students who have been charged or convicted of violating the law, even when the alleged delinquent or criminal behavior did not occur on school property or during school hours (Chicago Public Schools, 1998–1999; Ferkenhoff, 1997). These laws and regulations presume that principals will find out about non-school-based felony arrests and convictions of students from their closer relationship with police and prosecutors. This embrace is codified in a series of laws recently passed by the Illinois legislature that facilitate even greater exchange of information between law enforcement personnel, schools, and child welfare personnel.

The Illinois School Records Act (105 ILCS 10/6, 1999) permits state's attorneys and police officers unrestricted access to student records and further requires the school to make law enforcement requests part of the child's permanent record; other provisions (705 ILCS 405/5-325) require school officials to provide to the State's Attorney, upon request, information or a written report relating to the alleged commission of an offense; and Illinois Public Aid Code (305 ILCS 5/11-9, 1999) permits law enforcement access to certain public aid records without subpoena or notice requirements. The U.S. House of Representatives seeks to offer incentives to states to accommodate even greater exchange of information between schools and law enforcement by including in a proposed juvenile justice bill a provision that gives states additional funds if they make juvenile records available to schools (Juvenile Justice and Delinquency Prevention Act, 1999).

This wholesale relaxation of confidentiality protections for youth, protections that were a fundamental principle of the original Juvenile Court Act founders in Chicago in 1899, has further increased the incidence of suspensions/expulsions and of school-based arrests. Schools are routinely notified of a student's non-school-site arrests, probation, or detention. The knowledge that a student is in trouble or is a troublemaker may be a factor in a student's being more intensely scrutinized or being seen as a "bad kid".

It is worth noting that the school front door, as well as the exit door, has been transformed. School principals and administrators have wider discretion to refuse to enroll a student, even a public school student who resides in the appropriate district. This constricted eligibility for school registration is evident to those working with special education students, youth being released from juvenile detention or corrections, or youngsters in crisis who may manifest behavior problems. School enrollment and registration, once assumed to be a right, has become an arena of vast discretion and terrain for further educational exclusion.

Jane Addams and the other Hull House women, a century ago, were proponents of compulsory education, the abolition of child labor, and the creation of a separate court for children (Dohrn, 1999). These innovations were interrelated, for the primary goal was education and opportunity for children, not the exploitation of hazardous labor or incarceration with adults in prisons or adult poorhouses. Grace Abbott (1938) and her colleagues continued to document school attendance for decades as a bellwether for the well-being of children. What irony that 100 years after the establishment of the world's first juvenile court, schools and courts have again partnered, but this time to exclude, arrest, expel, and suspend children *from* school and to punish, prosecute, and imprison them in the criminal justice system.

Escalating Risks for Foster Children

Child welfare systems may have contributed to the entry of large numbers of adolescents into the juvenile justice system during the past decade. One aspect of increased risk, for example, is the triage of older adolescent foster kids out of the jurisdiction of state child welfare agencies. States have been lowering the age at which foster children, whom the state removed from parental custody because of abuse or neglect, can be "terminated" from the child welfare system and left on their own. In Illinois, for example, the age of termination was dropped from 21 years old in 1988 to 19 in 1991 (Illinois Juvenile Court Act, 1987, as amended). While wardship can continue past 19 upon a showing of "good cause," there is a significant disagreement among child welfare agencies and advocates as to what is meant by "good cause," and in practice, few cases challenge the automatic termination of foster children from the child welfare system. This extraordinary triage of tens of thousands of youth who are, by definition, victims of adult violence creates a pool of youngsters with slender preparation for higher education, living wage employment, or stable family life.

Each year nationwide, more than 20,000 youth are terminated from the foster care system—youth who have not been adopted or reunited with their biological family (Fagnoni, 1999). These are youngsters whom child welfare describes as "independent," prepared to be self-sufficient. Few have the life skills to complete basic education, become employed, or create stable families.

These youngsters are struggling to overcome educational deficits, multiple home placements, and past trauma. Teens in foster care are likely to have been in state custody for 7–8 years, to have endured an average of 10 placements each to different families and institutions, to have attended different schools, and to be at high risk for dangerous activities (Leathers &

Testam, 1999; Mech & Che-Man Fung, 1999). In the Chicago public schools, there are 18,000 foster children who are wards of the state; 16% of those kids have been kicked out or have dropped out of school (Illinois Department of Children and Family Services, 1999). With this profile, being terminated from foster care while still a teen bodes ill for genuine independence and adult citizenship.

The little research available indicates that nationwide, 2.5 to 4 years after exiting child welfare, 46% had not finished high school, 51% were unemployed, and 62% had not maintained a job for at least a year. In addition, 42% had birthed or fathered a child and 25% were homeless at least one night since their exit from foster care (Westat, 1991). A Wisconsin study of 113 former foster care youth, 12 to 18 months after their leaving the child welfare system, found a similar pattern (Courtney & Piliavin, 1998), and a California study also reports discouraging consequences (Barth, 1990).

Prior to termination, younger foster children, still within child welfare state custody but lacking stable foster families, are placed in institutions, group homes, independent living, or long-term foster care as young as 12 to 15. Some proportion of these children run from their placements, become subject to a warrant or "pick-up orders," and may land in detention. Both this group of foster children and the youngsters who are aging out of the foster care system, the forgotten children who have been designated with so-called Permanency Options such as "independent living" and "long-term foster care," are highly vulnerable to arrest and criminal prosecution.

Children who have been in foster care are more likely to be petitioned as delinquents than children who have not (Armstrong, 1998). There is limited data about the extent to which youth being petitioned as delinquents into juvenile courts have had experience in the child protection system, but researchers agree that child abuse and neglect increases a child's odds of future delinquency and adult criminality (Snyder & Sickmund, 1995). Recent studies indicate that maltreated children are at greater risk of involvement in the delinquency system (Carter, Sterk, & Hutson, 1999).

In New York City, the Vera Institute for Justice discovered that no one was tracking the arrest of foster kids and undertook a small study of youth admitted to two New York City juvenile detention centers. Vera found that 15% of the youth in detention were enrolled in the foster care system at the time of entering detention—eight times the rate of foster children in the 12- to 16-year-old age group in New York City. (Youth 12–16 in the child welfare system are 1.9% of all youth in that age group; Armstrong, 1998.) Vera gathered evidence indicating that foster care adolescents who are arrested and charged with a delinquency offense are more likely to remain in detention (because, in part, no parent arrives either at the precinct station or at the juvenile court hearing), more likely to be arrested from the site where they live, and therefore more likely to have no viable discharge site from detention (Armstrong, 1998).

In addition, the Vera studies demonstrated that certain child welfare agencies were more likely to call the police on adolescent wards in their custody than others. These youngsters, once arrested, charged, and released, recycle into the child welfare entry shelter, where they will be reassigned to a different placement at another agency group home or institution (Vera Institute of Justice, 1998). In other words, some agencies use arrest to rid themselves of difficult foster children, causing youth, who themselves have been victims, additional placements and the trauma of the juvenile justice experience. Vera has obtained the cooperation of the New York City child protection agency, the police, and the courts to design a project to interrupt this destructive system cycle that places foster children in the door of juvenile justice and detention.

Further compounding the problems for youth in foster care are recent policies permitting the child welfare system to reject or abandon children once they are arrested or appear in delinquency or adult criminal court. In Illinois, for example, the Department of Children and Family Services (DCFS) does not have to, and indeed may not be permitted to, provide services to any child aged 13 and older who has been adjudicated delinquent (20 ILCS 405/5(1)(1-1). The Seventh Circuit Court of Appeals and the Illinois Supreme Court recently held that DCFS is not required to provide to these children "specialized services" such as mental health, child welfare, and education (*David B. v. McDonald*, 1998; *In re A.A.*, 1998). Thus the assistance offered to children is dependent not on what the child needs, but instead on how he or she first comes to the attention of the child welfare system. Once the youngster's entry point is juvenile justice, the prospects are not for help, but for deeper penetration into juvenile and criminal incarceration, or homelessness and profound poverty. Thus child welfare systems join schools as accelerated feeder systems for juvenile and criminal prosecution and punishment.

Reviving Status Offenses

Offenses committed by youth that would not be crimes were they perpetrated by an adult are known as status offenses. They include truancy, runaway, liquor law violations, and incorrigible or ungovernable offenses (Rosenheim, 1976; Steinhart, 1996; see also curfew laws and girls, discussed separately below). Girls, historically and continuing today, constitute a substantial proportion of status offenders. In 1995, status offenses constituted 23.4% of girls' arrests; in 1996, more than half of those arrested for running away from home (a single-status offense) were girls (Chesney-Lind, 1999).

With the passage of the Juvenile Justice and Delinquency Prevention (JJDP) Act in 1974, there was a national commitment in the form of a mandate to remove status offenders from the definition of delinquency, as a result of persistent efforts to get troubled youth or minor offenders out of youth prisons because of the harmful effects of incarceration. Removal or deinstitutionalization of status offenders from juvenile correctional facilities became one of four mandates under the Act (Snyder & Sickmund, 1995; Coalition for Juvenile Justice, 1998). Illinois, for example, abolished status offender categories in 1975 (Illinois Trends and Issues, 1998). By the early 1990s, large numbers of status offenders had been successfully deinstitutionalized. What happened to them is another matter for inquiry, but at least they were no longer incarcerated with delinquent and criminal offenders.

In jurisdictions that continued to adjudicate status offenders in juvenile court, such as Massachusetts, categories or charges such as "stubborn children" or "unruly" are frequently used for children who are truants or have special needs. Although there is a reasonable-doubt standard for adjudication of these children, they most frequently plead guilty to the status offense; advocates and caseworkers see it as a tool to obtain services (Catherine Krebs, personal communication, June 1999).

Many children identical to those once considered status offenders are currently being relabeled and reenter the juvenile justice system under new categories. Beginning in the decade 1987–1996, the expansion of drug offenses resulted in an increased likelihood of formal handling (arrests and court filings), rising from 54% to 62%. "Public order" offenses, including disorderly conduct, liquor law violations, and weapons offenses, increased from 46% to 60%. The single largest increase in likelihood of formal handling was in the generic category called "other public order offenses," where the likelihood of formal processing increased from 29% to 54%! (Stahl, 1999).

Pending federal legislation would permit the incarceration of runaways and encourage the uses of contempt violations against status offenders as a path to detention and delinquency. This backlash against the once successful effort to abolish the incarceration of status offenders is an example of the continual pressure to unravel the progress of the JJDP mandates.

While the public and political focus has been fixed on youth homicides and violent offenses, there has been a substantial regrowth of revised versions of status offenses. This new wave of legal adjudications of frequent youth misbehaviors is largely invisible but impacts hundreds of thousands of youth, and their families, each year. In part, the attrition of informal, community, and civic methods of responding to the needs of youth—school attendance, youth centers, job apprenticeships—has created a vacuum. The abolition of truancy as a status offense in many jurisdictions, for example, was not accompanied by constructive programs for truants—in general, there were no additional resources for adolescents in crisis. Into that space, law enforcement, legal adjudication, and punishment stepped forward, in the name of "accountability" and "services." But the consequences for youth are dire.

Loitering, Curfew, and Association Offenses. Local municipalities, frequently authorized by state legislatures, have rushed to enact new curfew ordinances, some 1,000 since 1990 (Coalition for Juvenile Justice, 1998). Curfew laws, directed at youth to prevent youth crime in the late evening, fail to address the peak juvenile crime times, between 2 p.m. and 5 p.m. during the school year. Gang offending is similarly concentrated in mid to late afternoon (Sickmund et al., 1997).

In 1992, the Chicago City Council enacted the Gang Congregation Ordinance, which prohibits criminal street gang members from loitering with one another or with others in any public place (*City of Chicago v. Morales,* 1999). The ordinance created a criminal offense punishable by a fine of up to $500, imprisonment for not more than 6 months, and a requirement to perform up to 120 hours of community service. During the 3 years of its enforcement, police made more than 42,000 arrests and issued more than 89,000 dispersal orders. The ordinance was overturned by an appellate court, the Illinois Supreme Court, and the U.S. Supreme Court as unconstitutionally vague and failing to provide notice to the public about what conduct was illegal.

Curfew ordinances are notorious for being subject to racial and ethnic disparities in enforcement (Macallair & Males, 1998). Furthermore, arrests of girls for curfew violations increased by 155.2% between 1987 and 1996 (U.S. Department of Justice, 1997). Curfew violations have vastly widened the net of criminal involvement for youth, particularly youth of color and young women.

Young Women in Juvenile Justice

Each year, girls account for one in four arrests of youth in America, yet their presence in the juvenile justice system remains largely invisible. Young women have traditionally been arrested and incarcerated in large numbers for status offenses: arrests and prosecutions of young women declined after the JJDP of 1974 mandate to deinstitutionalize and divert youth charged with status offenses into programs providing alternatives to legal adjudication. But the past decade of criminalizing youth has resulted in increasing arrests of girls, once again, for status offenses or other minor violations of law.

Fully one quarter of all female delinquency arrests are for status offenses (as compared with less than 10% for boys), while another quarter of girls arrested are charged with larceny theft (basically, shoplifting)! Girls arrested for running away from home increased by 20.7%, and as noted above, curfew arrests of girls mushroomed an astonishing 155.2% (Chesney-Lind, 1999). Although media reports suggest that girls, as well as male delinquents, have become violent predators, the facts again belie this characterization of violence.

Arrests of girls for violent crime index offenses during the decade 1987–1996 did skyrocket, up 118.1%. Female delinquency charges for "other assault" increased 142.6% in the same period. Assault charges can range from conduct involving simple verbal aggression and threats, to minor school conflicts, nonserious disputes, and harmless fights; increasingly girls have been arrested for simple assault (Steffensmeier & Steffensmeier, 1980). Analysis suggests that much of the "tyranny of small numbers" (this phrase is attributed to Barry Krisberg, 1994) results from relabeling or bootstrapping—the practice by police, prosecutors, or judges that transforms a non-delinquency, noncriminal offense into an offense subject to incarceration (Chesney-Lind, 1997). Girls, for example, are more likely to be arrested for noninjury assaults (Currie, 1998) or as bystanders or companions to males involved in fighting. Virtually every person-to-person offense among girls in the Maryland juvenile justice system (97.9%) involved assault, and half of those were a fight with a family member, generally a parent (Mayer, 1994, cited in Chesney-Lind, 1999). This form of escalated charging is most pronounced against African American girls (Chesney-Lind, 1997).

Legislative erosion and organized opposition to the JJDP mandate against incarcerating children charged with status offenses has taken multiple forms, resulting in greater reincarceration of young women. In 1980, the definition of status offender in the federal law was amended to exclude children "who violated a court order" (Chesney-Lind, 1999; Public Law 96-509). Girls in foster care placements or group homes, for example, who run away, can be classified as delinquents and incarcerated, rather than characterized as status offenders who could be diverted away from court adjudication into specified programs for youth. This subversion of the original intent and purpose of JJDP falls most heavily on female delinquents, where the gender double standard results in judges sentencing girls to detention for contempt citations (violations of court orders) in far greater numbers than boys—apparently attempting to control and contain young women to protect them from themselves, in a manner that would not occur with young men. The 4.3% likelihood of incarceration for girls in juvenile justice accelerates to 29.9% when they are held in contempt (Bishop & Frazier, 1992; Chesney-Lind, 1999).

One consequence of the combination of traditional and contemporary juvenile justice pressures on young women is a racial, two-track system of justice, where White girls are institutionalized in private facilities and young women of color are detained in public facilities (Moone, 1997).

The numbers of girls held in private institutions has dramatically increased; 62% of incarcerated girls are being held in private facilities, and 85% of those are detained for "nondelinquent" offenses (such as violations of court orders, or status offenses) (Chesney-Lind, 1999).The number of young women detained in public detention facilities has remained steady (Krisberg, DeComo, Herrera, Steketee, & Roberts, 1991; Moone, 1997). Translated bluntly, this means that White girls are recommended for "treatment" whereas African American and Latina girls are detained (Chesney-Lind, 1999; Miller, 1995).

Pending federal legislation would encourage the uses of contempt violations as a path to detention and once again would permit the holding of children in adult jails. It is girls, frequently held in rural and small-town jails for minor infractions, who become most subject to violent abuse and suicide in such confinement (Chesney-Lind, 1998; Ziedenberg & Schiraldi, 1997).

Women have become the fastest growing sector of people in prison in the past decade; similarly, detentions of girls increased 23% between 1989 and 1993 (Poe-Yamagata & Butts, 1995). Girls remain in detention longer awaiting placement in private facilities or correctional institutions and are generally disliked by those working in the overwhelmingly male system of juvenile justice (Chesney-Lind, 1999). The failure to take into account past or current physical or sexual abuse and the lack of appropriate gender and cultural programming to address the needs of young women delinquents is pervasive.

Transgressions by girls have historically been treated differently from male misbehavior. It is profoundly disturbing that the combined invisibility and double standard paternalism/harshness against young females result in increasing loss of freedom for young women and inequality of response in programming. The women of Hull House would be dismayed and enraged by this backtracking on fundamental justice for children.

Probation/Supervision Violations

Youth who are on probation from a formal adjudication increased 24% between 1988 and 1992, drastically increasing the numbers of youth likely to violate the conditions of probation (Snyder & Sickmund, 1995). Probation violation leads to detention, absence from school, and greater risk of falling through the cracks. The gradual professional transformation of juvenile probation officers from allies and mentors of child defendants to law enforcement personnel has accompanied the increasingly punitive nature of juvenile justice in the past decade (Miller, 1995). Probation officers, often personally committed to youth development and success, nonetheless increasingly play prosecutorial roles in an expanded net of social control, scrutiny, and violations.

In Illinois, for example, the Juvenile Justice Reform Act of 1998 places probation officers in police stations to supervise youngsters who are not referred for a delinquency petition but receive instead "station adjustments." A station adjustment is an informal referral of the youngster to a youth or social service agency, instead of a referral to the state's attorney for a juvenile court petition of delinquency. No additional resources or funding streams accompany the station adjustment referral; in Illinois, there is no incentive for the agency to work with these youths and their families, and there is generally no follow-up by the police to see if the youngsters are attending a program. Yet the police keep a record of each youth's station adjustments, and a lengthy record may result in escalated charges if a delinquency petition is finally filed, in detention rather than return home pending trial, and in a more severe sentence after adjudication (the court decision of guilt or innocence).

Traditionally, probation officers became involved with a youth only after adjudication, during the period before disposition (the judicial determination whether the youth will be sent to a correctional facility, a specific placement, or return home on probation). Thus, involvement of probation officers at the earliest stage of youth trouble, even before the filing of a delinquency petition, is a new phenomenon.

As part of the new legislative revision of station adjustments in Illinois, the police officer is permitted to impose formal conditions on a minor if the officer has probable cause and an admission of involvement by the minor, with sanctions for failure to comply (Juvenile Justice Reform Act of 1998). The act further limits the number of station adjustments that precede referral to juvenile court, without prior approval of the state's attorney (Stevenson, 1999).

Again, the mechanisms of social control have tightened and the discretion and authority of police and prosecutors have expanded to make it an easier and more common practice to place youth under the mechanisms of law enforcement.

EXPANSION OF JUVENILE AND CRIMINAL JURISDICTION

As youth service systems (schools, foster care, probation, mental health) are scaling back, shutting down, or transforming their purpose, one system has been expanding its outreach to youth at an accelerated rate: the adult criminal justice system. All across the nation, states have been expanding the jurisdiction of adult criminal court to include younger children by lowering the minimum age of criminal jurisdiction and expanding the types of offenses and mechanisms for transfer or waiver of juveniles into adult criminal court. Barriers between adult criminals and children are being removed in police stations, courthouses, holding cells, and correctional institutions. Simultaneously, juvenile jurisdiction has expanded to include both younger children and delinquency sentencing beyond the age of childhood, giving law enforcement multiple options for convicting and incarcerating youngsters.

These multifaceted expansions of juvenile and criminal jurisdiction are another method by which the criminalization of children is proceeding. The age when a child is legally still considered a child (and when a child becomes culpable as an adult) has become a major element in the expansion of criminal court jurisdiction and the simultaneous constriction and extension of juvenile court jurisdiction. More youth are exposed to delinquency and criminal court for more types of behaviors at earlier ages. This expansion has occurred in a variety of ways.

Age Revisions

Age has become contested turf. Lowering the age at which children are considered to be criminally responsible has become pandemic. Common law provided that children under 7 could raise an infancy defense, which made them conclusively immune from criminal prosecution. Between 7 and 14, it was presumed that children were criminally irresponsible, a legal presumption that could be overcome by the prosecutor (Coalition for Juvenile Justice, 1998).

The majority of states have no set minimum jurisdictional age for delinquency court; the average age for those states that have established a minimum is 10 years of age (Griffin, Torbet, & Szymanski, 1998). Some states have gone even lower. Arizona allows delinquency petitions to be filed against children as young as 8 years old, Maryland's minimum age is 7, and North Carolina considers children culpable at the tender age of 6. The minimum jurisdictional age for juvenile court proceedings has been lowered by three states for the first time in 2 decades (Sickmund et al., 1997; Torbet et al., 1996).

At the same time that states are lowering the age of eligibility for juvenile court jurisdiction, they are also extending the maximum jurisdictional age for sentencing purposes. Some states have extended juvenile sentencing jurisdiction beyond the age of 21 and in a few cases provide for indefinite jurisdiction (National Criminal Justice Association, 1997). The retention of children for sentencing serves as a tool for making the delinquency system more punitive while avoiding the procedural protections required in adult court. Thus a child who is not eligible for adult sanctions at the time he or she is adjudicated delinquent may still be subject to the juvenile court's continued jurisdiction well beyond the date when he or she has reached the age of majority.

At the same time as they are lowering the age at which a child can be held accountable in juvenile court, states are simultaneously lowering the age at which children are excluded from juvenile court jurisdiction—and therefore subject to adult criminal court jurisdiction, irrespective of the alleged offense. Six states lowered the age of juvenile court exclusion between 1992 and 1995 (Sickmund et al., 1997). Although a majority of states continue to define a juvenile for delinquency (juvenile court) adjudication purposes as a person under 18, a growing number of states define a juvenile as under 17, and a handful define a juvenile as under 16 (Snyder & Sickmund, 1995). Despite the fact that children are not considered an adult for a variety of other purposes (i.e., drinking, driving, marrying, voting), children are being deemed adults at much earlier ages, not in recognition of their maturity, but for the purpose of imposing stiffer sanctions. The system responds to an immature and antisocial act by suddenly declaring a teen an adult.

Furthermore, federal law has promoted the state trend to try more children as adult criminals both by lowering the age for juvenile jurisdiction in the small number of federal juvenile cases and by encouraging state legislative policies that extend criminal court jurisdiction, providing fiscal incentives to states that comply. For example, in 1997 Congress appropriated $250 million for distribution among eligible states under the Juvenile Accountability Incentive Block Grants Program (JAIBG). In order to qualify for funds, a state was required to certify that it had adopted or was considering adopting laws, policies, and procedures designed to expand criminal court jurisdiction and enhance penalties for children. Laws were promoted that subjected children 15 years and older who were charged with violent offenses to adult criminal court jurisdiction, either by prosecutorial discretion or by operation of law, including violation of probation (Office of Juvenile Justice and Delinquency Prevention Fact Sheet #76, 1998).

In addition, bills in both the Senate and the House would give the U.S. Attorney, rather than a judge, sole discretion to determine whether a child

14 or older is to be tried as an adult (Violent and Repeat Juvenile Offender Accountability and Rehabilitation Act, 1999; Juvenile Justice Bill, 1999). The House bill goes furthest, allowing the prosecution of 13-year-olds as adults, with the approval of the Attorney General but with no judicial review. States have responded by expanding transfer laws to subject more children to adult criminal court jurisdiction.

Since 1992, the vast majority of states have amended their juvenile codes to encourage and increase the number of child delinquency cases going to adult criminal court through a variety of measures in addition to age. Most have added additional offenses to those eligible for waiver or transfer to adult criminal court, as well as to those automatically excluded from juvenile court jurisdiction (Torbet et al., 1996).

Waiver/Transfer to Adult Criminal Court

By 1995, at least 17 states had further expanded their statutes to mandate or permit waiver or transfer of children to adult criminal court (Lyons, 1995). Today, a child can find him- or herself in adult criminal court through a number of mechanisms. Four types of transfer or waiver are direct file, mandatory or automatic transfer, presumptive transfer, and discretionary transfer.

Direct file transfer permits the prosecutor to use his or her sole discretion in determining whether a child is to be charged in juvenile or adult court. So long as the child meets the minimum eligibility requirements for direct file (generally age and type of offense), there is no judicial oversight of the prosecutor's decision. As of 1998, 15 states had direct file provisions (Griffin et al., 1998). Such discretion by prosecutors is more invisible than exercises of judicial discretion that take place in open court, and prosecutorial discretion is not subject to review or appeal.

Mandatory or automatic transfers are just as common as direct file provisions, and they too are essentially dependent upon the discretion of prosecutors. While the name suggests legislative control or objective criteria, the reality is that transfers are, in large measure, governed by the prosecutors' charging decisions (McLean, 1998). Under mandatory transfer laws, a child meeting specified statutory requirements will be automatically transferred to adult criminal court on the state's motion. Typically, mandatory transfers apply to children of a certain age who are alleged to have committed certain crimes. Sometimes, there is an additional condition that the child has been adjudicated delinquent in the past. The judge has no discretionary authority to refuse the transfer, as long as the conditions have been met. While the prosecutor has no influence over a child's age or previous delinquency, his or her decision to charge attempted murder rather than aggravated battery, or to add that an offense was committed "in furtherance of gang activity," may govern whether the child goes to adult rather than juvenile court. These unreviewable prosecutorial determinations are susceptible to race and class bias and to other traditionally impermissible considerations under the law. Such discretion can result in disparate or inconsistent treatment of teens (Torbet et al., 1996).

Moreover, in making a charging decision, a prosecutor often does not have before him or her relevant information about a child's maturity level, social background, or history. Nor does the prosecutor generally have investigative evidence about the offense and the youth's alleged role. The child's social background and history, level of maturity, and psychological history are precisely the factors a judge considers when given the discretion to determine whether a child will be transferred to adult criminal court. It is troubling that prosecutors are permitted or expected to make this critical decision without consideration of the elements previously weighed by judges. Both mandatory transfer and direct file fail to consider a child's culpability or potential for rehabilitation (Drizin, 1999a).

As of 1998, 15 states had presumptive transfer statutes, and 46 had discretionary transfer provisions. Both allow for judicial oversight. In presumptive transfers, there is a rebuttable presumption that a child who meets statutory requirements must be transferred to adult criminal court. The state needs only to prove that the child meets that criteria. The child then bears the burden of demonstrating that waiver is not justified. In 4 of the 15 states, the child bears the burden of proving this by clear and convincing evidence (Torbet et al., 1996). Discretionary transfers allow for the greatest amount of judicial oversight, although the criteria established for judicial consideration are vulnerable to being legislatively restricted or changed.

These dramatic shifts from the original ideals and philosophy of the juvenile court become apparent through examination of recent amendments to the Illinois Juvenile Court Act. The 1998 amendments, reflecting nationwide trends, were promulgated by prosecutors after several highly publicized Chicago murder cases involving young teenage boys. Despite evidence indicating that juvenile crime was declining in Chicago and elsewhere, the Illinois legislature passed the bill, touted as a tough response to escalating juvenile crime (Parsons, 1998a). Unlike the original Juvenile Court Act, which identified the best interests of the child as a primary goal of the court, the new act repealed the best-interest standard and contains no such guiding reference.

For example, the primary focus in the purpose and policy section of the new Juvenile Justice Reform Act of 1998 is on "holding children accountable" and "making them understand that sanctions for serious crimes should be commensurate with the seriousness of the offense and merit strong punishment" (705 ILCS 405/5-101[1]). In transfers requiring judicial approval, the factors to be considered and the weight to be given those factors have changed. The court's focus is to be on the facts and nature of the alleged offense: how serious it is, whether the offense was committed in an "aggressive or premeditated manner," whether the child possessed or used a weapon at the time of the offense, and the child's potential level of culpability. The two factors that are given the greatest weight in considering whether to transfer a child are the seriousness of the offense and the minor's prior record of delinquency (705 ILCS 405/5-805[2] [3]).

This shift in focus ignores the qualities of the individual child before the court, his or her potential for rehabilitation with individualized intervention, his or her relative culpability and involvement, and the supportive factors in his or her character and environment. The nationwide expansion in transfer laws guarantees that the adult system will see an increase in children, not because more children are committing crimes (they are not), not because children are less amenable to rehabilitation (they are not), but because the lawmakers, the media, and the public have responded to sensationalism (Zimring, 1998).

Sentencing, Blended Jurisdiction, and Habitual Offenders

There are additional ways in which legislatures and courts are expanding jurisdiction over juveniles, subjecting them to longer and harsher sentences, with lifelong consequences. The Juvenile Justice Reform Act of 1998 is a practical guide to these methods, for it incorporates many of the changes in effect nationwide. The "Habitual Offender" provision commits a minor to the Illinois Department of Corrections, Juvenile Division, until the age of 21 if he or she has been adjudicated delinquent for three offenses that would be deemed felonies in adult criminal court (705 ILCS 405/5-815). A minor who is adjudicated twice for the equivalent of an adult, Class 2 felony that involves the threat of or actual physical force or violence against an individual, or the possession of a weapon, may be committed to the Juvenile Division of the Department of Corrections until the age of 21 (705 ILCS 405/5-820). Minors committed under either of these provisions are ineligible for parole before their 21st birthdays. Many states have "once an adult, always an adult" provisions, which specify that a child who has been prosecuted in an adult criminal court is automatically or presumptively waived to adult court for subsequent offenses (Torbet et al., 1996).

Also included in the new Illinois act is an increasingly popular provision that essentially allows for the exercise of dual jurisdiction over a minor

(705 ILCS 405/5-810). Blended or extended jurisdiction is seen as a way to enhance penalties for youth, or as an alternative to transfer (Zimring, 1998). The schemes of blended sentencing vary among the states, but are consistent in their focus on lengthier sentences. In Illinois, for example, the extended jurisdiction provision permits the judge to impose two sentences on the youthful offender, the first a juvenile sentence, the second, an adult. The adult sentence is tolled (or suspended) while the juvenile serves his or her first sentence. If the minor successfully serves the juvenile sentence, the adult sentence is vacated. Should the minor violate any of the conditions of the first sentence, however, the state's attorney can file a motion to impose the adult sentence. The prosecution then bears the burden of proving beyond a preponderance of the evidence that the conditions have been violated. If the violation involves the commission of any offense, be it something as minor as disorderly conduct, the judge *must* impose the adult sentence, regardless of whether it is appropriate in light of the juvenile's behavior since the time it was originally imposed. The judge is given some discretion when the violation does not involve the commission of an offense (705 ILCS 405/5-810).

Children in Adult Criminal Courts

Crucial questions are going unasked as children are increasingly appearing in adult criminal courts. Criminal courts operate on guilty pleas, and informed, competent decisions to plead guilty may not be possible for many children. Adult courts fail to acknowledge the youth of the child, to take into account the child's age, developmental capacity, or experience when assessing culpability. Adult courts impose adult sentences, which differ from delinquency sentences in two critical ways: they are determinate, and they are significantly longer. Determinate sentences result in extended incarceration of children, beyond a time when they may be rehabilitated. Longer sentences mean that a child will ultimately be incarcerated in an adult prison, where they may be subject to physical abuse, suicide, and an education from adult offenders, rather than rehabilitation for a future productive life. Youth sent to the adult criminal system are essentially cut off from educational and counseling programs, from juvenile probation officers, and from appropriate medical and mental health services (Parsons, 1998b). Sending children to prison encourages more sophisticated criminal behavior (Stansky, 1996). There is ample evidence that children respond better to positive prevention programs than they do to punitive legislative measures (Krisberg, Currie, & Onek, 1995; Zierdt, 1999).

THE EROSION OF CIVIC RESPONSIBILITY FOR CHILDREN

Addressing the needs of both public safety and positive youth development requires an active and participating public. If the only popular cry is for short-term fixes—"get them out of the neighborhood," "lock them up and throw away the key," and "something must be done"—society will continue on its current course of escalating punishment for children and increasing adult abdication of responsibility. If schools are not for learning from mistakes, if child welfare is not for protecting children who have been harmed, if health systems are not geared to healing youth—further reliance on exclusion, punishment, and prison becomes the likely option. Tens of thousands of productive adults who passed through the juvenile justice system in their youth are witness to the healing and redemptive effect of getting a second chance: the program, the judge, the probation officer who made a difference and allowed them to turn their life around (Criminal Justice Institute, 1999; Dohrn & Drizin, 1999).

The real adult problem is masked by our social focus on the "youth problem." In scapegoating kids, we reveal that as a society, we don't like adolescents very much. Youth, being the intelligent people they are, are vividly aware of the angry popular and policy backlash directed against them. They are keenly alert to issues of fairness (which are at the heart of justice); they observe the adult world around them with a laserlike ability to identify hypocrisy. They see that their voices, their opinions, and their interests are largely ignored, as are their rights as future citizens.

The use of the law to enforce a legal-educational-political system that harms the aspirations and best intentions of youth cannot be good for society. Holding children accountable for protracted social failures reeks of expediency and runs counter to developing international human rights standards for children around the world. Adult citizens are engaged in the social neglect and abuse of children, both in public fiscal policy and in the absence of the commitment of our own precious time and imagination.

Criminalizing youth behaviors, policing schools, punishing children by depriving them of an education, constricting social protections for abused and neglected youth, and subjecting youth to law enforcement as a "social service"—these trends smack of social injustice, racial inequity, dehumanization, and fear-filled demonization of youngsters, who are our prospective hope. At stake here is the civic will to invest in our common future by seeing other people's children as our own.

Acknowledgment. Invaluable attention, critical thought, and research assistance were provided by Christina Gabriel Kanelos and Catherine Stewart. A decade of ongoing collaboration and intelligent passion was provided by Bruce Boyer, Steven Drizin, Cheryl Graves, Thomas Geraghty, and Toni Curtis, as well as the whole Children and Family Justice Center team.

REFERENCES

Abbot, G. (1938). *The child and the state* (Vols. 1 and 2). Chicago: University of Chicago Press.

Ambosia, T-J., & Schiraldi, V. (1997, February). *From classrooms to cellblocks: A national perspective*. Washington, DC: The Center on Juvenile and Criminal Justice.

Ariès, P. (1962). *Centuries of childhood: A social history of family life*. New York: Vintage Books.

Armstrong, M. L. (1998, May). *Adolescent pathways: Exploring the intersections between child welfare and juvenile justice, PINS, and mental health*. New York: Vera Institute of Justice.

Ayers, W. (1997). *A kind and just parent: The children of juvenile court*. Boston: Beacon Press.

Ayers, W., & Dohrn, B. (1999, November 21). Have we gone overboard with zero tolerance? *Chicago Tribune*, Op-ed.

Barth, R. P. (October, 1990). On their own: The experiences of youth after foster care. *Child and Adolescent Social Work, 7*(5), 419–440.

Bell, J. (1998, September/October). Shadowboxing with the apocalypse: Race and juvenile justice. *Youth Law News,* 19–21.

Bishop, D., & Frazier, C. (1992). Gender bias in the juvenile justice system: Implications of the JJDP Act. *Journal of Criminal Law and Criminology, 82*(4), 1162–1186.

Blumstein, A. (1995). Youth violence, guns, and the illicit drug industry. *Journal of Criminal Law and Criminology, 86*(10), 10.

Canada, G. (1995). *Fist, stick, knife, gun: A personal history of violence in America*. Boston: Beacon Press.

Carter, J., Sterk, C., & Hutson, R. Q. (1999). Evidence of a link between maltreatment and delinquency: A literature review [On-line]. Available: *WWW.gahsc.org/ jcarter/litreview.htm*

Chesney-Lind, M. (1997). *The female offender: Girls, women, and crime*. Thousand Oaks, CA: Sage.

Chesney-Lind, M. (1998). Girls in jail. *Crime & Delinquency, 34*(2), 150–168.

Chesney-Lind, M. (1999, July). Challenging girls' invisibility in juvenile court. *Annals of the American Academy of Political and Social Science, 564,* 185–202.

Chicago Police Department statistics, Robeson High School, 1996–1997/1998.

Chicago Public Schools. Uniform Discipline Code. (1998–1999). pp. 14–20.

Children's Law Center of Massachusetts. (1999, June). Interview with Catherine Krebs, attorney.

City of Chicago v. Morales. (1999). 527, U.S. 41.

Coalition for Juvenile Justice. (1998). *A celebration or a wake? The juvenile court after 100 years.* 1998 Annual Report, Washington, DC: Author.

Convention on the Rights of the Child. G.A. Res. 44/25, U.C. GAOR, 44th Sess. U.N. Doc. A/RES/44/25 (1989).

Criminal Justice Institute and Children and Family Justice Center. (1999). *Second chances: 100 years of children's court: Giving kids a chance to make better choices.* Washington, DC: Author.

Currie, E. (1998). *Crime and punishment in America.* New York: Metropolitan Books.

Courtney, M. E., & Piliavin, I. (1998, July). Foster youth transitions to adulthood: Outcomes 12 to 18 months after leaving out-of-home care. Madison: School of Social Work and Institute for Research on Poverty, University of Wisconsin–Madison.

David B. v. McDonald. 156 F.3d 780 (7th Circ. 1998).

Devine, J. F. (1996). *Maximum security: The culture of violence in inner-city schools.* Chicago: University of Chicago Press.

DiIulio, J. J., Jr. (1995, December 15). Moral poverty. *Chicago Tribune,* Op-ed sec. 1, p. 31.

Dohrn, B. (1999). Justice for children: The second century. In G. H. McNamee (Ed.), *A noble social experiment? The first 100 years of the Cook County juvenile court 1899–1999* (pp. 98–102). Chicago: Chicago Bar Association.

Dohrn, B., & Drizin, S. (1999, March 4). A second chance: Juvenile delinquents who transformed themselves and history. *Chicago Tribune,* Op-ed.

Drizin, S. (1998, April 27). Should we demand juveniles to cry us a river? *Chicago Tribune* [Commentary], p. 15.

Drizin, S. (1999a, April 27). Net of "automatic transfer" growing too wide. *Chicago Daily Law Bulletin, 145*(80), 4.

Drizin, S. (1999b, May 24). Race, class, religion, politics cloud juvenile justice. *Chicago Sun Times,* p. 31.

Fagnoni, C. M. (1999, May 13). Challenges in helping youths live independently. U.S. General Accounting Office. Testimony before the Subcommittee on Human Resources, Committee on Ways and Means, House of Representatives.

Ferkenhoff, E. (1997, May 1). City schools clamp down on violence by students. *Chicago Tribune,* Sec. 2, p. 7.

Few clues to unravel the riddle "why?" "We wanted to for a long time." (1999, April 22). *Chicago Tribune,* p. 1.

Fifty teens arrested at Roosevelt High. (1994, December 14). *Chicago Sun Times,* p. 20.

Gangi, R., Schiraldi, V., & Ziedenberg, J. (1998, December). *1988–1998 New York state of mind? Higher education vs. prison spending in the Empire State.* Washington, DC: Center on Juvenile and Criminal Justice.

Geraghty, T. F. (1999, January). The centennial of the juvenile court: What would Jane Addams think? *CBA Record,* p. 50.

Griffin, P., Torbet, P., & Szymanski, L. (1998, December). *Trying children as adults in criminal court: An analysis of state transfer provisions.* U.S. Dept. of Justice, Office of Juvenile Justice and Delinquency Prevention, Transfer Report.

Gun Free Schools Act of 1994, 20 U.S.C. §8921(e).

Hart, P. D. (1998, December). *Children's court centennial: Attitudes toward youth and juvenile justice.* Washington, DC: Research Associates.

Illinois Department of Children and Family Services Forum on Education and Child Welfare. (1999, September). Chicago.

Illinois Public Aid Code, 305 ILCS 5/11-9. (1999).

Illinois School Student Records Act, 105 ILCS 10/6. (1999).

Illinois School Records Act, 705 ILCS 405/5-325.

Illinois Trends and Issues. (1998). Chicago: Illinois Criminal Justice Information Authority.

In re A.A., 181 Ill.2d 32, 690 N.E.2d 980 (Ill. 1998).

In re Gault, 357 U.S. 1 (1967).

Judge upholds expulsions. (2000, January 12). *Chicago Tribune,* p. 1.

Juvenile Court Act of 1987. Abused, neglected, and dependent minors (as amended), 705 ILCS 405/2-31. Originally P.A. 85-601, Art. II, sec.2-31, eff. 1/1/88. Relevant portion amended by P.A. 87/14, Art 2, sec 2-6, effective 7/24/91.

Juvenile Justice Bill, H.R. 1501 [House of Representatives Bill]. (1999).

Juvenile Justice and Delinquency Prevention Act, H.R. 1501, reauthorizing H.R. 1150 (1999, June).

Juvenile Justice Reform Act of 1998. (1999). 705 ILCS 405/5-101(1).

Kenwood reaps beepers in sweeps. (1994, November 1). *Chicago Tribune,* p. 1.

Klonsky, M. (1998). *Small schools: The numbers tell a story. A review of the research and current experiences.* Chicago: The small schools workshop at the University of Illinois at Chicago.

Krisberg, B. (1994). Youth violence: What are the facts? Presentation at the Conference on Children in a Violent America, Chicago.

Krisberg, B., Currie, E., & Onek, D. (1995, Summer). What works with juvenile offenders: A review of "graduated sanction" programs. *Criminal Justice, 10,* 20–61.

Krisberg, B., DeComo, R., Herrera, N. C., Steketee, M., & Roberts, S. (1991). *Juveniles taken into custody: Fiscal year 1990 report.* San Francisco: National Council on Crime and Delinquency at 43; Joseph Moone, *Id.* at 1.

Leathers, S., & Testam, M. (1999). *Older wards study: Caseworkers' reports on the status of DCFS wards aged seventeen and one-half years old and older.* Unpublished report distributed at Making the Transition from Foster Care to Adulthood, a conference hosted by the Jane Addams Center for Social Policy and Research, May 25, 1999.

Lincoln Park High searches prompt suit. (1999, November 19). *Chicago Tribune,* p. 2c, Metro Chicago sec.

Lubow, B. (1999, April 8). An overview of comprehensive detention systems reform. Speech before National Training Conference on Juvenile Detention Reform. Chicago, IL.

Lyons, D. (1995, November). National conference of the state legislatures, state legislate report: 1995 juvenile crime and state enactments.

Macallair, D., & Males, M. (1998). *The impact of juvenile curfew laws in California.* San Francisco: Justice Policy Institute.

Macallair, D., Taqi-Eddin, K., & Schiraldi, V. (1998, September). *Class dismissed: Higher education vs. corrections during the Wilson years.* Washington, DC: Center on Juvenile and Criminal Justice.

Males, M. (1996). *The scapegoat generation: America's war on adolescents.* Monroe, ME: Common Courage Press.

Massachusetts Department of Education data sheet. (1996–97). Student characteristics.

Mauer, M. (1999). *Race to incarcerate: The Sentencing Project.* New York: New Press.

McLean, G. (1998, January 28). Re-evaluate juvenile justice act. [Commentary]. *Chicago Tribune,* p. 14.

Mech, E. V., & Fung, C. C. (1999, March). Placement restrictiveness and educational achievement among emancipated foster youth. *Research on Social Work Practice,* (9), 213.

Miller, J. (1995, October 12). JDAI National Conference Speech, Baltimore.

Moone, J. (1997). 1991–1995 juveniles in private facilities. Washington, DC: Department of Justice.

Mulligan, A. E. (1997, Winter). Alternative education in Massachusetts: Giving every student a chance to succeed. *The Boston University Public Interest Law Journal,* 6(2).

Milloy, C. (1999, May 2). A look at tragedy in black, white. *The Washington Post,* p. c1.

National Center for Education Statistics, U.S. Department of Education, Fast Response Survey System. (1997). Principal/school disciplinary survey on school violence. FRSS 63.

National Center for Education Statistics. (1998). *Violence and discipline problems in U.S. public schools: 1996–97.* Annual Report on School Safety. Washington, DC: U.S. Department of Justice. NCES 98-030.

National School Safety Center. (1998, Updated June). Total school-associated violent death count: July 1992 to present.

Oberman, M. (1994). Turning girls into women: Reevaluating Modern Statutory Rape Law. *Journal of Criminal Law and Criminology, 85,* 15.

Office of Juvenile Justice and Delinquency Prevention. (1998, April). Fact sheets #76 and #104. Washington, DC: U.S. Department of Justice.

One strike and you're out! Advocating for children facing suspension or expulsion from Massachusetts' public schools, training materials. (1998 March). Children's Law Center of Massachusetts, Inc.

Pardo, N. (1999, June). All work, less play in public schools. *Chicago Reporter,* 28(6), 7.

Parsons, C. (1998b, January 14). Youths could face new system of justice, Reform plan targets juvenile offenders. *Chicago Tribune,* p. 1, Metro Chicago.

Parsons, C. (1998a, February 4). Tougher sentencing for youths awaits Edgar ok. *Chicago Tribune,* p. 10.

Phinney D. (1999, July). Prison funding explodes in growth. ABC News.com.

Poe-Yamagata, E., & Butts, J. A. (1995). *Female offenders in the juvenile justice system.* Pittsburgh, PA: National Center for Juvenile Justice.

Polakow, V. (1992). *The erosion of childhood.* Chicago: University of Chicago Press.

Polakow, V. (1993). *Lives on the edge: Single mothers and their children in the other America.* Chicago: University of Chicago Press.

Pressman, P. (1995, October). *State law challenges to school discipline: An outline of claims and case summaries* (3rd ed.). Boston and Washington, DC: Center for Law and Education.

Public Law 96-509. (1980). U.S. Statutes at Large, Ninety-Sixth Congress, 2nd Session, December 8. Washington, DC: U.S. Government Printing Office.

Puritz, P. (1995, December). *A call for justice: An assessment of access to counsel and quality of representation in delinquency proceedings.* Washington, DC: American Bar Association, Juvenile Justice Center, Juvenile Law Center, and Youth Law Center.

Puritz, P., & Scali, M. A. (1998). Beyond the walls: Improving conditions of confinement for youth in custody. Washington, DC: American Bar Association, Juvenile Justice Center, OJJDP.

Rosenheim, M. K. (1976). Notes on helping juvenile nuisances. *Pursuing justice for the child* (pp. 43–66). Chicago: University of Chicago Press.

Safe School Act of 1994. (2000). 20 U.S.C. 5961.

Schiraldi, V. (1998, March). *Is Maryland's system of higher education suffering because of prison expenditures?* Washington, DC: Justice Policy Institute.

Schiraldi, V., Donahue, E., & Ziedenberg, J. (1998). *School house hype: School shootings and the real kids face in America.* Washington, DC: The Justice Policy Institute.

Search ends in arrest of 66 students. (1995, May 3). *Chicago Sun-Times,* p. 21.

Sickmund, M., Snyder, H. N., & Poe-Yamagata, E. (1997). *Juvenile offenders and victims: 1997 update on violence, statistics summary.* Washington, DC: Office of Juvenile Justice and Delinquency Prevention.

Snyder, H. N., & Sickmund, M. (1995). *Juvenile offenders and victims: A national report.* Washington, DC: Office of Juvenile Justice and Delinquency Prevention.

Stahl, A. L. (1999, April). *1987–1996 juvenile court processing of delinquency cases.* OJJDP Fact Sheet No. 104. Washington, DC: U.S. Department of Justice, Office of Juvenile Justice and Delinquency Prevention.

Stansky, L. (1996, November). Age of innocence—More and more states telling teens: If you do an adult crime, you serve the adult time. *American Bar Association Journal, 82,* p. 60, quoting Jeffrey Fagan and Mark Soler.

Steffensmeier, D. J., & Steffensmeier, R. H. (1980). Trends in female delinquency: An examination of arrest, juvenile court, self-report, and field data. *Criminology, 18,* 62–85.

Steinberg, J. (1999, January 3). The coming crime wave is washed up. *The New York Times,* p. 4-1.

Steinhart, D. J. (1996, Winter). Status offenders: The future of the juvenile court. *David and Lucille Packard Foundation, 6*(3), pp. 86–89.

Stevenson, P. (1999, June). Trends and issues update, the Juvenile Justice Reform Act. *Illinois Criminal Justice Information Authority, 1*(2), 2.

Tanenhaus, D. S., (1998/1999, Winter). Justice for the child. The beginning of the juvenile court in Chicago. *Chicago History*, pp. 4–19.

Torbet, P., et al. (1996, July). *State responses to serious and violent juvenile crime.* Pittsburgh: National Center for Juvenile Justice.

Tragedy in Colorado, Growing gap between teens, adults creating a cultural divide in relationships. (1999, April 22). *Los Angeles Times*, p. 16.

U.S. Department of Education and U.S. Department of Justice. (1998). *Annual Report on School Safety*. Washington, DC: Author.

U.S. Department of Justice, Office of Juvenile Justice and Delinquency Prevention. (1997). *Female offenders in the juvenile justice system, statistics summary* (Report prepared by Poe-Yamagata, E., & Butts, J. A. of the National Center for Juvenile Justice). Washington, DC: Author.

U.S. Department of Justice, Office of Juvenile Justice and Delinquency Prevention. (1996, July). *State responses to serious and violent juvenile crime*. Washington, DC: Author.

Vera Institute. (1998, April). *Overlap study report: Adolescents in child welfare and juvenile detention*. New York: Author.

Violent and Repeat Offender Accountability and Rehabilitation Act, S. 254 [Senate Bill]. (1999).

Weiss, J. (1999, April 29). Jumbled values steer some kids to dark path, today's mixed messages pose danger to teens, experts say. *Dallas Morning News*, p. 1A.

Westat, Inc. (1991). *A national evaluation of Title IV-E foster care independent living programs for youth*. Washington, DC: Department of Health and Human Services.

Wylie, N., Scheft, J., & Abramson, J. (1993, November). Search and seizure in schools: Commonwealth v. Carey and Commonwealth v. Snyder. *Municipal Law Newsletter*.

Ziedenberg, J., & Schiraldi, V. (1997). *The risks juveniles face when they are incarcerated with adults*. Washington, DC: Justice Policy Institute.

Zierdt, C. (1999, Spring). The little engine that arrived at the wrong stations: How to get juvenile justice back on the right track. University of San Francisco, Law Rev. 33-401.

Zimring, F. E. (1996, August 19). Crying wolf over teen demons. *Los Angeles Times*, p. B-6.

Zimring, F. E. (1998). *American youth violence*. New York: Oxford University Press.

CHAPTER 8

Throwaway Children: Conditions of Confinement and Incarceration

JAMES BELL

As we approach the 100th anniversary of the juvenile court there are serious questions about the court's survival and the treatment of children in trouble with the law. Although juvenile crime is currently decreasing significantly, the numbers of juveniles being confined is growing at an alarming rate.[1] The phenomenal increase in youth incarceration is resulting in overcrowded conditions, stretching the capacity of most facilities to the breaking point. The combination of more young people being confined for longer periods of time in more crowded facilities increases the chances of suicide or violence in many juvenile facilities. In this chapter I will describe and analyze the conditions of confinement found in secure confinement facilities nationwide with an emphasis on the rights and responsibilities of juveniles and staff.

THE SOCIAL CONTEXT OF JUVENILE SECURE CONFINEMENT

Shortly after the establishment of the first juvenile court, in 1899, W. E. B. Du Bois, one of the most significant American thinkers of this century, wrote in his seminal work *The Souls of Black Folk* that "the problem of the 20th Century is the problem of the color line."[2] Similarly, around that time the term *adolescence* was coined by psychologist G. Stanley Hall. He described it as a period between 12 and 20 that encompassed a developmental state unique from other periods of life.[3] Today, the nexus of color and adolescence have converged in a way that has juveniles being confined in numbers that cannot be accounted for by criminal activity alone and should give pause to any civil society. In California, for example, minority youth make up 86% of those incarcerated in long-term treatment facilities, and Texas has 76% of its facilities containing youth of color.[4]

There are societal factors that contribute mightily to the marginalization and incarceration of minority youth that cannot be ignored. Implicit messages prevalent throughout the juvenile system legitimize treating minority youth as beyond rehabilitation, thereby making it permissible to warehouse them in conditions of confinement not fit for members of any civilized society.

Institutional racism, present throughout the juvenile justice system, manifests itself in subtle but telling ways. If one were to divide the juvenile justice system into subparts, there would be several places where decisions are made regarding minority youth and their families that widen the net for youth of color—decisions about where to patrol, whom to arrest, charge, and prosecute. Is there deliberate, knowing racism in each decision? Probably not in the majority of cases, yet the fact still remains that minority youth are represented in juvenile justice systems in numbers that cannot be accounted for by law violations exclusively. So although it is the case that racism may not be documented in each decision, the cumulative effect is the same.

Throughout the system there are examples of ways of thinking that contribute to the extraordinary numbers of youth of color in the system. Some juvenile court judges, probation officers, and others in the system believe that minority families are dysfunctional and that it is a waste of valuable resources to provide services to folks who are already programmed for failure. This results in a funneling of resources to "good families," who are often not from communities of color.

Similarly, there are assumptions about youth of color that contribute to their overrepresentation in the system. These beliefs hold that minority youth are prone to violence and criminal activity, they are not in school or working, and worst of all they expect to be incarcerated and therefore are not uncomfortable with being securely confined. Such assumptions reflect an expectation of failure that in turn is internalized by the young people who do in fact fail.

Jeremy Rifkin, in his important book *The End of Work*, introduces the concept of economic irrelevance.[5] Economic irrelevance refers to those segments of our population that have no possibilities of contributing to society because they have neither desirable skills nor significant purchasing power. Many of the minority youth in the juvenile justice system are the living embodiments of policy decisions in support of a social structure that does not include them in a productive future.

A vivid example of this point is the symbiotic relationship between supposed intellectuals espousing essentially racist theories about criminal predisposition among youth of color[6] and politicians' use of this pseudoscience to create a political climate in which it is acceptable as part of policy debates to hear Senators Jeff Sessions and Orrin Hatch refer to young people as "superpredators" on the floor of the United States Senate.

Most young people growing up in the marginalized core centers of our cities are law abiding and trying desperately to make some sense of their lives. But they are caught up between a small group of chronic law violators and a society that ignores their potential and has written them out of the future. These kids live in a world where politicians tolerate racial segregation in housing, dysfunctional schools, and an economic system that has no place for them, thus effectively sealing off their escape routes from the killing zones. More important, two generations are turning inward and away from the old institutions in the community and the larger society and are participating in destructive behaviors that have adults frightened and confused.

Self-destructive behavior manifests itself in the internalized troika of self-hatred, self-doubt, and justifiable rage. Self-hatred results in behavior that is destructive of the youth and all those around them. Self-doubt locks young people into a narrow visions of limited possibilities. Young people can never envision themselves *really* living the good life. They feel incompetent to compete academically and don't believe that life has anything more to offer them than what they see around them.

Finally, the rage involved in this marginalized life of limited possibilities makes its own logic. That logic states that what much of society thinks is wrong is actually right in this world. In this world, humanity does not prevail, but instead twisted rules regarding respect, reputation, and turf govern behavior and attitudes.

Legislation is a crucial part of the social context impacting conditions of confinement. Legislatures all over the country are enacting laws that are supposed to "get tough" on juvenile crime. This usually takes the form of lowering the age at which children can be sent into the adult system. For example, a case receiving notoriety recently involved 13-year-old Nathaniel Abraham, who was prosecuted as an adult and convicted of second-degree murder for a crime committed when he was 11 years old.[7] Statutes recently passed by legislatures in a variety of states around the country that are not informed by data or research will have a devastating impact on the number of youth of color in the system. Approximately 30 states now impose mandatory minimums for certain crimes, and 42 states permit release of a minor's name, address, and picture to a variety of agencies and disclosure of information that is supposed to be confidential to the general public.[8]

Juvenile justice professionals should raise their voices in opposition to the legislative agendas that continue to demonize young people of color. Public officials must be challenged to envision the impact on the community of refusing to try to rehabilitate thousands of young people in our community by putting them in adult courts and adult prisons.

As the forces mentioned above coalesce to increase incarceration of young people, a majority of juvenile detention facilities are becoming increasingly overcrowded. In the following section I will describe the various types of facilities that house young people and advocate appropriate standards for humane confinement.

DESCRIPTION OF JUVENILE FACILITIES

Adult Jails

Adult jails are secure confinement facilities that are constructed for adults who will be confined for a maximum of one year. These facilities are commonly referred to as county jails and are characterized by multiple-occupancy cells, small recreational yards, no classrooms, and some form of commissary selling essential items. Adult jails usually confine both male and female adults. They have a small section for isolation and one or more cells that are used for detoxification from alcohol or drugs. In the past, they were not constructed with the detention of juveniles in mind, resulting in a variety of problems when young people have been detained.

Juveniles detained in these facilities are mostly preadjudication youth (i.e., they have not been found to have committed a delinquent act) proceeding through the court processes. One of the major problems with confining children in adult jails is that often there is nothing for the children to do during the day. They become bored and may continually demand attention or destroy property. There is also the possibility that children will be physically or sexually abused at the hands of the jailers or other inmates.

In order to protect children while they are in the jail, jailers often isolate them from the general population in dark dreary isolation cells. This results in increased fear and depression for the child, as evidenced by suicide rates that are eight times higher in adult jails than in juvenile detention centers. Further, many children exposed to a jail environment view themselves as criminals and begin to act accordingly, increasing the likelihood of reincarceration. Adult jails are no place for children and every effort should be made to assure some form of alternate confinement.

Detention Centers

Juvenile detention centers are the appropriate place for children to be confined. They provide a single room for the youth and have classrooms, day rooms, and a gymnasium or some other type of indoor recreation space. Staff at detention centers are supposed to be specifically trained to deal with the unique needs of detained youth.

The conditions of detention centers are usually substantially better than those of adult jails, although a majority of these facilities are chronically overcrowded and services provided to youth are being reduced. The chronic crowding has placed many detention centers in crisis with judges and probation and detention center staff as children stay longer and violence increases within the facility.

Training Schools

Juvenile training schools are long-term treatment centers where juveniles are sent after the court finds that they have committed a delinquent act. These places are usually located away from the urban areas of the state and require commitments of approximately 18 months. Such facilities are characterized by large land areas and clusters of cottages or residential units.

Programmatically, their mandate is to implement treatment interventions that address the problems contributing to young people's decisions to violate the law. Training schools provide the most opportunity for young people to receive long-term intensive treatment for a variety of problems. Training schools, unfortunately, are the only institutions in which youth of color are most likely to get meaningful therapy or counseling on a consistent basis. Generally, the problem with training schools is that they are often far away from the population centers, making visitation and contact with the community difficult. Similarly, training schools often have problems transitioning young people back into the community after their release.

Boot Camps and Outdoor Experiential Facilities

"Boot camp" is a catchall phrase that can apply to several different types of outdoor experiential programs. A common characteristic of the program is that there is usually some type of intense physical requirement or guided activity that requires teamwork. Some programs impose a military atmosphere with strict discipline and constant interaction between the staff and detainees. Others place young people in situations that require trust and teamwork in order to accomplish goals or gain program rewards.

These programs have varying levels of success depending upon whether the program and the young person are appropriately matched. It should be noted that boot camps of all varieties have not turned out to be the "magic bullet" they are often touted to be. In fact, their recidivism rates are not significantly different from traditional correctional facilities.

A common thread running through all of these types of facilities is that they reflect institutional models that have little ability to change the lives of young people in trouble with the law. In the following section I will discuss many of the living conditions prevalent in a significant number of facilities.

CONDITIONS OF CONFINEMENT

In order to discuss conditions of confinement, it is important to understand the sources of law that establish the minimum levels of humane conditions required to securely confine children in trouble with the law. The first source is the United States Constitution, which is interpreted through case law regarding conditions. Similarly, children may be entitled to additional protection under state laws or regulations. For example, most states have laws giving children a right to treatment and rehabilitation. In addition, many states have laws requiring that children be placed in the least restrictive environment consistent with public safety needs. Some states also have laws or regulations setting standards for maximum population, physical conditions, health and safety requirements, and programming.

Moreover, professional standards establish minimum criteria for juvenile corrections conditions. Standards applicable to secure confinement of juveniles include the American Correctional Association (ACA) Standards for Juvenile Correctional Facilities and the National Commission on Correctional Health Care (NCCHC) Standards. Professional standards reflect the collective wisdom of people working in the profession, and courts often use them as a guide to determine whether the Constitution has been violated.

A useful mnemonic device to analyze conditions of confinement is C.H.A.P.T.E.R.S. This stands for classification, health/mental health, access, programming, training, environment, restraints and discipline, and safety. Many of these conditions were addressed specifically in the case of *Alexander S. v. Boyd.*[9] *Boyd* represents the most recent and comprehensive litigation on conditions of confinement of juvenile facilities. The case involved a challenge to South Carolina's juvenile institution's conditions of confinement. The findings in *Boyd* and other cases like it will be discussed in the section that follows.

Classification

Classification is the process of assigning a young person to a living unit for the duration of his or her stay at the facility. Most states have laws or regulations requiring certain forms of classification, such as separating males from females, adults from children, abused and neglected children from children who are law violators, or preadjudication from postadjudication inmates. Most facilities have their own written regulations along these lines, and most have additional regulations on separation of individuals accused of violent offenses, individuals with infectious diseases, and individuals with violent propensities.

The problem in many juvenile facilities is that there are often not enough rooms to separate different young people adequately. For example, in one case a facility had a White separatist accused of burning down the home of an African American family in the same room as an African American youth. In order to prevent clashes, the African American youth was put in solitary confinement for his "own safety."

In *Martarella v. Kelley,* the court enumerated minimum classification requirements:

> All relevant factors including his maturity, emotional development, emotional and psychiatric history, findings of fact, or, if they are known, the charges against him, and evidence of drug use and [classification] shall not be made on the basis of age, size and aggressiveness only.[10]

Issues that arise often in juvenile detention pertain to the separation of violent from nonviolent offenders and separation by gender. Children in secure confinement have a right to be free from unreasonable threats to their physical safety. Facilities must have a system for screening and separating aggressive juveniles from more passive ones. Additionally, factors to be considered when classifying are age, experience, sophistication, gender, race, and potential infectious diseases. Similarly, the failure to protect children from the sexual behavior of other confined children may result in liability.[11]

Separation by gender can sometimes be confusing. Many states allow boys and girls to mix in the daily program at the facility. In some jurisdictions boys and girls are kept on different sleeping units. Alternatively, in some jurisdictions boys can sleep on the same units as girls, but there can be no mingling of the genders in the same rooms. Thus, there is much wider latitude for young people regarding classification than exists for adults. However, there are still problems. Sometimes girls and boys on the same units flirt and expose themselves to one another while staff are not watching.

Today, problems arise when staff assigned to monitor young people are from opposite genders, although there have been no juvenile cases on this issue. In looking at cases where adult penitentiaries house males, the courts have found that although prisons are required to hire and assign female guards throughout the facility, male inmates retain constitutional protection against invasion of their privacy by members of the opposite sex.

Male inmates are entitled to a reasonable accommodation of their privacy interest to prevent unnecessary observation of their naked bodies by female officers.[12] However, the established policy in juvenile facilities is that no male should be allowed to administer to adolescent females without a female staff person present.

But policies are not always followed. I learned this lesson the hard way through a case in Idaho. There, girls were serving inordinately long periods of seclusion in isolation because they failed to awaken and conduct early morning unit activities. After asking questions about isolation procedures, I offhandedly joked that the girls could avoid all this hassle if they just got a good night's sleep. One girl quipped back that they would get a good night's sleep if they didn't have to stay up at night "screwing the guards."

Health/Mental Health

Included in the analysis of health and mental health is the issue of the intake or initial screening the facility provides when a young person first enters. Minimally, every facility should have a screening mechanism for new detainees that looks for (1) communicable diseases, (2) alcohol or drug intoxication, (3) pregnancy, and (4) necessary medication for an ongoing condition (e.g., epilepsy, diabetes, and asthma). Youths with any of the first three conditions should not be placed in the general youth population, but should receive specific medical treatment. For longer term stays, children should also have their vision, teeth, and hearing checked.

The screening should be done by *trained* personnel, not necessarily by a physician, but at least a nurse practitioner or a physician's assistant. Routinely, many facilities have detention staff with little or no medical training in the correct way to conduct an intake screening. For example, in a case I litigated in Tucson, Arizona, a young boy was never asked if he had asthma on intake. He went into seizures at 3:00 a.m. on a weekend and nearly died because late-night staff had no idea what was happening to him or, more important, what to do about it.

The National Commission on Correctional Health Care and the courts have addressed this issue. Both require that the initial screening include gathering information on the following:[13]

1. Current illness and health problems, including sexually transmitted and other infectious diseases
2. Dental problems

3. Use of alcohol and other drugs, which includes types of drugs used, mode of use, amounts used, date or time of last use, and side effects after stopped use
4. Immunization history

In addition, observation should be made of:

1. Behavior that includes state of consciousness, mental status, appearance, conduct, tremors, and sweating
2. Condition of skin, including trauma markings, bruises, lesions, jaundice, rashes and infestations, and needle marks.

Often children referred to detention for violations of the law have traditionally had poor medical screening. Unfortunately for many it is while they are incarcerated that they receive their first health assessment. It is important for the health of the staff as well as other detainees that this job be done professionally at the earliest time possible.

Not only should juveniles be screened; children in confinement have a right to medical care.[14] Minimally, case law and standards require daily access to medical facilities, including the provision of a 24-hour nursing service.[15] There should be a qualified health professional on site at all times, with a physician on call; transportation to medical services at other locations if necessary; a system of daily sick-call that does not substitute staff judgment for medical judgment; and medical supervision for children detoxifying from drugs or alcohol.[16]

There is no question that juvenile secure confinement facilities are encountering children with serious emotional problems in more frequent numbers than in the past. Many experts point to the failure of the public school and mental health systems as well as the prevalence of drugs, violence, and other factors. Nevertheless, secure confinement facilities are required to humanely house these young people and provide mental health screening and services.

It is crucial therefore that facilities screen minors for mental health problems, there be provisions for emergency psychological services, there be established procedures for dealing with suicidal youngsters, medications be prescribed and administered by qualified medical personnel, there be provisions for children to request psychological care, and there be adequate staffing for ongoing psychological services.

Children should have a basic initial psychological screening upon entry into detention. This screening instrument should be developed by mental health professionals. Additionally, the mental health professionals should train detention workers on the use of the instrument and expected responses they elicit from minors. The form at a minimum should address issues of depression, potential suicidal behavior, and psychological history of the young person.[17]

This point was made clear in a case I litigated in Indiana. A girl was arrested for stealing suntan lotion from a drug store where she stopped on her way to work. Her parents did not have a telephone, and it took approximately 2 hours for them to be contacted and arrive at the facility. Upon admittance into the facility the girl was interviewed by untrained staff who did not ask if she was depressed or suicidal. She was both, and by the time her parents arrived, she had hanged herself.

Similarly, if a minor is going to be detained for some period of time after the detention hearing, then a mental status examination should be given. Additionally, there must be 24-hour access to psychological services.[18] Although the law does not require that there be ongoing counseling or therapy sessions provided by the institution, the appropriate practice would provide opportunities for the children to talk about their problems as part of the daily program.

Additionally, detained children who are going to be confined for a long period of time should be given a developed treatment plan and related ongoing services.[19] In that vein, if psychotropic drugs are a part of that treatment, they must be administered carefully. The staff must be trained in the dispensation and should recognize adverse effects. Record keeping involves a log that specifies the name of each child, name of medication, amount of dosage, and frequency of administration. These records should be regularly monitored by the prescribing psychiatrist.

Traditionally, mental health providers and correctional staff have not coordinated services well. As more facilities become crowded with children with serious emotional disturbances, these two service providers will have to find ways to work together to serve the needs of children in trouble with the law.

Access

These issues involve the right of access by youth in confinement to family and other important people in their lives. Many people underestimate how important visits are to young people and their families while they are going through the court system. Access issues are critical for youth who are being securely confined before any findings of guilt or innocence. Moreover, it is important to keep in mind that the juvenile justice system encourages treatment and rehabilitation of children and therefore access should only be limited where necessary for institutional security or other appropriate reasons.

Visitation. The right of the detained minor to visitation is constitution-ally protected.[20] However, the courts do not specifically state the amount of visitation allowed, the time for visits, nor who is allowed to visit. Al-though there is no constitutional minimum for visitation, institutions hous-ing children must provide for "reasonable" visitation.

Children should have at least as much opportunity for visitation as adults. Visits should be available during several hours of the day, with provi-sion of alternative visiting times for parents who are unable to schedule visits during the normal hours. Approved visitors should include adult rela-tives and family friends. Younger brothers, sisters, and others should be allowed to visit with approval of the minor's probation officer or counselor. Unfortunately, punitive attitudes, understaffing, and limited physical areas for visiting have resulted in narrowly restricted visiting opportunities for youth in confinement.

It should be noted that the right to visitation, like any other right, is not absolute and the institution may cancel visits or refuse to allow certain parties to visit if there is a reasonable belief they are bringing in contraband or there is a safety or security justification to deny such a visit.

Telephone Use. The courts have not established an absolute require-ment for telephone use. As with visitation, the facility must provide "reason-able" access to telephones.[21] Standards have established some procedures for facilities. For example, ACA standards require that a young person be allowed to make two telephone calls at the time of initial detention.[22] Simi-larly, a youth should be allowed a minimum of two calls per week that cannot be taken away for disciplinary purposes.[23] The calls may be made to parents, other relatives, and attorneys.

Mail. Sending and receiving mail is a protected constitutional right.[24] Therefore secure confinement facilities serving youth have an obligation to provide writing materials and stamps. Mail is categorized into two types: privileged and nonprivileged.

Privileged mail is between the child and his or her attorney, a judge, a legislator, or some other public official. Privileged mail is usually desig-nated as such (e.g., "legal mail") on the envelope. Privileged mail may not be opened by staff, except to inspect it for contraband. [25]

Nonprivileged mail is all other mail. Mail from someone outside the facility to a child may be inspected for contraband, but may only be read by staff if there are grounds to believe that the mail contains escape plans, plans for criminal activity, obscenity, or that it constitutes a violation of the law (e.g., a death threat to someone). Even then, the staff must be able to articulate those grounds in order to open and read the mail. It is not enough for staff to just have a feeling or a hunch; unless they can demonstrate some factual basis to support their feelings, the mail may not be read. There must be a particularized showing, based on the specific detainee's record or other facts related to institutional security.

As a practical matter, the facility should do its inspection for contraband in the presence of the minor or assign a minor in conjunction with staff to inspect the mail. Otherwise, when children receive letters that have been inspected out of their presence, the facility is leaving itself open for complaints that staff did more than inspect for contraband. The handling of outgoing mail should be the same. Minors should be able to seal their mail when they give it to staff for mailing. This ensures that there is no room for argument about staff reading the mail when they inspect it before sealing.

Oftentimes facility administrators do not pay attention to this important constitutional issue. For example, in one facility each staff member had a different criteria for what he or she thought was offensive. Some staff allowed profanity but no sexual references. Others said sexual references were all right as long as there was no profanity. Others edited out any information about the daily routine of the facility. It is exactly this kind of arbitrary enforcement of individual censorship that the courts address in their decisions.

Secure confinement staff should know that mail may be censored if they have a suspicion that children are planning escapes, planning violent acts, promoting gang activity, or contacting victims. The law lists these criteria for censorship:

1. Whether the connection between the regulation and the justification is so remote as to render it arbitrary or irrational
2. Whether there are alternative means for inmates to exercise their right
3. Whether accommodation of the right will have an impact on other inmates and staff
4. Whether there is an obvious, easily available alternative to the regulation that accommodates the inmate's rights at little cost to penological interests

It is important to understand that access issues are to be looked at in their entirety, the key point being that there must be contact with the outside world for children in confinement. Therefore, facilities should examine all policies regarding visitation, telephone use, and mail to assure themselves that children can contact someone outside the walls if they are being threatened or harmed.

Programming

Programming involves the daily schedule of the institution. It includes such issues as education and recreation. A secure facility for young people should be a place where the daily activity assists in rehabilitation efforts. Too often in many facilities young people sit in "forced idleness" while absolutely nothing is done to reorient them toward being positive members of the community after their release. Good detention practice keeps children busy and active.

Education. Education is the cornerstone of any good rehabilitative program. The requirements are similar in preadjudication detention centers and in long-term training schools. State law requires children to attend school until a certain age and juvenile institutions must comply with state law requirements. It may also be the single most important service that institutions can provide, since many children in institutions are far behind in their studies or have actually dropped out of school.

Incarcerated juveniles have a constitutional right to an adequate educational program.[26] This includes education before and after adjudication as well as special education services.[27] Juveniles placed in detention prior to a hearing are entitled to educational services. Denial of education during pretrial detention constitutes punishment before trial and is, therefore, a violation of the juvenile's due process rights under the Fourteenth Amendment.[28]

The Washington Supreme Court has held that state compulsory education laws require the provision of an educational program for juveniles in detention awaiting adjudication. Further, such a program should be provided to juveniles "within a few days of detention."[29] Oftentimes facilities will not begin a school program for young people until they have been there at least a week. There is no good justification for this practice, but it is quite typical. Facility administrators seem to believe that leaving a child in his or her room for a week following the initial arrival at the facility somehow makes that child better prepared to attend the school program.

Although reluctant to dictate what form the program should take, the Washington Court suggested a set of guidelines. It recommended the prompt evaluation of the child to determine whether, and in what areas, he or she is academically deficient. After this assessment, the child should be placed in a remedial program to learn basic reading, spelling, and math skills. Additionally, vocational training should be available to help the young person learn skills he or she could pursue once out of detention.

Regarding juveniles in a long-term detention facility, the federal courts have held that the Eighth Amendment prohibition against cruel and unusual punishment requires states to provide "treatment" to juveniles subject to long-term detention, which the court defined as detention that lasts 30 days or longer.[30] This treatment must include appropriate educational services.

The form that these educational services should take was specified in *Morgan v. Sproat*. There, the court ordered a state institution to implement an educational plan that would achieve the following goals:

(1) to provide a complete educational assessment of each incoming student, (2) to provide special education services and programs to all students who are diagnosed as needing such services, (3) to establish an in-service training program for all teaching staff, (4) to hire a teaching staff certified to teach in the fields to which they are assigned, (5) to bring their high school programs into compliance with state requirements for public high schools, (6) to institute a periodic testing program to determine the educational progress made by individual students, and (7) to obtain sufficient instructional materials to run an individualized program of instruction that provides rewards for academic progress.[31]

The court found these elements necessary for an educational program, since a program lacking these characteristics was "fundamentally deficient."

In addition to providing general education services, secure confinement facilities must provide special education services as well.[32] Children may be eligible for special education services if they suffer from severe vision or hearing problems, orthopedic impairments, chronic illness, mental retardation, speech or language impairment, attention deficit disorder, serious emotional disturbance, or learning disabilities (a disorder in understanding or using language manifested as an impaired ability to listen, think, speak, read, write, spell, or do mathematical calculations).[33] Research indicates that anywhere from 20% to 60% of detained children are special education eligible.[34] Some of these children come into detention with a well-documented history of special education services, and others have disabilities that have gone undetected or unaddressed by the school system.

The courts have made it clear that children in correctional facilities are entitled to the benefit of special education laws and that appropriate services must be provided.[35] Special education–eligible children are entitled to a broad range of assessment, evaluation, educational, and related services (including transition services) under the Individuals with Disabilities Education Act (IDEA) of 1997.[36] Federal time lines for assessment and implementation apply, even though the child is in "temporary" detention. Institutions confining children must also refrain from discriminating against educationally disabled children under the Rehabilitation Act of 1973.[37]

The requirements of federal law are quite explicit regarding services to be provided to youth with special needs in secure confinement. Indeed, the court in *Boyd* held that

> the purpose of the IDEA is to assure that all children with disabilities have available to them a free and appropriate education. The regulations make clear that the reference includes state correctional facilities.[38]

However, children often go without identification of their special education needs and the related services mandated by law.

Recreation/Exercise. Exercise, recreation, and access to fresh air are important for both the health and development of children, but also because it enables them to get rid of tension and frustration that otherwise might result in misbehavior. We know that time moves very slowly for an incarcerated child, and recreation and exercise help the time to pass more quickly.

It is especially important that children have access to fresh air for at least one hour on a daily basis if weather permits. This is true even in cold climates. Detention centers should have sweatshirts and coats so that children may go outside when it is not inordinately cold. I have litigated cases against facilities where children get no access to the outdoors if the temperature is below 50 degrees Fahrenheit, resulting in their not getting fresh air for weeks and months.

The cases vary greatly on what exercise must be provided, but at a minimum, children should have an opportunity for outdoor large-muscle exercise that ranges from 1 to 3 hours daily, weather permitting.[39] Facilities should also provide structured indoor activities consisting of games and books to occupy the children's time in the evenings. All too often "recreation" consists of an entire unit watching movies or daytime talk television. In one facility I inspected, the children and staff in the "sex offender" unit were watching the *Jerry Springer Show,* which that day featured "I am a stripper and proud of it." Of course the show featured the requisite bump and grind necessary for ratings. Good facilities do not include television as a significant part of the recreation program.

Oftentimes children on discipline are denied recreation and large-muscle exercise. This is a violation of the minor's rights. The facility should provide supervised exercise for children who pose escape risks and who are minors with disciplinary problems. Simply having a child walk up and down the unit is not large-muscle exercise and does not comply with the law.

Training of Staff

Workers at a secure confinement institution for juveniles should not be placed in the unenviable position of working with children in detention without training. Facility administrators have a duty to hire qualified people, train them adequately, and supervise them to insure that they are implementing the training.

The courts have not articulated exactly what levels of training are necessary; however, they have imposed liability for failure to hire properly qualified staff and failure to adequately train and supervise staff. The ACA has adopted standards for juvenile facilities that outline minimum training criteria.[40] Typically a staff member should receive 40 hours of preservice training and 40 to 80 hours of in-service training. Similarly, part-time staff and volunteers should get the amount of training appropriate to their assignment.

Training subjects recommended include

Security procedures
Supervision of juveniles
Signs of suicide risk
Suicide precautions
Use-of-force regulations and tactics
Report writing
Juvenile rules and regulations
Rights and responsibilities of juveniles
Fire and emergency procedures
Key control
Interpersonal relationships
Social and cultural lifestyles of population
Adolescent growth and development
Communication skills
First aid and CPR

The key to any good secure confinement facility is the quality of the line staff and their immediate supervisors. Properly trained and supervised staff usually exercise good judgment and provide safe, caring, and humane confinement. It is widely known throughout the field that any examination of a well-run facility reveals excellent staff. The examples of staff mistreating young people are too numerous to mention, but they range from activities such as staff members taunting youth who are smokers and in withdrawal by smoking cigarettes outside their rooms and blowing smoke in their faces, to drinking, partying, and having sex with girls in facilities.

Environment

This subject of environment encompasses all of the physical and space issues in juvenile facilities. Since juvenile facilities are often overcrowded,
the physical plant suffers from significant overuse and resulting disrepair.
There has been a great deal of litigation over environmental issues in both
adult and juvenile facilities. Professional standards usually get quite specific
about the physical plant requirements associated with these issues.

Fire Safety. This is a critical area in juvenile facilities, since the outbreak of fire where people are securely confined can result in tremendous
loss of life. At a minimum, the facility must have (1) smoke detectors or
similar monitoring devices, (2) a written evacuation plan, with posted dia-
grams, available to youths and staff, (3) at least two means of escape from
the facility in case of fire, (4) *working,* fully charged fire extinguishers, and
(5) smoke lights marking the exits in the event of fire.[41]

Most of the cases dealing with fire safety involved adult corrections
facilities; however, the consent decree in *Robyn A. v. McCoy*[42] approved
an even higher degree of fire safety than what is required for adults. The
decree required the facility to do the following: Establish an evacuation
plan approved by the city fire marshal; only hire staff who have demonstrated familiarity with the evacuation plan; teach all children the evacuation procedures upon admission to the facility; conduct fire drills at least
once per week; install electronic locking hardware on all doors; have fire
safety inspections performed at least once per quarter; and implement all
recommendations from these inspections within the time required by the
inspector.

The key analysis on adequacy of fire safety is whether the equipment
is properly located, that it is functional, and that staff know how to use
it. Assuring that those questions are answered appropriately will reduce
significantly the chance of loss of life during a fire emergency.

Lighting. The courts have not required specific levels of candlepower,
but professional standards require that lighting be sufficient for detainees
to comfortably read books in their cells without eyestrain.[43] Facilities should
also encourage designs that allow access to natural light so that young people will not be in dark solitary rooms.

Ventilation. Air flow in the room is important, particularly in small,
cramped rooms where the children may have to eat their meals in close
proximity to the toilet. Poor ventilation makes for terrible living conditions.
For example, in one facility I inspected, the mesh grating covering the win-

dow was torn and there was graphic sexual and violent graffiti on the walls as well as semen on the radiators, which emitted terrible odors.

Institutions often have significant temperature differences within the facility. While the courts will defer to the administration in the keeping of healthful levels of circulation, the consent decree in *Robyn A. v. McCoy*[44] established temperature ranges no lower than 64 or higher than 84 degrees Fahrenheit.

Food. In juvenile secure confinement facilities food must be nutritionally adequate; courts have, however, imposed further requirements that meals be served at regular intervals, and the inmates be provided with snacks between meals.[45] The facility should prepare a balanced diet for youths, with food properly prepared (not consistently overcooked or undercooked) and with three full meals each day, and juveniles should receive some type of snack between dinner and breakfast the next morning. Food may never be withheld for disciplinary reasons.

Restraints and Discipline

Restraints. Restraints are difficult to write about, since there are no standards or rules that mandate or prohibit certain practices. Therefore, there is a wide range of policies and practices being used around the country. Each individual situation should be handled on a case-by-case basis. There are some general guidelines, however, that are important to delineate. Hard restraints (metal handcuffs) should not be used on children except for transportation from one place to another. They should never be used to restrain a young person to a stationary object. For example, one facility I sued had a routine practice of handcuffing children to a fence with their arms elevated above their heads for a minimum of 6 hours.

If children must be restrained, staff should use soft leather restraints. Restraints of any type should never be used as punishment, and they should only be used for as long as the child is out of control. There should be constant monitoring of children in restraints. Some courts have allowed restraints to be used for a limited period to prevent injury of the minor to him- or herself or to others.[46] Courts have held that restraints may not be used for longer than 30 minutes without authorization of qualified professionals or institutional administrators.[47]

In addition to mechanical restraints, juvenile facilities are currently using chemical restraints. These agents are known as Mace, tear gas, or pepper spray. Pepper spray, the most common in juvenile facilities, is a generic name for a variety of commercial inflammatory agents utilizing oleoresin capsicum (oc), an oily resin extracted from the cayenne pepper plant. The spray causes immediate swelling and burning of the eyes, a burning sensation of the skin, loss of upper body control, and paralysis of the larynx, which may render the victim temporarily unable to speak. When inhaled, it causes inflammation of the respiratory tract and breathing passages resulting in coughing, gagging, and gasping for breath.

Proponents of the spray contend that it is safer than other methods of subduing unruly detainees because it avoids the physical contacts that can lead to serious injury. While this may be true, it is also true that pepper spray poses risks for a variety of long-term injuries, particularly for asthmatics. In addition, the potential for abuse, even with stringent safeguards, is great. Indeed, we have encountered cases where youth have been pepper sprayed so much that they have permanent scars or eye damage.

In a case from the state of Washington[48] challenging the use of chemical agents on youth, the court held that spray could be used to protect a substantial amount of valuable property or to prevent substantial injury to persons under the following restrictions:

1. There must be a credible threat of a specific injury.
2. The only legitimate intended result of pepper spray use is the incapacitation of a dangerous person and *not* the infliction of pain.
3. The spray shall not be used for punishment and can only be used to incapacitate a dangerous person.
4. Spray should only be used when absolutely necessary.

Some facilities use tear gas to break up fights or control unitwide behavior. In South Carolina the court found improper the use of tear gas on children to "enforce orders."[49] The court found that the gas could be used only when there was a serious risk of bodily harm to another, and less intrusive means of restraint were not available. Thus, juvenile facilities using chemical restraints run the risk that children, especially those with underlying health conditions such as asthma or heart problems, or children who are taken into custody while intoxicated, may suffer injury or death.

Isolation. Most institutions use isolation for out-of-control individuals as punishment for breaking rules. Even though isolation is commonly imposed as a sanction in juvenile institutions, some courts have found that children may only be placed in isolation when they pose an immediate threat to themselves or other people, that they must be monitored closely, and that they must be released as soon as they have gained control of themselves.[50]

Some facilities overuse isolation because they lack adequately trained staff to more appropriately handle out-of-control or acting-out minors. We have litigated practices where children have to stand with their nose to the wall in isolation for 4 hours without moving. Other cases have children in isolation for 5 days for violations as minor as talking during meals. Worse, some children are sent to adult jails because they cannot be handled by juvenile confinement staff. Administrators should scrutinize isolation policies to assure that young people are not languishing in their rooms for inappropriate periods of time.

Due Process. Due process involves minors being treated fairly when they are being disciplined.[51] As part of this fair treatment, every minor should have the rules explained in his or her primary language. Thus every detainee should know what the rules are and what types of behavior violate the rules.

Additionally, prior to imposition of discipline, minors have a right to be heard regarding their version of events. They have a right to a due process hearing *prior* to serving all of the time imposed for the misbehavior. The hearing does not have to be elaborate, but a minor should not have served all of his or her time in isolation before receiving a hearing. This makes common sense and helps ensure that minors and staff are treated fairly.

Grievance Procedures. Grievance procedures enable a child to register complaints about daily life issues that do not involve discipline (e.g., food quantity or quality). The basic elements of adequate procedures are notice to the children of the availability, a clear and simple procedure through which the child may present his or her grievance to staff, prompt investigation of the grievance (usually 3 days) and an opportunity for the child to present the grievance to a staff member who was not involved in the incident, notice to the child of the decision of the impartial person, and a decision and final action taken.

CONCLUSION

As juvenile justice facilities increasingly fill with youth of color, there is a tendency for insufficient resources to be directed toward providing adequate services. The work of juvenile corrections personnel is clearly important as society grapples with the increasing number of children in trouble with the law. However, instead of existing as large, violent warehouses of human misery, juvenile corrections institutions should provide individualized and comprehensive interventions (not overly standardized "treatment" protocols) that hold young people accountable and help give them the necessary personal, educational, and technical skills designed to help them make the transition to becoming responsible adults.

At the same time it is equally important that community-based organizations be given the ability to assume more direct responsibility for their own youth, thereby reducing the rapid growth and encroachment of large impersonal institutions.

We need to shift the focus from the young person's deficits to his or her strengths. There is no question that youth have the capacity—with sufficient guidance, support, and positive intervention—to achieve, thrive, and become responsible contributing members of their communities. Additionally, it is my experience that with proper support and encouragement, young people can help address the needs of their community and participate in peer-to-peer support activities.

It is this orientation toward positive outcomes that is so sorely lacking in our juvenile justice policies. We act out our worst impulses on young people who, given the chance, can change their lives. We are punitive, retributive, and dismissive. Our juvenile institutions are worse than those of any other industrialized nation and are simply unacceptable.

Recently we celebrated the 50th anniversary of the Declaration of Human Rights. One of the leaders in getting that document enacted and signed was Eleanor Roosevelt. In advocating for passage of the declaration, Mrs. Roosevelt said, "Where, after all, do universal human rights begin? In small places, close to home. Such are the places where man, woman and child seek equal justice, equal opportunity and equal dignity." Here in the United States we must work tirelessly to insure that our juvenile facilities meet that standard.

NOTES

1. Dale Parent et al., *Conditions of Confinement: Juvenile Detention and Corrections Facilities, a Research Report.* (Washington, DC: Office of Juvenile Justice and Delinquency Prevention (OJJDP), August 1994).

2. W. E. B. Du Bois, *The Souls of Black Folk* (New York: Dodd Mead, 1903).

3. G. Stanley Hall, *Adolescence—Its Psychology and Its Relations to Physiology, Anthropology, Sociology, Sex, Crime, Religion and Education* (New York: D. Appleton, 1969).

4. California Youth Authority (CYA), *Summary Fact Sheet* (January 1999); Texas Youth Commission, *Texas Youth Commission Population Demographics* (January 1999).

5. Jeremy Rifkin, *The End of Work* (New York: Putnam, 1995).

6. Richard J. Herrnstein and Charles Murray, *The Bell Curve: Intelligence and Class Structure in American Life* (New York: Free Press, 1994).

7. L. L. Brasier, "Rally protests Abraham ruling," *Detroit Free Press*, November 24, 1999.

8. Office of Juvenile Justice and Delinquency Prevention (OJJDP), *State legislative responses to violent juvenile crime* (Patricia Torbet, Linda Szymanksi, November 1998).

9. *Alexander S. v. Boyd*, 876 F. Supp. 773 (D.S.C. 1995).

10. 359 F. Supp. 478, 485 (S.D.N.Y 1973).

11. *Alexander S. v. Boyd; Guidry v. Rapides Parish School Board*, 560 So.2d 125 (La. Ct. App. 1990).

12. *Canedy v. Boardman* 16 F.3d 183 (7th Cir. 1994).

13. National Commission on Correctional Health Care Standards for Health Services in Juvenile Detention and Confinement Facilities 1995 Y-35.

14. *Estelle v. Gamble*, 429 U.S. 97 (1976).

15. *Inmates of Boys' Training School v. Affleck*, 346 F. Supp. 1354 (D.R.I. 1972).

16. *Robyn A. v. McCoy* CIV-90-1151-FR (1992).

17. American Correctional Association Standards for Juvenile Detention Facilities 1991, 1-JDF-4C-35.

18. National Commission on Correctional Health Care Standards for Health Services in Juvenile Detention and Confinement Facilities 1995 Y-36.

19. *Gary W. v. Louisiana*, 437 F. Supp. 1209 (E.D. La. 1976).

20. *Ahrens v. Thomas*, 434 F. Supp. 873 (W.D. Mo. 1977), *aff'd*, 570 F.2d 286 (8th Cir. 1978); *Thomas v. Mears*, 474 F. Supp. 908 (E.D. Ark. 1979); *Gary W. v. State of Louisiana*, 437 F. Supp. 1209 (E.D. La. 1976); *D.B. v. Tewksbury*, 545 F. Supp. 896 (D. Or. 1982), *Taylor v. Armontrout*, 888 F.2d 555 (8th Cir. 1989).

21. *Gary W. v. Louisiana*, 437 F. Supp. 1209 (E. D. La. 1976).

22. American Correctional Association Standards for Juvenile Detention Facilities 1991, 1JDF-5A-11.

23. *Doe v. Holladay*, 1982.

24. *Turner v. Safley*, 482 U.S., 107 S.Ct. 2254 (1987).

25. See *Wolff v. McDonnell*, 418 U.S. 539, 574-77, 94 S.Ct. 2963 (1974).

26. *Inmates of the Boys' Training School v. Affleck*, 346 F. Supp. 1354, 1370 (D.R.I. 1972).

27. *D.B. v. Tewksbury*, 545 F. Supp. 896, 905 (D. Or. 1982); *Martarella v. Kelley*, 359 F. Supp. 478, 481 (S.D.N.Y. 1973); *Green v. Johnson*, 513 F. Supp. 965, 976 (D. Mass. 1981).

28. *D.B.*, 545 F. Supp. at 905.

29. *Tommy P. v. Board of County Commissioners*, 645 P.2d 697, 701-704 (Wash. 1982).

30. *Martarella v. Kelly* 359 F. Supp. 478, 481.

31. 432 F. Supp. 1130 (S.D. Miss. 1977).

32. *Alexander S. v. Boyd*, 876 F. Supp. 773 (D.S.C. 1995).

33. 20 U.S. Code §§ 1401(a)(1)(A), 1401 (a)(15), 34 Code of Federal Regulations § 300.7.

34. See "The Prevalence of Disabilities in the Juvenile Court Population," chap-

ter II-A in Loren Warboys et al., *California Juvenile Court Special Education Manual* (San Francisco: Youth Law Center, 1994).

35. *Green v. Johnson,* 513 F. Supp. 965 (D. Mass. 1981); *Donnell C. v. Illinois State Board of Education,* 829 F. Supp. 1016 (N.D. Ill. 1993).

36. 20 U.S. Code, §§ 1401(a)(16), 1401(a)(17), 1401(a)(19), 34 Code of Federal Regulations §§ 300.16, 300.17, 300.18.

37. 29 U.S. Code § 504 *et seq.*

38. *Alexander S. v. Boyd,* 876 F. Supp. 773, 801 (D.S.C. 1995).

39. *D.B. v. Tewksbury,* 545 F. Supp. 896 (D. Or. 1982); *Morgan v. Sproat,* 432 F. Supp. 1130 (S.D. Miss. 1977); *Baker v. Hamilton,* 345 F. Supp. 345 (W.D. Ky. 1972); *Thomas v. Mears,* 474 F. Supp. 908 (E.D. Ark. 1979); *Martarella v. Kelley,* 359 F. Supp. 478, 485 (S.D.N.Y. 1973); *Inmates of Boys Training School v. Affleck,* 346 F. Supp. 1354, 1369-70 (D.R.I. 1972), Civil No. 4529 (D.R.I. Jan. 15, 1979) (final order); *Ahrens v. Thomas,* 434 F. Supp. 873 (W.D. Mo. 1977), *aff'd in part,* 570 F.2d 286 (8th Cir. 1978).

40. American Correctional Association Standards for Juvenile Detention Facilities 1991, 3-JDF-3B-01.

41. *Ahrens v. Thomas,* 434 F. Supp. 873 (W.D. Mo. 1977), *aff'd* in part, 570 F.2d 286 (8th Cir. 1978).

42. Civ. No. 90-1151-FR (1992).

43. *Ahrens v. Thomas,* 434 F. Supp. 873 (W.D. Mo. 1977), *aff'd* in part, 570 F. 2d 286 (8th Cir. 1978); *Inmates of Boys Training School v. Affleck,* 346 F. Supp. 1354, 1369-70 (D.R.I. 1972), Civil No. 4529 (D.R.I. Jan. 15, 1979) (final order). *Ramos v. Lamm,* 639 F. 2d 559 (10th Cir. 1980), cert. denied 450 U.S. 1041 (1981).

44. See n. 16.

45. *Inmates of Boys' Training School v. Affleck,* 346 F. Supp. 1354 (D.R.I. 1972).

46. *Milonas v. Williams,* 691 F.2d 931 (10th Cir. 1982), cert. denied, 460 U.S. 1096 (1983).

47. *Gary W. v. Louisiana,* 437 F. Supp. 1209 (E.D. La. 1976).

48. *Horton v. Williams,* Case No. C94-5428 RJB.

49. *Alexander S. v. Boyd,* 876 F. Supp. 773 (D.S.C. 1995).

50. *H.C. v. Jarrard,* 786 F.2d 1080 (11th Cir. 1986).

51. *Wolff v. McDonnell,* 418 U.S. 539, S.Ct. (1974).

Afterword

"You see," says Ivan Karamazov in Fyodor Dostoevsky's novel, "I must repeat again, it is a peculiar characteristic of many people, this love of torturing children, and children only. To all other types of humanity these tortur-
ers behave mildly and benevolently, like cultivated and humane Europeans;
but they are very fond of tormenting children, even fond of children in that
sense. It's just that defenselessness that tempts the tormentor." This book
treats those generally thought to be "cultivated and humane" Americans,
and the violations of children over the years, violations concealed by a presumed regard for human rights, individual freedom, equity. Our country is
thought to be, after all, the world's greatest democracy. And a democracy,
after all, is conceived to be a community devoted to the worth and promise
of every human being, old and young.

Pondering the essays in this book (essays that evoke Emile Zola's greatest protest, called "J'accuse"), we are not only reminded of the homeless
children in our past, the ragpickers, the excluded ones, the beaten ones.
The drawn faces of the children in Charles Dickens' novels come to mind,
or (earlier) William Blake's little chimney sweepers. Blake knew most
clearly that the suffering was not mainly due to the cruelty of genteel individuals; it was systemic, due in large measure to the inhumanity of the
economic system and the moral or religious codes that sustained it and
justified its injustices, its neglect, and (yes) its savagery.

We know that the system did not come automatically into being, that
it is the consequence of multiple acts of exploitation, property seizure, ma-
nipulation. The schools, too, were often complicit in violating the rights of
children, in rendering thousands invisible. Today we can clearly see how
the triumph of the "free market" carries with it rationales for treating children as "resources" rather than as persons. If they are useless, if they inter-
fere somehow with the mechanisms of technology, if their vitality is at odds
with the shapes of the "virtual" realities, they can (if only in the interests
of efficiency) be criminalized or cast aside. Poverty, racial discrimination,
class difference—all become forces in the service of pecuniary accumulation, greed, shameless and faceless power.

For F. Scott Fitzgerald, shameless power led to carelessness. "They
were careless people, Tom and Daisy—they smashed up things and crea-

tures and then retreated back into their money or their vast carelessness, or whatever it was that kept them together, and let other people clean up the mess they had made." For Valerie Polakow, the wonderful and insightful editor of this text, systemic violence has led to a "terrifying blindness" and the failure to act against "savage policies." And that suggests the painful questions the writers here force us to ask: Who will clean up the mess? Where do we start? What is there to do?

Not only does this book disclose truths too many choose to deny. Not only, as the philosopher says, does it "unconceal." It appeals. It should appeal at once to our indignation and to our freedom, our freedom to break with the assumed, with the taken for granted, with the comfortable denials. It should appeal to our capacity to summon up a better state of things, to come together to transform. New commitments are required, a new passion of concern, new forms of advocacy. Yes, and a renewed involvement with political science, history, poetry, philosophy, whatever can enable us to name the world around somewhat more bravely, somewhat more accurately—and to act somehow, to repair.

I choose to end with Dostoevsky and with what Ivan calls his "rebellion." Perhaps we can read "harmony" as "profitability" or "technological primacy"—and it may hold meanings that move us to move. "Listen! If all must suffer to pay for the eternal harmony, what have children to do with it, tell me please? It's beyond all comprehension why they should suffer, and why they should pay for the harmony. . . . But what pulls me up here is that I can't accept that harmony." These wise and outraged essays may move us to accuse and, in time, to refuse. Moving past the facts, reaching towards new possibility, the readers of this important book may find their own lives changed.

Maxine Greene
Teachers College
Columbia University

About the Editor and
the Contributors

Valerie Polakow is a professor of education at Eastern Michigan University. She is the author of *The Erosion of Childhood* (University of Chicago Press, 1982, 1992) and *Lives on the Edge: Single Mothers and Their Children in the Other America* (University of Chicago Press, 1993), which won the Kappa Delta Pi Book of the Year Award in 1994. She has written numerous articles and book chapters about women and children in poverty, welfare policies, child care policies, child and family homelessness, and educational advocacy. She has been active in local and national advocacy groups that support the legal and educational rights of welfare recipients and homeless children. During 1995 she was a Fulbright scholar in Denmark, researching welfare and child care policies. Forthcoming publications include *Diminished Rights* (with T. Halskov & P. Schultz Jørgensen) and *International Perspectives on Homelessness* (with C. Guillean).

James Bell has been a staff attorney at the Youth Law Center in San Francisco for 17 years, representing children confined in adult jails, juvenile detention centers, and training schools. He has written articles analyzing the death penalty for children and testified before Congress on federal legislation that impacts adolescents. He has worked extensively with policy makers and community organization across the country on issues such as violence prevention and alternatives to incarceration. In the international arena he has assisted the African National Congress in the administration of the juvenile justice system in South Africa, worked with Palestinians and Israelis on alternatives to juvenile incarceration, and trained lawyers on the human rights of children in Cambodia. He is the recipient of many awards, including the Livingston Hall Award for Outstanding Juvenile Advocacy of the American Bar Association, the Clinton White Attorney of the Year Award from the Charles Houston Bar Association, and the Advocate of the Year from the Office of Juvenile Justice.

Sue Books, a former journalist, is now an associate professor in the Department of Educational Studies at the State University of New York at New

Paltz. She has studied and written about children, poverty, and schooling throughout her academic career, and is the editor of *Invisible Children in the Society and Its Schools* (Erlbaum, 1998).

Bernadine Dohrn is director of the Children and Family Justice Center at Northwestern University School of Law and Legal Clinic and has three sons. The center is a holistic children's law center, where 10 clinical faculty with 60 law students provide legal representation for children in matters of education and adoption, delinquency and immigration, child neglect/abuse and domestic violence, health and disability, and constitutional rights. The CFJC is a national policy center for the comprehensive needs of adolescents and their families, providing critical analysis of youth law and the administration of justice, educating the public, and preparing professionals who advocate for children. The center strives for a community-involving approach to the crises confronting millions of youngsters who find themselves in courts in America each day.

Barbara Finkelstein is a professor in the Department of Education, Policy, Planning, and Administration and director of the International Center for the Study of Education Policy and Human Values at the University of Maryland, College Park. She has received an array of awards—Senior Research Fellowship from the Japan Society for the Promotion of Sciences, the Henry Alan Moe Prize for the Arts, an NEH Senior Fellowship, the Distinguished International Service and the Woman of the Year Awards at the University of Maryland—for work on the historical and cultural dimensions of childhood and cultural education policies and practices. She has been president of the History of Education Society and of the American Educational Studies Association and vice president of Division F of the American Educational Research Association; currently edits the Reflective History Series, Teachers College Press; and serves on the international advisory boards of *Pædagogica Historica, History of Education Journal,* and *Journal of Educational Policy.*

James Garbarino is the co-director of the Family Life Development Center and the Elizabeth Lee Vincent Professor of Human Development at Cornell University. His research focuses on the causes, consequences, and prevention of youth violence, and he is the author or co-author of 17 books, including *Lost Boys: How Our Sons Turn Violent and How We Can Save Them* (Free Press, 1999).

Assistant professor **LynNell Hancock** is an education writer and editor who has served on the full-time faculty of Columbia University's Graduate

School of Journalism since 1995. She developed the school's curriculum on covering children's issues as director of the Prudential Fellowship for Children and the News. Prior to Columbia, Hancock served as national education editor for *Newsweek* magazine, education-beat reporter for *The New York Daily News,* and investigative reporter for *The Village Voice.* She continues to contribute to *Newsweek, U.S. News & World Report, Columbia Journalism Review,* and other publications. She is author of *Hands to Work,* an upcoming William Morrow book on welfare reform.

Pedro A. Noguera is a professor in the Graduate School of Education at Harvard University, where he serves as the Dimon Chair in Community and School Leadership. Previously he was a professor in social and cultural studies at the Graduate School of Education and the director of the Institute for the Study of Social Change at the University of California, Berkeley. His research focuses on the ways in which schools respond to social and economic forces within the urban environment.

Sasha Polakow-Suransky is a senior at Brown University, where he is pursuing a BA in history and urban studies. He recently returned from Paris, where he was studying history and economics at the Institut d'Etudes Politiques and Université de Paris 8. He is the author of *Access Denied: Mandatory Expulsion Requirements and the Erosion of Educational Opportunity in Michigan* (Student Advocacy Center of Michigan, 1999) as well as articles in the *Michigan Administrative Law Quarterly* and *Tikkun* magazine. He currently serves as an editor for *The College Hill Independent,* and has been selected as a 2000 National Truman Scholar.

Joseph A. Vorrasi is a graduate research assistant at the Family Life Development Center and a graduate student of Human Development at Cornell University. He is pursuing a doctoral degree in developmental psychology, and his research focuses on the developmental implications of childhood risk, stress, abuse, and trauma. He has published papers on war-exposed children, psychological and physical child maltreatment, and poverty and violence.

Index

Abbott, Grace, 167
Abraham, Nathaniel, 190
Abramson, J., 164
Access, during confinement, 197-199
Accumulation of risk models, 62-63, 75
Achenbach, T. M., 64
Addams, Jane, 167
Adler, J., 86
Adult jails, 191
African Americans
  environmentally induced damage and, 45, 46, 48
  mass media and, 91-92
  poverty among, 50-51
  zero-tolerance policies and, 104-105, 106, 107, 165
Aid to Families with Dependent Children (AFDC), 2, 34
Alexander S. v. Boyd, 193, 202
Allis, S., 89, 90
Alternative education
  state programs, 122-123
  zero-tolerance policies and, 109-111, 121-123
Amazing Grace (Kozol), 9
Ambosia, T-J., 159
American Civil Liberties Union, 86, 119
American Correctional Association (ACA), 193
American Federation of Teachers (AFT), 123
American Indian/Alaskan Natives
  corporal punishment in schools, 27
  environmentally induced damage and, 45
American Lung Association, 44, 51

American Youth Violence (Zimring), 88
Amnesty International, 11
Anderson, N., 91
Annin, P., 90
Apple, M. W., 23, 24
Applebome, P., 150
Ariès, P., 22, 24, 160
Arizona, 195
Arkansas, 132
  Jonesboro incident, 86, 91-92, 94-95, 101, 164
Arkow, P., 22
Armstrong, M. L., 168-169
Ascione, F. R., 22
Asian/Pacific Islanders, environmentally induced damage and, 45
Asimov, N., 133, 134
Association offenses, 171
Asthma, 44, 47-50, 51, 52, 53, 195, 206
Ayers, W., 158, 165

Babbit, Duane, 131-132
Bai, M., 79
Bandura, A., 71
Barocas, R., 62
Barry, D., 132
Barth, R. P., 168
Bassuk, E. L., 7
Bassuk, S. S., 7
Beals, G., 90
Begley, S., 51
Behair, R., 89
Belkin, L., 45
Bell, C., 133
Bell, E., 131, 133

Bell, James, 14–15, 158, 188–210
Bellamy, C., 23
Belluck, P., 49, 52, 53
Berkeley Media Studies Group, 92, 94
Bernstein, N., 48
"Best interest of the child" approach,
    29, 33
Bickerstaff, S., 123
Biesecker, G. E., 47
Bishop, D., 173
Blake, William, 211
Blanc, S., 68
Bliesner, T., 63
Blount, W. R., 71
Blumstein, A., 158
Body-bag journalism, 92–94
Bogos, P. M., 104, 121
Books, Sue, 12, 21–23, 31, 42–58
Boot camps, 192–193
Brace, C. L., 22
Brant, M., 90
Brasier, L. L., 209 n. 7
Brayfield, A. A., 6
Bremner, R. H., 29
Brody, I. N., 23
Bronfenbrenner, U., 60
Brown, A., 93–94
Brown, R. H., 28
Browne, A., 7
Brown v. Board of Education, 124
Buckner, J. C., 7
Bureau of Indian Affairs, 27
Burleigh, N., 89
Burton, Eve, 93
Butterfield, F., 10
Butts, J. A., 173

California, 14, 92, 119–120, 168, 189
    alternative education program, 122
    East Los Angeles, 49
    student perceptions of violence,
        136–152
Campbell, D., 89
Campbell, D. Ross, 26
Canada, G., 157
Carpenter, J., 83

Carra, J., 46, 47
Carter, J., 168
Caspar, L. M., 6
Ceci, S., 60
Centers for Disease Control and Preven-
    tion, 45, 47–48, 51–52
Ceo, Jack, 105, 121–122
Chase, M., 51
Chesney-Lind, M., 158, 164, 170, 172,
    173
Chicago, 12–13, 61, 64, 73
    child welfare system, 167–168
    Englewood incident, 78–79, 80–85,
        87, 93
    first juvenile court, 159, 166
    Gang Congregation Ordinance,
        171
    policing of schools in, 163–164
    school suspensions and exclusions,
        166
Chicago Sun-Times, 81, 83
Chicago Tribune, 80, 82, 84–85, 93
Child Behavior Checklist, 64
Child care, 32–33, 87
Child Development Block Grants, 35
Childhood
    age of legal, 159–160, 175–177
    historical perspective on, 21–22
Children Now survey, 87
Children's Aid Society, 23
Children's Bureau, 23, 34
Children's Defense Fund, 3–4, 6–11,
    22, 23, 43, 47, 50–51, 59–61
Children's Law Center of Massachu-
    setts, 165–166
Child saving, 29–30, 32–34
Child welfare, premises of, 33
Chomsky, N., 37
Cicchetti, D., 63
City of Chicago v. Morales, 171
Clark, Kenneth, 9
Classification, for incarceration,
    193–195
Clemetson, L., 79
Click Health, 51
Clinton, Bill, 2, 36

Coalition for Juvenile Justice, 89, 159, 170, 171, 175
Cobb, Lyman, 25
Cole, John, 122-123
Cole, W., 81
Coleman, J., 135
Colorado
  alternative education policies, 123
  Columbine High incident (Littleton), 79, 86, 91, 95, 101, 125, 130-131, 132, 135, 157-158, 162, 164
  school-discipline laws, 125
Columbine High incident (Littleton, Colorado), 79, 86, 91, 95, 101, 125, 130-131, 132, 135, 157-158, 162, 164
Commission on Civil Rights, U.S., 103, 109
Cone, M., 43, 48, 49
Confinement and incarceration, 188-210
  access to family and friends, 197-199
  adult jails, 191
  boot camps, 192-193
  classification, 193-195
  detention centers, 191-192
  due process, 207
  environment, 204-205
  grievance procedures, 207
  health/mental health, 195-197
  isolation, 195, 206-207
  outdoor experiential facilities, 192-193
  programming, 200-202
  restraints, 205-206
  social context of, 188-191
  training of staff, 203
  training schools, 192
Convention on the Rights of the Child, 11, 160
Coriell, K. B., 125
Corporal punishment
  religious tradition and, 26-27
  in schools, 23

Cortez, A., 121, 123
Cost, Quality, and Outcomes Study, 6
Courtney, M. E., 168
Crenson, M. H., 23, 33
Criminal court
  age of legal childhood and, 159-160, 175-177
  blended jurisdiction with juvenile court, 179-180
  children in, 180
  waiver/transfer from juvenile court, 177-179
Criminalizing behavior of children, 157-187
  age of legal childhood, 159-160, 175-177
  blended jurisdiction, 179-180
  children in adult criminal courts, 180
  erosion of civic responsibility for children and, 181
  gender and, 171-173
  habitual offenders, 179-180
  policing of schools in, 161-167
  probation/supervision violations, 173-174
  reviving status offenses, 169-171
  risks for foster children, 167-169
  school exclusion and, 162, 165-167
  sentencing, 179-180
  waiver/transfer to adult criminal court, 177-179
Criminal Justice Institute, 181
Crouse, Mary Ann, 29
Cuban, L., 30
Curfew, 171
Currie, E., 150, 172, 180
Curtis, G. C., 71

Daniel, P. T. K., 125
David B. v. McDonald, 169
Day nurseries, 32-33
Dead-baby beat, 92-94
Death penalty, 101-102
Declaration of Human Rights, 23, 208
DeComo, R., 173
Deich, S., 6

Delpit, L., 53
deMause, L., 21, 22, 24
Denmark, 60
DeParle, J., 3, 7
Department of Education, U.S., 101, 103, 162–163
Department of Housing and Urban Development, U.S., 46
Department of Justice, U.S., 87–88, 121, 123, 171
Detention centers, 191–192
Detroit Free Press, 93
Devine, John F., 150, 164
Dickens, Charles, 211
DiIulio, John J., Jr., 89–90, 91, 157
Direct file transfer, 177–179
Discretionary transfer provisions, 178
Dohrn, Bernadine, 14–15, 102, 157–187, 160, 165, 167, 181
Doi, D., 87
Donahue, E., 158
Doner, E., 24, 33, 34, 37
Dorfman, L., 80, 94
Dostoevsky, Fyodor, 211, 212
Drizin, S., 158, 178, 181
Drucker, Ernest, 45, 55
Drugs
    youth violence and, 72–74
    zero-tolerance policies and, 102
Du Bois, W. E. B., 188, 208 n. 2
Dubrow, N., 61
Due process
    during confinement, 207
    and zero-tolerance policies, 118–120
Duignan-Cabrera, A., 89
Dunst, C., 63
Durkheim, E., 151

Ebb, N., 6, 7
Economic inequality, perception of, 67–70
Edelbrock, C., 64
Edelman, Marian Wright, 24, 133
Education. *See also* Schools
    alternative programs, 109–111, 121–123

during confinement, 200–202
    training of confinement institution staff, 203
Education Commission of the States, 9
Eftimiades, M., 89
Eggleston, P., 49
Elliot, D. S., 72
End of Work, The (Rifkin), 189
England, R., 135–136
Englewood incident (Chicago), 78–79, 80–85, 87, 93
Environmentally induced damage to children, 42–58
    asthma, 44, 47–50, 51, 52, 53, 195, 206
    and distribution of power and wealth, 53–56
    lead poisoning, 46–47, 51–52, 53
    responses to, 50–52
    tuberculosis, 45–46, 50, 55
Environmental racism, 50
Erickson, E., 149
Eron, L. D., 71
Even Start, 35
Exercise, during confinement, 202

Fagnoni, C. M., 167
Family Leave Act (1994), 36
Family violence, impact of exposure to, 70–72
Federal Interagency Forum on Child and Family Statistics, 6
Ferguson, Cathy, 84
Ferkenhoff, E., 166
Fine, M., 21, 22
Finkelstein, Barbara, 11–12, 21–41, 22, 23, 24, 26, 27, 28, 29, 30, 31, 33, 34, 35, 37
Fiore, F., 91
Fire safety, during confinement, 204
Fitzgerald, F. Scott, 211–212
Fontaine, Lamar, 26
Food, during confinement, 205
Food stamps, 4
Fortas, Abe, 160
Foster children, 167–169

Foucault, M., 150
Fox, James Alan, 89, 90
Framing Youth (Males), 87
Frank Porter Graham Child Development Center, 6
Fraser, M. W., 69
Fraser, N., 52-53
Fraternal Order of Police, 122
Frazier, C., 173
Freedom Forum, 91
Fuentes, A., 88, 101-102
Fung, C. C., 168

Galtung, Johan, 10
Gangi, R., 159
Gannon, Mary, 103
Garbarino, James J., 10, 12, 21, 59-77, 60-63, 69, 73
Gatsonis, C. A., 47
Gegax, T. T., 79, 86
Gellene, D., 51
Gelles, R., 70
Gender
   family roles and, 33
   as issue in incarceration, 194-195
   juvenile justice system and, 171-173
   status offenses and, 169-170
General Accounting Office, U.S., 6, 46, 51
George, T., 86
Georgia, 132
Geraghty, T. F., 159
Gest, T., 90
Ghandi, Mahatma, 69-70
Gilberto, Jesus, 50
Gilliam, Franklin D., 92
Gilligan, J., 68-69
Giroux, H., 35
Giuliani, Rudolph, 3
Glaser, B., 136
Glaser, G. H., 70-71
Glassner, B., 132
Glenn, M. C., 23, 27
Glick, D., 79
Goffin, S. G., 119
Goldman, L. R., 46, 47

Goldstein, A., 45
Gordon, D., 79
Gordon, Linda, 21, 33, 34, 35
Goss v. Lopez, 119
Goulding, S. C., 89
Grace, J., 81
Great Britain, 101
Greene, Maxine, 211-212
Greenhouse, J. B., 47
Greenspan, S., 62
Greven, Philip, 21, 24, 26
Grievance procedures, during confinement, 207
Griffin, P., 175, 177
Grubb, W. Norton, 23, 28, 29, 31, 33, 35-36, 54
Gun Free Schools Act (1994), 13, 103, 104, 165
Gutman, Laura, 45

Hale, Edward Everett, 28
Hall, G. Stanley, 188, 208 n. 3
Hancock, LynNell, 12-13, 78-98, 94
Harrigan, M. M., 162
Harris, Eric, 101
Harris, Ryan, 78, 80, 81, 83, 85
Hart, P. D., 165
Hatch, Orrin, 90, 190
Haubrich, V. F., 23, 24
Hawes, J. M., 22, 23
Hawkins, M., 6
Head Start, 35
Health insurance, 7-8
Heide, K. M., 71
Helburn, S., 6
Helfer, M. E., 22
Herbert, B., 49
Herrera, N. C., 173
Herrnstein, Richard J., 54, 208 n. 6
Hewlett, S. A., 37
Hispanics
   environmentally induced damage and, 45, 46, 48
   mass media and, 91-92
   poverty among, 50-51
   zero-tolerance policies and, 165

Historical perspective, 21-41
 age of legal childhood, 159-160
 attitudes toward childhood, 21-22,
  160
 federal government and, 29-31
 local government and, 23-24
 political traditions in, 24-25, 28-31
 religious traditions in, 24, 25-27
 social action and strategy, 22-23
 socioeconomic traditions in, 25,
  31-37
Hofferth, S. L., 6
Homeless children, 9-10
Homicides, youth violence and, 60-61,
 87, 170-171
How to Really Love Your Child (Campbell), 26
Hudson, J. G., 123
Huesmann, L. R., 71
Hull House, 167
Huston, A. C., 22, 31, 34
Hutson, R. Q., 168
Hyman, I. A., 23, 26, 35

Idaho, 195
Illinois. *See also* Chicago
 blended jurisdiction, 179-180
 child welfare system, 167-168, 169
 habitual offenders, 180
 juvenile transfer to criminal court,
  178-179
 probation laws, 174
 sentencing, 179
 zero-tolerance policies, 103
Illinois School Records Act (1999), 166
Incarceration. *See* Confinement and incarceration
Indiana, 119-120, 197
Individuals with Disabilities Education
 Act (IDEA; 1997), 201-202
In re A.A., 169
In re Gault, 160
Institutional racism, 189-190
Intercultural Development Research Associates, 123

Intergenerational transmission of violence, 71
International Covenant of Civil and Political Rights, 11
Isolation, during confinement, 195,
 206-207
Iyengar, Shanto, 92

Jacklin, B., 135
Jackson, Jesse, 103
Jackson, R. J., 51-52
Jail. *See* Confinement and incarceration
Jenkins, E., 133
Jenkins, P., 22, 23, 35
Jensen, M. A., 119
Johnson, D., 103
Jones, R., 103
Jonesboro, Arkansas incident, 86, 91-
 92, 94-95, 101, 164
Jonesboro Sun, The, 91-92
Joyner-Kersee, Jackie, 52
Juvenile Accountability Incentive Block
 Grants Program (JAIBG), 176
Juvenile court. *See also* Confinement
 and incarceration
 age of legal childhood and, 159-160,
  175-177
 blended jurisdiction with criminal
  court, 179-180
 education during confinement and,
  201-202
 as journalistic beat, 93-94
 origins of, 159, 166, 188
 stereotypical thinking and, 189
 waiver/transfer to adult criminal
  court, 177-179
Juvenile Justice and Delinquency Prevention Act (1974), 170
Juvenile Justice and Delinquency Prevention Act (1999), 166
Juvenile offenders, 10-11

Kahn, P., 7
Kamlani, R., 89, 90
Kannapell, A., 51

Kantrowitz, B., 88
Karas, J., 118–119
Karvelis, Bryan, 54
Keene-Osborn, S., 79
Keleher, T., 103
Kelley, Florence, 32
Kelley, Frank, 122
Kempe, R. S., 22
Kentucky, 132
Kerber, L. K., 25
Kett, J. J., 22, 23, 33
King, C. R., 54
Kinkel, Kip, 101
Klaidman, D., 79
Klebold, Dylan, 101
Klonsky, M., 163
Knapp, M. S., 9
Koebel, L. L., 121
Korbin, J. E., 22
Kostelny, K., 61
Kotlowitz, Alex, 80–81, 91–92
Kozol, Jonathan, vii–viii, 8, 9, 42–44,
    49, 50
Krebs, Catherine, 170
Kresnak, Jack, 93
Krisberg, Barry, 172, 173, 180
Krugman, R., 22
Kunkel, D., 87

Labi, N., 86
Lacayo, R., 88–89
Ladson-Billings, G., 151
Lang, S. S., 74
Larson, E., 132
Lasch, C., 23
Lawrence, C., 83
Lazerson, Marvin, 23, 28, 29, 31, 33,
    35–36, 54
Lead poisoning, 46–47, 51–52, 53
Leary, W. E., 49
Leathers, S., 168
Lefkowitz, M. M., 71
Leon, S. H., 123
Lerner, Barron, 45
Lewin, T., 101

Lewin, Y., 102
Lewis, C., 31
Lewis, D. O., 70–71
Lighting, during confinement, 204
Lively, D. E., 46, 47, 50
Loitering, 171
Los Angeles Times, The, 81
Losel, F., 63
Lubow, B., 158
Lueng, Kameryan, 102
Lyons, D., 177

Macallair, D., 159, 171
Mace, 205
Mail, during confinement, 198–199
Males, Mike A., 22, 87, 158, 171
Mann, C., 3
Marcus, Stephen, 51
Martarella v. Kelley, 194
Marusza, J., 21, 22
Marx, Karl, 68
Maryland, 123
Massachusetts, school suspensions and
    exclusions, 165–166
Mass media, 78–98
    body-bag beat, 92–93
    Columbine High incident (Littleton,
        Colorado), 79, 86, 91, 95
    Englewood incident (Chicago), 78–
        79, 80–85, 87, 93
    fear versus facts and, 88–89
    Jonesboro, Arkansas incident, 86,
        91–92, 94–95
    juvenile court beat, 93–94
    racial issues and, 85, 91–92
    superpredator approach and, 89–92,
        157
    zero-tolerance policies and, 102–103
Mathis, D., 86
Matter of Jackson, 122
Matter of P.J., 118
Mauer, M., 159
May vs. Anderson, 8
McClelland, P., 60
McCollum, Bill, 90

McLean, G., 177
Mech, E. V., 168
Medicaid, 4, 46, 51
Medical screening, 195-196
Meier, D., 151
Meier, K., 135-136
Messner, S. F., 67
Michel, S., 21, 31-36
Michigan, 3, 7, 13
  zero-tolerance policy, 103, 104-126
Michigan Association of Chiefs of Police, 122
Michigan Association of Secondary School Principals, 121
Michigan Federation of Teachers (MFT), 121
Michigan Police Legislative Coalition, 122
Mikulski, B., 36
Miller, J. G., 90, 173, 174
Mink, Gwendolyn, 7-8
Minnesota, 123
Mississippi, 132
Missouri, 123
Moen, P., 60
Moone, J., 173
Morain, D., 106
Morganthau, T., 90
Morgan v. Sproat, 201
Morse, Eric, 80
Mourad, R., 24, 33, 34, 37
Mulligan, A. E., 165-166
Munzer, Alfred, 44
Murray, Charles, 54, 208 n. 6

National Association of Colored Women, 32
National Association of State Boards of Education, 121
National Center for Education Statistics, 9, 123, 162
National Center for Juvenile Justice, 89
National Center for Missing and Exploited Children, 23
National Clearinghouse for the Defense of Battered Women, 7

National Coalition for the Homeless, 3-4, 7
National Commission on Correctional Health Care (NCCHC), 193, 195-196
National Criminal Justice Association, 176
National Institutes of Health (NIH), 48, 49
National Law Center on Homelessness and Poverty, 10
Nebraska, 119-120, 123
Needleman, H. L., 47, 51-52
New Jersey, 27, 123
Newsweek magazine, 86, 88, 90
New York (state), 123, 159
New York City, 3, 5-6, 27, 73
  Brooklyn, 54
  Children's Health Fund, 48-49
  East Harlem, 53
  foster children in, 168-169
  school violence in, 150
  South Bronx, 9, 43, 45, 49-50, 55
New York Daily News, 86, 93-94
New York Times, The, 102, 135
Noble, H. B., 47-48
Noddings, N., 28
Noguera, Pedro, 13-14, 130-153, 150
North Carolina, 175
Norton, M. B., 25
Norvell, S., 89
Nossiter, A., 44, 49
Nuñez, Ana, 55

Oberman, M., 160
O'Brien, E., 101
O'Connell, M., 6
O'Driscoll, P., 86
Office of Juvenile Justice and Delinquency Prevention (OJJDP), 59, 158, 176
Ohio, 123
O'Neil, J., 47
Onek, D., 180
Oregon, 132
  Springfield incident, 101

O'Rourke, L. M., 91
Outdoor experiential facilities, 192–193

Pardo, C., 61
Pardo, N., 164
Parens patriae, 28–29
Parent, Dale, 208 n. 1
Parental authority, 30–31
Parrot, S., 3
Parsons, C., 178, 180
Patterson, Orlando, 135
Pederson, D., 86
Pennsylvania, 28–29
Pepper spray, 205–206
Perry, Bruce, 71–72
Personal Responsibility and Work Opportunity Reconciliation Act (1996), 2, 35, 36–37
Peterson del Mar, D., 21, 22
Phinney, D., 159
Piliavin, I., 168
Pincus, J. H., 70–71
Pinkney, D. S., 44, 45
Pitts, Jim, 10, 101–102
Piven, F. F., 3
Plotz, J., 22
Podesta, J. S., 89
Poe-Yamagata, E., 87–91, 157–159, 161, 171, 173, 175, 176
Polakow, Valerie, 1–18, 6, 7, 9, 10, 54, 160, 212
Polakow-Suransky, Sasha, 13, 101–129
Police Officers Association of Michigan, 122
Political traditions, 24–25, 28–31
Pollack, M., 132
Pope, V., 90
Possley, Maurice, 80–85, 93
Poverty
    extent of, 50
    increased levels of, 59–60
    international comparisons, 68
    racism and, 68–69
    youth violence and, 59–61, 63–64
Power, distribution of, 53–56
Pressman, P., 164

Prison. *See* Confinement and incarceration
Probation violations, 173–174
Prothrow-Stith, D., 10
Psychological screening, 196–197
Public policies, 2–8
Puente, T., 85
Purdy, M., 53
Puritz, P., 158, 160, 161

Racism
    environmental, 50
    institutional, 189–190
    poverty and, 68–69
    zero-tolerance policies and, 104–105, 106, 107, 165
Radbill, S. X., 23
Rafferty, Y., 10
Raichle, D. R., 23, 27
Recreation, during confinement, 202
Redfield, J. H., 27
Redlener, Irwin, 48, 49
Rehabilitation Act (1973), 201
Relative deprivation, 68
Religious traditions, 24, 25–27
Restraints, during confinement, 205–206
Rheinberger, M., 23
Riess, J. A., 47
Rifkin, Jeremy, 189, 208 n. 5
Rizley, R., 63
Roberts, S., 173
Robinson, Larry Keith, 131–132
Robyn A. v. McCoy, 204–205
Rodriguez, R., 90
Roosevelt, Eleanor, 208
Rosen, J. F., 46, 47
Rosenheim, M. K., 159, 169
Rosenstreich, David, 49
Ruben, D., 45, 46

Safe School Act (1994), 165
Salomon, A., 7
Sameroff, A., 62, 63, 75
Sandifer, Yummy, 80–81
Saramago, José, 1, 15

Scali, M. A., 158, 161
Scheft, J., 164
Schiraldi, V., 157, 158, 159, 173
Schlossman, S. L., 21–23, 33
Schools. *See also* Education; Zero-tolerance policies
  at-risk students and, 9
  corporal punishment in, 23
  education during confinement,
    200–202
  increase in suspensions and expulsions, 162, 165–167
  limits on teacher authority, 30–31
  overcrowded, 9
  policing, 161–167
  school-based arrests, 162–165
Schulze, Joseph, 118–119
Script-based knowledge, 71
Scudder, R. G., 71
Seifer, R., 62
Self-destructive behavior, 190
Sentencing, 179–180
Sessions, Jeff, 190
Sexton, J., 54
Shakespeare, William, 161
Shanok, S. S., 70–71
Shaw, Clay, Jr., 7
Sherman, A., 3, 4, 42
Shogren, E., 132
Sickmund, M., 87–91, 157–159, 161,
    170, 171, 173–176
Siemaszko, C., 86
Silver, R., 135
Silverman, I. J., 71
Simmons, Brent, 119, 120, 124
Sizer, T., 151
Smartt, Kimberly, 102
Smith, D., 46
Smith, V. E., 90
Snyder, Howard N., 87–91, 94–95,
    157–159, 161, 170, 171, 173–174,
    175, 176
Social learning theory, 71
"Socially toxic" worlds, 12
Social Security Act (1935), 2, 34, 35
Social Security Act (1962), 35

Social toxicity, 61–62
Socioeconomic traditions, 25, 31–37
Souls of Black Folk, The (Du Bois),
    188
South Carolina, 206
Spivak, H., 133
Springfield, Oregon incident, 101
Stahl, A. L., 158, 170
Stanley, M., 28
Stansky, L., 180
Starke, Jeffrey, 45
Status offenses, 169–171
Steffensmeier, D. J., 172
Steffensmeier, R. H., 172
Steinberg, J., 158
Steinbock, M., 7
Steinhart, D. J., 169
Steinmetz, S., 3
Steketee, M., 173
Sterk, C., 168
Stevens, J., 80
Stevenson, P., 174
Stewart, J., 135–136
Stodghill, R., II, 81
Stone, D. H., 109
Straus, M., 70
Strauss, A., 136
Stuart B. McKinney Act (1990), 9–10
Student Advocacy Center of Michigan,
    105–118
Styfco, S. J., 6
Sullivan, L., 46
Sullivan, W. M., 28
Super, D., 3
Superpredator approach, 89–92, 157,
    189–191
Supervision violations, 173–174
Suplee, C., 45
Swadener, B. B., 9
Swarns, R., 6
Sweden, 60
Szymanski, L., 175, 177

Tanenhaus, D. S., 159
Taqi-Eddin, K., 159
Tear gas, 206

Telephone use, during confinement, 198
Temporary Assistance to Needy Families (TANF), 2, 37
Ten Bensel, R. W. T., 23
Tennessee, 123
Testam, M., 168
Texas, 10
    alternative education program, 122-123
There Are No Children Here (Kotlowitz), 80-81
Time magazine, 81, 86, 90
Tips, Nancy, 51
Tobin, M. J., 47
Toby, J., 133, 149
Toch, T., 88
Tolan, Patrick, 64
Torbet, P., 175, 177-178, 179
Training schools, 192
Trennert, R. A., 27
Trivette, C., 63
Tsuneyoshi, R., 31
Tuberculosis, 45-46, 50, 55

UNICEF, 23
United Nations Declaration of Human Rights, 23, 208
U.S. News & World Report, 88-89, 90

Vardin, P. A., 23
Ventilation, during confinement, 204-205
Vera Institute of Justice, 168-169
Verso, Wendy, 6
Violence. *See also* Youth violence
    context of, 134-136
    as integral to American history, 132
Violent and Repeat Juvenile Offender Accountability and Rehabilitation Act (1999), 177
Violent Youth Predator Act (1996), 90
Virginia, alternative education program, 122

Visitation, during confinement, 198
Vorrasi, Joseph A., 12, 59-77

Wagenheim, Wendy, 119
Walder, L. O., 71
Wallack, L., 80
Walter v. School Board of Indian River County, 122
War against Poverty, 35
Washington (state), 200
Wealth, distribution of, 53-56
Weapons, zero-tolerance policies and, 102-126
Webber, T., 103
Weekly Standard, 89-90
Weinreb, L. F., 7
Weinstein, J., 3
Weis, L., 21, 22
Welfare state, 2-8
    recent changes in, 2, 35, 36-37
West, C., 37
Westat, Inc., 168
Wetherington, E., 60
WIC (Special Supplemental Food Program for Women, Infants, and Children), 46
Wilkinson, Richard G., 55
Williams, K., 86
Willwerth, J., 88-89
Wilson, John Q., 89
Wilson, R. A., 43
Wilson, W. J., 60
Wilson-Brewer, R., 135
Wing, B., 103
Wisconsin, 168
Wise, J. H., 23, 26, 35
Wishy, Bernard, 25-26
Wolfner, G. D., 70
Wolford, B. I., 121
Wollons, R., 21
Woodruff, K., 92
Wylie, N., 164

Yardley, J., 131-132
Youth violence, 59-77. *See also* Mass media; Zero-tolerance policies

Youth violence (*continued*)
  accumulation of risk model, 62-63,
    75
  case study, 64-66
  Columbine High incident (Littleton,
    Colorado), 79, 86, 91, 95, 101,
    125, 130-131, 132, 135, 157-
    158, 162, 164
  death penalty and, 101-102
  drugs and, 72-74
  Englewood incident (Chicago), 78-
    79, 80-85, 87, 93
  exposure to family violence and,
    70-72
  homicides, 60-61, 87, 170-171
  Jonesboro, Arkansas incident, 86,
    91-92, 94-95, 101, 164
  overall crime rate and, 60
  participation in illicit economy and,
    72-74
  perception of economic inequality
    and, 67-70
  poverty and, 59-61, 63-64
  responding to threat of, 149-
    152
  social toxicity and, 61-62
  Springfield, Oregon incident, 101
  student perspectives on, 136-
    149
  superpredator approach to, 89-92,
    157, 189-191

Zax, M., 62
Zero-tolerance policies, 101-129
  age of students expelled, 106-107
  drugs and, 102
  due process and local control in,
    118-120
  Gun Free Schools Act (1994), 13,
    103, 104, 165
  in Illinois, 103
  increase in suspensions and expul-
    sions, 162, 165-167
  interviews of expelled students,
    111-118
  and lack of alternative education,
    109-111, 121-123
  mass media and, 102-103
  in Michigan, 103, 104-126
  in other states, 125
  racial bias and, 104-105, 106, 107,
    165
  rise of, 102-103
  and struggle for readmission,
    107-108
Ziedenberg, J., 158, 159, 173
Zierdt, C., 180
Zigler, E., 6
Zimring, Franklin E., 88, 91, 157, 158,
    179-180
Zirkel, P., 102
Zoglin, R., 89, 90
Zola, Emile, 211